Data Management in
Machine Learning Systems

Synthesis Lectures on Data Management

Editor
H.V. Jagadish, *University of Michigan*

Founding Editor
M. Tamer Özsu, *University of Waterloo*

Synthesis Lectures on Data Management is edited by H.V. Jagadish of the University of Michigan. The series publishes 80–150 page publications on topics pertaining to data management. Topics include query languages, database system architectures, transaction management, data warehousing, XML and databases, data stream systems, wide scale data distribution, multimedia data management, data mining, and related subjects.

Data Management in Machine Learning Systems
Matthias Boehm, Arun Kumar, and Jun Yang
2019

Non-Volatile Memory Database Management Systems
Joy Arulraj and Andrew Pavlo
2019

Data Exploration Using Example-Based Methods
Matteo Lissandrini, Davide Mottin, Themis Palpanas, and Yannis Velegrakis
2018

Data Profiling
Ziawasch Abedjan, Lukasz Golab, Felix Naumann, and Thorsten Papenbrock
2018

Querying Graphs
Angela Bonifati, George Fletcher, Hannes Voigt, and Nikolay Yakovets
2018

Query Processing over Incomplete Databases
Yunjun Gao and Xiaoye Miao
2018

Natural Language Data Management and Interfaces
Yunyao Li and Davood Rafiei
2018

Human Interaction with Graphs: A Visual Querying Perspective
Sourav S. Bhowmick, Byron Choi, and Chengkai Li
2018

On Uncertain Graphs
Arijit Khan, Yuan Ye, and Lei Chen
2018

Answering Queries Using Views
Foto Afrati and Rada Chirkova
2017

Databases on Modern Hardware: How to Stop Underutilization and Love Multicores
Anatasia Ailamaki, Erieta Liarou, Pınar Tözün, Danica Porobic, and Iraklis Psaroudakis
2017

Instant Recovery with Write-Ahead Logging: Page Repair, System Restart, Media Restore, and System Failover, Second Edition
Goetz Graefe, Wey Guy, and Caetano Sauer
2016

Generating Plans from Proofs: The Interpolation-based Approach to Query Reformulation
Michael Benedikt, Julien Leblay, Balder ten Cate, and Efthymia Tsamoura
2016

Veracity of Data: From Truth Discovery Computation Algorithms to Models of Misinformation Dynamics
Laure Berti-Équille and Javier Borge-Holthoefer
2015

Datalog and Logic Databases
Sergio Greco and Cristina Molinaro
2015

Big Data Integration
Xin Luna Dong and Divesh Srivastava
2015

Instant Recovery with Write-Ahead Logging: Page Repair, System Restart, and Media Restore
Goetz Graefe, Wey Guy, and Caetano Sauer
2014

Data Management in Machine Learning Systems

Matthias Boehm, Arun Kumar, and Jun Yang

ISBN: 978-3-031-00741-5   paperback
ISBN: 978-3-031-01869-5   ebook
ISBN: 978-3-031-00096-6   hardcover

DOI 10.1007/978-3-031-01869-5

A Publication in the Springer series
SYNTHESIS LECTURES ON DATA MANAGEMENT

Lecture #57
Series Editor: H.V. Jagadish, *University of Michigan*
Founding Editor: M. Tamer Özsu, *University of Waterloo*
Series ISSN
Print 2153-5418   Electronic 2153-5426

Data Management in Machine Learning Systems

Matthias Boehm
Graz University of Technology

Arun Kumar
University of California, San Diego

Jun Yang
Duke University

SYNTHESIS LECTURES ON DATA MANAGEMENT #57

ABSTRACT

Large-scale data analytics using machine learning (ML) underpins many modern data-driven applications. ML systems provide means of specifying and executing these ML workloads in an efficient and scalable manner. Data management is at the heart of many ML systems due to data-driven application characteristics, data-centric workload characteristics, and system architectures inspired by classical data management techniques.

In this book, we follow this data-centric view of ML systems and aim to provide a comprehensive overview of data management in ML systems for the end-to-end data science or ML lifecycle. We review multiple interconnected lines of work: (1) ML support in database (DB) systems, (2) DB-inspired ML systems, and (3) ML lifecycle systems. Covered topics include: in-database analytics via query generation and user-defined functions, factorized and statistical-relational learning; optimizing compilers for ML workloads; execution strategies and hardware accelerators; data access methods such as compression, partitioning and indexing; resource elasticity and cloud markets; as well as systems for data preparation for ML, model selection, model management, model debugging, and model serving. Given the rapidly evolving field, we strive for a balance between an up-to-date survey of ML systems, an overview of the underlying concepts and techniques, as well as pointers to open research questions. Hence, this book might serve as a starting point for both systems researchers and developers.

KEYWORDS

ML systems, data management, data science, ML lifecycle, ML training, ML serving, in-database analytics, linear algebra, optimizing compilers, distributed machine learning, hardware accelerators, data access methods, resource elasticity, data cleaning, model management, benchmarking

Contents

Preface

Machine learning (ML) systems can be defined in a narrow or broad sense. First, there is a variety of ML applications like classification, regression, and clustering algorithms, as well as other tasks of the entire knowledge discovery or data science lifecycle. In a narrow sense, an ML system is simply the software system that executes these ML applications. Second, these software systems employ and extend techniques from multiple research communities. This includes: (1) compilation techniques from high performance computing (HPC), programming language compilers, and query compilation; (2) runtime techniques—for execution and data access—from database systems, operating systems, and distributed systems; as well as (3) hardware accelerators from computer architecture. Thus, in a broad sense, an ML system comprises the ML applications as well as the entire software and hardware system and its infrastructure.

The data management community and related fields have been working for over a decade on challenging ML workloads and dedicated ML systems. In modern ML systems, data management is central because: (1) ML applications benefit from high-quality and high-quantity input data; (2) data access is often a performance bottleneck whose repetitive workload characteristics can be optimized via classic data management techniques; and (3) common system architectures range from ML in database (DB) systems, through DB-inspired ML systems, to ML lifecycle systems. Especially in the last few years, many new ML systems have been introduced. These systems cover a range of very different architectures but also employ a number of common concepts and techniques. This rapidly evolving field, many discussions with team members from emerging systems, as well as our own experience with building such ML systems—like *RIOT*, *SystemML*, *Bismarck*, *Cumulon*, *Columbus*, *Hamlet*, and *Morpheus*—inspired us to give an overview of systems and techniques as well as research challenges and opportunities in the form of a SIGMOD 2017 tutorial.

The goal of this book is to expand on that effort by systematically structuring the up-to-date literature on ML systems and by providing an overview of the underlying techniques. In detail, we aim to survey the major categories of ML systems, as well as their key concepts and techniques at different levels of the system stack from programming model, through compilation and optimization, to runtime backends. The survey also includes orthogonal aspects such as resource elasticity and different tasks in the ML lifecycle. We hope this structure will also foster a discussion on common system architectures and components of ML systems. Such a consolidation of terminology and concepts could help systems researchers and developers alike to avoid inevitable redundancy when building end-to-end systems, identify baselines and research opportunities, and adopt recent advances of the field. Finally, the material of this book might also serve as the basis for advanced courses on the architecture and implementation of ML systems at undergraduate or graduate level.

Matthias Boehm, Arun Kumar, and Jun Yang
February 2019

Acknowledgments

First of all, we want to thank H. V. Jagadish for encouraging and supporting us to extend our SIGMOD 2017 tutorial *Data Management in Machine Learning: Challenges, Techniques, and Systems* into this book project. Although we certainly underestimated the effort of writing this book, retrospectively, we are glad to have invested this effort. Furthermore, we are grateful for having worked on a variety of academic and industrial ML systems as part of larger teams. Hence, this book draws tremendously from ideas, contributions, and discussions of many people—too many to be named—from different communities. Obviously, the trend of open source ML systems and early sharing of system internals was an essential basis for the material in this book as well. Finally, we thank Bettina Kemme (and her students Joseph Vinish D'silva and Hanfeng Chen), Sudip Roy, and Zack Ives, for their valuable comments and suggestions on an early draft of this book.

Matthias Boehm, Arun Kumar, and Jun Yang
February 2019

CHAPTER 1

Introduction

Machine learning (ML) and, in general, artificial intelligence (AI) techniques, are undoubtedly changing many aspects of our lives and societies, even though often unnoticed. Applications of ML and AI are ubiquitous in almost every domain and they leverage (1) a diverse set of algorithms from clustering, classification, regression, time series analysis, recommendations, and reinforcement learning, together with (2) application-specific pipelines that connect these algorithms with steps for preparing data, incorporating domain knowledge, interpreting results, and applying insights.

ML and AI are undergoing rapid and profound changes themselves as well, in terms of new paradigms and algorithms, new system architectures and hardware accelerators, as well as new techniques for preparing data and managing models. In pursuit of performance and productivity, data scientists and engineers have come to rely on a myriad of data and ML systems, old and new. These systems have different architectures and provide different levels of abstraction to their users. They often combine ideas and techniques from multiple computing disciplines, including not only ML and AI, but also data management, operating and distributed systems, high-performance computing (HPC), programming languages, and algorithms.

In this book, we take a view of ML systems from the vantage point of data management research. We explore how the principles and techniques of declarative specification and automatic optimization—pillars underlying the success of data management systems—can be applied to building ML systems. We survey existing ML systems in terms of their architecture, as well as compilation and execution techniques, and explain how many systems share similar designs and optimizations. Given the rapid evolution of this field, the increasingly complex stack, and diversity of user communities, designing appropriate programming models and well-defined system architectures are of utmost importance; they provide a sufficient separation of concerns between modeling and computation, between algorithmic and system details, as well as between various components or layers within an ML system.

1.1 OVERVIEW OF ML LIFECYCLE AND ML USERS

Before diving into data management aspects of ML systems and applications, we start by giving a birds-eye view of the end-to-end lifecycle of an ML application. Figure 1.1 illustrates this lifecycle, which typically involves an ML user or developer known by the terms *data scientist* or *ML engineer*. We divide this lifecycle into three major processes: *Source*, *Build*, and *Deploy*.

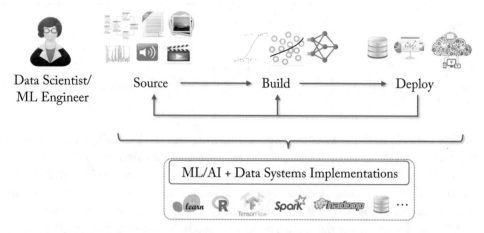

Figure 1.1: High-level illustration of the end-to-end ML lifecycle in a typical data-driven application. The underlying ML/AI or data system may also be a cloud-native service.

Source: The data scientist has to start with large volumes of potentially heterogeneous forms of data that reside in a classical database management system (DBMS), data warehouse, or a raw "data lake" based on a distributed file system such as Hadoop Distributed File System(HDFS). How does one convert these data sources to a well-defined set of useful features for an ML model to even start learning from? What if training labels are not available or not enough for a prediction task to start with? What if the data has quality issues such as inconsistent values or wrongly coded features? Recent surveys of data scientists show that they often spend up to 80% of their time wrestling with such data-related issues even before starting their ML modeling [1, 2].

Build: Once the training dataset is well defined, the data scientist has to steer the process of *model selection* to pick which trained prediction functions to deploy. This process typically involves substantial exploratory analysis combining data slicing and dicing with training numerous ML models, as well as tuning hyper-parameters to improve accuracy. Since different ML models have different pros and cons in terms of their accuracy, runtime, and interpretability, data scientists typically also perform "algorithm selection" to choose between models at this stage. In the "inner loop" of model selection are the core tasks of efficient and scalable ML training and inference, which have been the focus of a large body of ML systems research. The data scientist also has to debug the trained ML models, if any accuracy-related issues arise.

Deploy: The trained prediction functions have to be deployed into production to serve predictions for the application. While this process is often simple for offline environments involving data systems, in online Web-based applications and data streaming environments like the Internet of Things (IoT), such *model serving* workloads raise new systems concerns. Moreover, ML models are seldom static, since the data they are built upon and the application they serve are not static either. As the application evolves, so does the data and so should the ML models. Thus, monitoring and maintaining the freshness of ML models is also a part of this process.

Kinds of ML Users: Most ML applications have multiple ML users with different roles in the ML lifecycle and different levels of ML expertise. The commonly used term *data scientist* typically refers to ML users with enough technical background in ML and statistics to massage the data and build ML models for the application. They either use existing ML tools like *Scikit-learn* and *SparkML* to apply well-known ML algorithms or create custom ML algorithms tailored to their application in different ML programming models and tools such as linear algebra scripts in R-like environments and neural computational graphs in *TensorFlow*. They typically work closely with *data engineers*, who help corral various data sources across data systems to construct training data for ML, possibly including transforming the data with custom scripts in SQL, Python, or other languages. The term *ML engineer* is sometimes used to denote a role that combines the above two roles, i.e., people with expertise in both ML modeling and data engineering. *Domain experts*, who include subject-matter experts and business analysts, typically help data scientists craft prediction objectives, understand the data deeply, and set the interpretability and accuracy expectations for the ML application. Such users typically do not have much ML expertise and prefer to use automated scripts created by data scientists or visual dashboards for their own analyses. Finally, *ML DevOps engineer* is a role in production settings, especially at Web companies and many enterprise companies that use cloud services, that involves monitoring multiple deployed user-facing ML applications and responding to alerts on the behavior of ML models to help data scientists and ML engineers fix potential issues.

1.2 MOTIVATION

The recent success of ML is likely attributed to a combination of better algorithms, improved data acquisition, and general hardware advancements. In the following, we make a case for why data management is central from different perspectives.

Application Perspective: We see an increasing number of data-driven applications in important domains such as e-commerce, healthcare, finance, transportation, and production. The ubiquity of sensors, mobile devices and services enables automated data collection and feedback loops for label acquisition using incentives, user tracking, or other means. These large data collections with abundant labeled data then enable training more complex models—in terms of their numbers of parameters—while still providing good generalization. However, it is challenging to manage these large, potentially heterogeneous and distributed, data collections and leverage them in ML pipelines. While representation learning (e.g., with deep learning architectures) can alleviate some need for feature engineering on homogeneous input data (e.g., image, speech, or text), many real-world applications rely on multiple heterogeneous sources of data and knowledge (e.g., combinations of image, speech, text, structured data), and may have different interpretability requirements.

Workload Perspective: In many ML pipelines, data access is the performance bottleneck because many ML algorithms rely on operations with low operational intensity (such as matrix-vector multiplication) and are thus, I/O- or memory-bandwidth bound. However, ML algorithms are often iterative with repeated data access until model convergence. The same applies to end-to-end ML workflows, which may repeatedly access data for training over different feature subsets, tuning hyper-parameters, or learning ensembles. Such access patterns can be exploited via classic data management techniques such as caching, compression, partitioning and replication, and tailor-made index structures. Furthermore, there are numerous opportunities for alternative physical operator implementations and data layout decisions, which draw from similar ideas in relational database systems. Finally, with higher-level knowledge of processes inherent in the use of ML, opportunities for reusing computations with materialized views also arise.

Systems Perspective: From a systems perspective, we see three major categories of data-centric systems. First, motivated by data-centric applications and workloads and the fact that many enterprise ML workloads leverage data stored inside database systems, there are strong incentives to integrate ML algorithms into these systems to avoid unnecessary data transfer. Second, many existing ML systems are inspired by database systems and HPC compilers. For example, they often employ automated techniques for domain-specific simplification rewrites, operator selection and placement, and physical data layout decisions. Third, end-to-end ML pipelines span data acquisition, preparation, training and scoring, and model management, with various kinds of feedback loops. Managing such complex ML lifecycles calls for a unified, higher-level approach toward managing data, models, and their dependencies.

Together, these three perspectives cover the entire technology stack from systems to applications driven by data, which motivates a data-centric view of ML and a closer look at the challenges and opportunities for data management in ML systems. The end-to-end ML lifecycle poses a myriad of challenges that touch upon various areas of data management, including languages and interfaces, query execution and optimization, physical database design, parallel and distributed dataflows, data integration and cleaning, provenance management, and visual analytics.

1.3 OUTLINE AND SCOPE

Our overall goal is a comprehensive review of systems and techniques that tackle data management challenges in the context of ML workloads. We categorize existing systems and survey state-of-the-art techniques in order to convey major design principles of common system architectures, describe effective optimization and runtime techniques, and provide an overview of open research problems.

Structure: We structure our coverage of existing systems and techniques middle-out: starting from the integration of ML into database systems, over database-inspired ML systems, to ML lifecycle systems.

- **ML Support in Database Systems:**

  - Chapter 2 describes how various ML primitives and algorithms can be realized in database systems, focusing on the opportunities and limitations of leveraging standard database query and extensiblility features. A series of examples will provide some background on linear algebra and iterative ML algorithms.

  - Chapter 3 then provides an overview of deeper integration of ML into database systems. This includes learning over joins, approaches for deep integration, and specialized database systems.

- **DB-Inspired ML Systems:**

  - Chapter 4 turns to the internals of ML systems and surveys common optimization scopes and objectives, logical and physical rewrites, logical and physical operator selection, operator fusion, and the runtime adaptation.

  - Chapter 5 descends one level to execution strategies and compares the three predominant models of execution: data-parallel, task-parallel, and parameter server. This chapter also includes a discussion of hybrid execution strategies and hardware accelerators.

  - Chapter 6 then discusses data access methods that are often essential in ML systems, such as caching, memory management, lossless and lossy compression, NUMA-aware partitioning, and index structures.

  - Chapter 7 then broadens the view to ML in a cloud and specifically addresses management of heterogeneous and elastic computing resources and well as optimization for monetary costs.

- **ML Lifecycle Systems:**

  - Chapter 8 finally surveys other major tasks in the ML lifecycle ranging from data sourcing and preparation, over model selection and debugging, to model deployment and serving.

Scope: As already mentioned, our primary focus is on data management in ML systems. Although this broad definition could also cover general-purpose data flow systems [36, 84] and graph-focused systems [362, 363], they are beyond the scope of this book. Similarly, we also exclude recent lines of work on leveraging ML for data management problems such as cost model learning [228, 314], parameter tuning [27], workload prediction [223, 265], query optimization [229], as well as learned index structures and other other query execution components [191, 192].

CHAPTER 2

ML Through Database Queries and UDFs

This chapter explores various options for performing ML using a database system. Before we start, a valid question is why—at first glance, the relational model and query language seem to be a poor fit with ML, as most ML algorithms look very different from and oftentimes far more complicated than database queries. Thus, database systems have traditionally served as a data store for ML; the ML algorithm would pull the data out from the database, transform it into the appropriate format (e.g., matrices, tensors, or dataframes), and then analyze it using programs written in a different programming language. On the other hand, there are a number of compelling arguments for doing ML inside a database system.

The first argument is convenience. Why deal with multiple platforms with different languages if we can work with a single one for the entire data analysis pipeline? Database systems are well equipped to store, manage, transform, and query data; if they can also support other tasks in the "source-build-deploy" ML lifecycle (more in Chapter 8)—such as selecting, training, deploying, updating, and managing ML models—database systems would serve as a convenient, end-to-end ML platform.

The second argument is efficiency. Copying massive amounts of data from one system to another is costly; we can gain efficiency by moving analysis (into database systems) instead of data (out from database systems). Conducting data analysis inside database systems also readily benefits from their wide array of efficient and scalable data processing techniques. Finally, having all tasks in the ML lifecycle within a single system opens up opportunities to optimize across all tasks.

The third argument is declarativeness. Database systems pride themselves in providing declarative task specifications. Declarativeness not only simplifies development but also enables automatic optimization, which is crucial to achieving efficiency and scalability while shielding programmers from low-level details that can be complex, uncertain, and/or evolving. While database systems have been a proven success for structured data management, it remains to been seen whether they are adequate for ML, and if not, what extensions will be required.

On the topic of declarativeness, it is worth noting that many other platforms also allow declarative specification of data analysis and ML programs. MATLAB and R, for example, innately support matrices and linear algebra, which are in fact more natural than SQL for many ML workloads. These platforms have interpreted languages and do not fully exploit declarativeness to perform aggressive optimizations (such as rewriting linear algebra expressions). However, more recent systems, such as *RIOT* [381, 385], *pandas*, and *Spark*, while remaining interpreted, use deferred evaluation to build up larger expressions and optimize them much like relational queries. Chapter 4 will provide a more in-depth discussion of such optimization scopes.

Roadmap: We begin with a series of examples of implementing ML algorithms in database systems. The approaches range from simply leveraging SQL, to progressively more complex uses of the standard database extension mechanisms of *UDTs, UDFs,* and *UDAs* (*User-Defined Types, Functions, and Aggregates*), to modifying the language and internals of a database system to support ML. While some of these approaches discussed in this chapter have started showing their age, they still serve as good background for understanding the opportunities and limitations for doing ML within database systems. We conclude this chapter with a broader discussion of how various ML systems leverage database systems or techniques; some of these approaches will be covered in more detail by subsequent chapters. We also point out connections to several topics that the database research community has worked on.

2.1   LINEAR ALGEBRA

Many ML algorithms can be naturally expressed in the language of matrices and linear algebra. In this section, we explore ways to represent matrices as database tables, and to express linear algebra operations in SQL. To illustrate, let us consider a simple but interesting problem—supporting matrix-matrix multiply in SQL. We shall start with the most straightforward approach, and then examine a series of improvements.

Example 2.1   Matrix Multiply with Sparse Representation   Consider the product $\mathbf{C}$ of an $m \times \ell$ matrix $\mathbf{A}$ and an $\ell \times n$ matrix $\mathbf{B}$, where $c_{ij} = \sum_{k=1}^{\ell} a_{ik} b_{kj}$. Suppose we represent each matrix using a separable table whose tuples store individual elements of the matrix, i.e., $\mathbf{A}$ is represented by a table A(i, j, val), where val stores the value of the element positioned at (i, j).[1] With this representation, we can compute $\mathbf{C} = \mathbf{A} \times \mathbf{B}$ using the following SQL query:

```
SELECT A.i, B.j, SUM(A.val*B.val)
FROM A, B
WHERE A.j = B.i
GROUP BY A.i, B.j;
```

Note that for a sparse matrix, we can omit its 0-valued elements in its table representation, and the above SQL query still works. Also, by specifying the order of attributes i and j when declaring the primary key for the table, we can simulate either row-major (i, j) or column-major storage (j, i) order for the matrix.

---

[1]On a related note, while this triple-based sparse representation is quite natural from the perspective of a matrix, data in matrices often start out in database tables where individual features are stored as columns. In that case, some preprocessing (using an "unpivot" operation) would be needed to convert data into this sparse representation.

Another technicality worth noting is that when writing element-wise operations (e.g., $\mathbf{A} + \mathbf{B}$) in SQL under this representation, a full outer join would be required. Had we used an inner join instead in that case, we would lose result elements at positions where one of the input matrix has a 0 element.   ∎

This straightforward approach, considered in *RIOT-DB* [381] and *MAD* [81], works quite well for sparse matrices, but it is rather inefficient for dense matrices. First, we need to store two extra integers i and j for each element, resulting in considerable storage (and hence processing) overhead compared with a more compact, array-based representation that requires no explicit storage of i and j. Second, when executing the above query, a database system will likely be unable to match the performance of highly optimized linear algebra libraries such as BLAS. On the other hand, despite these inefficiencies, this straightforward approach can still beat implementations that only optimize in-memory computation when data cannot all fit in main memory, thanks to database systems' built-in support for massive data.

We can further eliminate the inefficiencies noted above using the extensibility features found in modern database systems, which allow users to define new, more complex data types and functions (UDTs and UDFs, respectively). The UDFs can call highly optimized linear algebra libraries for computation. For example, by defining a UDT for vectors and a UDF that efficiently computes the dot product of two vectors, we arrive at the following approach.

Example 2.2   Matrix Multiply with Vector Representation   Using a vector UDT, we represent matrix $\mathbf{A}$ as a table A(i, row), where the vector-typed row stores the i-th row of $\mathbf{A}$. Similarly, we represent matrix $\mathbf{B}$ as a table B(j, col), where the vector-typed col stores the j-th column of $\mathbf{B}$. Suppose the UDF dotprod($\mathbf{v}_1$, $\mathbf{v}_2$) computes the dot product of two vectors. Then, we can compute $\mathbf{A} \times \mathbf{B}$ using the following SQL query:

```
SELECT A.i, B.j, dotprod(A.row, B.col)
FROM A, B;
```

Note that we can encapsulate a considerable amount of optimization inside the UDT and UDF. For example, depending on the sparsity of a vector, it can be stored using either densely (as an array of values) or sparsely (as pairs of indices and non-zero values); dotprod can operate differently based on the input representations, and calling the appropriate BLAS routines for computation.   ∎

This approach, considered also in *MAD* [81] and used in many systems such as *Bismarck* [115] and *BUDS* [118], avoids the two inefficiencies of the approach in Example 2.1, by using a more compact representation for dense matrices and by leveraging highly optimized libraries. However, this approach is not without its own issues. First, it exposes different representations to users—$\mathbf{A}$ is by row, $\mathbf{B}$ is by column, while $\mathbf{A} \times \mathbf{B}$ is produced in a sparse representation. It is not difficult to write SQL code to convert between representations, but having to do so runs counter to the mantra of "physical data independence" endeared by database systems.

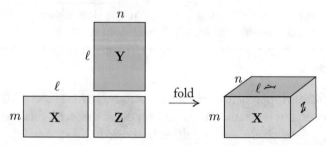

Figure 2.1: Illustration of the compute-to-I/O ratio for matrix multiply $\mathbf{Z} = \mathbf{X} \times \mathbf{Y}$. The volume of the cuboid on the right is proportional to the amount of computation while the surface area is proportional to the amount of I/O.

The second issue is performance. Multiplying rows and columns may not be the most efficient way to multiply two matrices. To see why, note that multiplying an $m \times \ell$ matrix with an $\ell \times n$ matrix involves $\ell \times m \times n$ element-wise multiplications (assuming a simple algorithm, not those with subcubic running time such as Strassen), as well as reading/writing $m \times \ell + \ell \times n + n \times m$ elements. As illustrated in Figure 2.1, these two quantities correspond to the volume and (one half of) the surface area of a cuboid formed by "folding" the two input matrices together with its product. When multiplying two large matrices that do not fit in available fast memory, we need to partition them into submatrices to multiply—which can be viewed as dividing the big cuboid into small cuboids to process. Processing each small cuboid requires I/Os proportional to its surface area. Intuitively, to minimize I/Os, we would like to minimize the surface-to-volume ratio of these cuboids, by making them as close to a perfect cube as possible; a $c \times c \times c$ cube has a surface-to-volume ratio of only $\Theta(c^2/c^3) = \Theta(1/c)$. In contrast, multiplying rows by columns would result in cuboids of dimension $1 \times \ell \times 1$, with a surface-to-volume ratio as high as $\Theta(1)$—in other words, we are not getting much computation done for each chunk of data we bring into fast memory.

To resolve the above issues, we need a more flexible matrix representation that can give us "blockier" submatrices, as used in *RIOT* [381] and *SimSQL* [221].

Example 2.3   Matrix Multiply with Blocked Representation   Suppose we have a UDT for (small) matrices or 2d arrays, a UDF `matmult` that multiplies two matrices of compatible dimensions represented in this UDT, and a UDA `matsum` that (element-wise) sums up matrices of identical dimensions represented in this UDT. To represent a large matrix, we divide it into a collection of blocks (submatrices), and store them in a table $(\underline{i}, \underline{j}, block)$, where the UDT-typed `block` stores the submatrix in the `i`-th row and `j`-th column (of the submatrices). Given $\mathbf{A}$ and $\mathbf{B}$ represented this way using blocks of compatible dimensions, we can compute $\mathbf{A} \times \mathbf{B}$ using the following SQL query:

```
SELECT A.i, B.j, matsum(matmult(A.block, B.block))
FROM A, B
WHERE A.j = B.i
GROUP BY A.i, B.j;
```

Typically, we make the blocks square-shaped, identically sized, and large enough for efficient data transfer and to let UDFs such as `matmult` take advantage of high-performance non-SQL library routines. Some padding and/or additional metadata may be needed to handle matrices whose dimensions are not perfect multiples of the default. While non-squared, non-uniform blocking is theoretically possible, in practice it becomes very complicated because it needs to handle possibly different block dimensions alignment across matrices. ∎

A traditional database system will do pretty well with the above approach, but there is still room for improvement. For example, given enough fast memory to accommodate many blocks, we should group multiple blocks into larger square submatrices to multiply in memory. A traditional database optimizer will fail to recognize this grouping strategy because it has no knowledge of the semantics of matrix multiply. Teaching a database (or database-style) optimizer how to handle linear algebra will be a topic we cover in Chapter 4. We will also revisit matrix blocking in Chapter 5 when discussing data-parallel execution, and Chapter 6 when discussing access methods.

While we have considered only matrix multiply thus far, many other linear algebra operations can be handled by SQL with similar approaches. SQL queries can be composed together to process complex linear algebra expressions.

Example 2.4 Ordinary Least Squares   We are given data $(\mathbf{X}, \mathbf{y})$ consisting of n observations, where the i-th observation includes a response y_i and values of p predictors $x_{i1}, x_{i2}, \ldots, x_{ip}$. Consider a linear regression model $\mathbf{y} = \mathbf{X}\boldsymbol{\beta} + \boldsymbol{\epsilon}$, where $\boldsymbol{\beta}$ is a $p \times 1$ vector of parameters that we wish to learn from data, and $\boldsymbol{\epsilon}$ is an $n \times 1$ vector of errors. Suppose we wish to find $\boldsymbol{\beta}$ to minimize the sum of squared errors, i.e., $(\mathbf{y} - \mathbf{X}\boldsymbol{\beta})^\top (\mathbf{y} - \mathbf{X}\boldsymbol{\beta})$. Under a number of reasonable assumptions, the optimal $\boldsymbol{\beta}$ value, called the *Ordinary Least Squares* estimator, can be computed explicitly by:

$$(\mathbf{X}^\top \mathbf{X})^{-1} \mathbf{X}^\top \mathbf{y}.$$

This linear algebra expression involves only multiplies, transposes, and an inverse. We have already seen how to do matrix multiplies in SQL; matrix-vector multiply is similar. Transpose is straightforward in SQL. Here, inverse is applied to $\mathbf{X}^\top \mathbf{X}$, a $p \times p$ matrix, which is likely not too big as p denotes the number of predictors/parameters. Thus, we can treat $\mathbf{X}^\top \mathbf{X}$ as a "value" and use a UDF `inverse` that invokes a non-SQL library routine to invert a memory-resident matrix [81, 141, 221]. ∎

As the above example illustrates, many linear algebra operations are conveniently expressible in SQL with a little help from "scalar" UDFs—i.e., those that operate on individual values (possibly of UDTs). However, there are also other operations that are harder to express. For example, inverting a large matrix using SQL is more difficult. To invert a matrix $\mathbf{M}$ in a block-wise fashion, let $\mathbf{M} = \begin{bmatrix} A & B \\ C & D \end{bmatrix}$. Then, inverting $\mathbf{M}$ can be reduced to inverting $\mathbf{A}$ (which can be done in memory by choosing a small enough $\mathbf{A}$) and then inverting $(\mathbf{D} - \mathbf{CA}^{-1}\mathbf{B})$, the Schur complement of $\mathbf{A}$ (which has the same size as $\mathbf{D}$ and can be solved recursively). Coding this procedure would require some recursion or looping construct, which still can be done using more powerful, non-scalar UDFs that can operate on whole database tables, but some of SQL's simplicity and optimizability would be lost.

2.2   ITERATIVE ALGORITHMS

As discussed at the end of the last section, we always have the option of implementing complex algorithms using UDFs coded in procedural extensions of SQL or even other languages such as Python or R. Oftentimes, it is beneficial for UDFs to limit themselves to providing high-level execution control, while pushing much of data processing down into the database system by issuing appropriate queries; such UDFs are called "driver" UDFs in [141]. Many iterative algorithms in ML can be implemented as driver UDFs.

Beyond driver UDFs, certain computation patterns commonly found in ML, such as iterating over a large dataset, can leverage better support from database systems. In particular, UDAs have shown to be a surprisingly flexible tool when implementing ML algorithms inside database systems. Briefly, a user can define a UDA by specifying three functions.

- Init(*state*) initializes the state so it is ready to receive data to aggregate. For example, to implement AVG as a UDA, we will maintain the sum s and count c of data items seen thus far, and initialize the state (s, c) as $(0, 0)$.

- Accumulate(*state*, *data*) updates the state with the new *data* item. For example, for AVG, we simply increment s by the value of *data* and increment c by 1 (ignoring NULL values).

- Finalize(*state*) computes the final result from the state. For example, for AVG, we return s/c (or NULL if $c = 0$).

Optionally, if the aggregation can be computed over different subsets of the data independently and combined together, the user can supply a fourth function.

- Merge(*state*$_1$, *state*$_2$) merges state values computed over disjoint input subsets into one. For example, for AVG, we merge (s_1, c_1) and (s_2, c_2) into $(s_1 + s_2, c_1 + c_2)$.

Merge enables a database system to perform additional optimizations automatically, e.g., partitioning the input data and executing the UDA in parallel.

Let us now examine some examples of using UDAs (often with additional help of driver UDFs) to implement ML algorithms.

Example 2.5   Gradient Descent   Gradient descent (GD) is a popular and effective method for solving a variety of convex optimization problems that arise in ML, e.g., linear and logistic regression, support vector machines, conditional random fields, graphical models, etc. Given a model with parameters w, we want to learn from data D, i.e., minimizing a loss function $F(w; D)$, which is typically the sum of loss over all training data plus some regularization term. Intuitively, GD starts with some initial guess w_0 and improves it iteratively until some stopping condition is met. Informally, in each step $t + 1$, GD updates w in the direction of the gradient of the loss function at w_t, i.e., $F'(w_t; D)$. Under certain (commonly held) conditions, GD converges to a local minimum; if F is convex, it is the global minimum.

We can implement the gradient computation in each iteration of GD as a UDA over D (given the current w_t). On the other hand, the outer loop, which updates w until a stopping condition is met, is more conveniently implemented by a driver UDF.

Interestingly, a popular variant of GD, stochastic gradient descent (SGD), presents more opportunities for leveraging UDAs. Suppose that $F(w; D)$ is *linearly separable* over the set of data points $D = \{d_i\}_i$, i.e., we can write $F(w; D) = \sum_i f(w; d_i)$ where d_i iterates over D. Instead of updating w using the "full" gradient computed over the entire D in each GD step, SGD just chooses a single point d_i in D and use $f'(w; d_i)$ to approximate $F'(w; D)$. Remarkably, for convex loss functions, SGD also converges to the global minimum, even if we process data points in a fixed, arbitrary order.

Since each SGD iteration examines a single data item, we can implement it in `Accumulate`, by using the data item to update the parameter values kept as part of the UDA state. This approach is taken by *Bismarck* [115] and *MADlib* [141]. The overall SGD algorithm consists of multiple *epochs*, where each epoch involves calling the UDA to iteratively update the parameters, and testing the stopping condition at the end. The stopping condition may itself be implemented as a UDA. The overall control flow can be implemented by a driver UDF.

SGD iterations are sequential, so the `Merge` optimization for the UDA is not directly applicable. However, it has been observed that by averaging models trained on different parts of the data, one can still achieve good results overall; therefore, by implementing model averaging in `Merge`, SGD can benefit from automatic parallelization by the database system [115].

It is worth noting that there are other variants of GD. For example, a popular variant is *mini-batch*, which we will discuss more in Chapter 5. It splits D into small batches to calculate the gradients used for updating the model. In practice, it often makes the gradient signal less noisy and offers higher computational efficiency.   ∎

Example 2.6 k-Means Clustering k-means is a popular method for cluster analysis. Given n data points, we want to find k centroids to minimize the sum of squared distances between each data point and its closest centroid. The problem is known to be NP-hard, and an iterative algorithm in the style of expectation-maximization is often used.

1. Pick initial k candidate centroid locations.

2. Assign each data point to the closest candidate.

3. Reposition each candidate as the centroid of its assigned points.

4. Repeat 2–3 above until assignment changes no more (or very little).

Each iteration (2–3) of the above algorithm can be implemented as a UDA over all data points. Given k candidate locations, this UDA computes the k updated candidate locations. The UDA state is a list $\{\langle loc_i, cnt_i, sum_i \rangle\}_{1 \le i \le k}$, where loc_i is the location of the i-th candidate centroid, cnt_i is the number of data points assigned to this candidate, and sum_i is the (component-wise) sum of the coordinates of these data points.

- Init: given each candidate location loc_i, we initialize cnt_i and sum_i both to 0.

- Accumulate: given a data point p, we find the candidate i closest to p; we then increment cnt_i by 1 and add p's coordinates to sum_i.

- Merge: given state values $\{\langle loc_i, cnt'_i, sum'_i \rangle\}_{1 \le i \le k}$ and $\{\langle loc_i, cnt''_i, sum''_i \rangle\}_{1 \le i \le k}$, we return $\{\langle loc_i, cnt'_i + cnt''_i, sum'_i + sum''_i \rangle\}_{1 \le i \le k}$.

- Finalize: for each i, we compute the updated candidate location as sum_i / cnt_i.

One SQL query with this UDA gives one iteration of the k-means algorithms. For the next iteration, the UDA will be initialized with the k locations computed from the previous iteration. A driver UDF can be used for overall execution control. The stopping condition can be evaluated in SQL as well. This approach has been taken in *GLADE* [74, 296] and *MADlib* [141].   ∎

From the two examples above, we see that database systems are quite flexible at supporting iterative algorithms. A driver UDF can conveniently implement the overall control flow of the algorithm while still leveraging the underlying database system for data processing. Moreover, a sweet spot is the use of UDAs for specifying computation that iterates over a large dataset, a task often found at the core of many ML algorithms and one that database systems are particularly adept at.

2.3   SAMPLING-BASED METHODS

Sampling underpins many ML algorithms. For example, in Bayesian ML, we start by assuming that observable data are generated by a stochastic process whose parameters are uncertain. Our goal is to combine our prior briefs about the parameters with the observed data to arrive at a better understanding of these parameters, i.e., their posterior distribution. Oftentimes, the posterior distribution is difficult to derive analytically, so a common approach is to sample from this distribution using Monte Carlo simulation. With these samples, we can then perform various useful tasks, such as marginal inference or computing maximum posteriori estimates.

By storing samples in tables, database systems can facilitate fast querying and analysis of a large number of samples. More interestingly, by extending databases systems with UDFs that support generations of samples, we can simplify the specification of sampling procedures and allow further optimization of sampling and inference. We use an example to illustrate these opportunities.

Example 2.7 Markov Chain Monte Carlo   Much of the time in Bayesian analysis, sampling directly from posterior distributions is difficult, so Markov Chain Monte Carlo (MCMC) is often the sampling method of choice. With MCMC, a sampler generates a Markov chain of samples, whose stationary distribution is the target posterior. One popular MCMC sampler is the Gibbs sampler. Suppose we have an n-variate distribution, but the conditional distributions are easier to sample from. A Gibbs sampler begins with some initial sample $\mathbf{z}^{(0)}$. To obtain the $(t + 1)$-th sample $\mathbf{z}^{(t+1)}$, we sample each component $z_i^{(t+1)}$ conditioned on all other components sampled most recently, i.e., from $p\left(z_i^{(t+1)} \mid z_1^{(t+1)}, \ldots, z_{i-1}^{(t+1)}, z_{i+1}^{(t)}, \ldots, z_n^{(t)}\right)$. This process repeats until a desired number of samples are obtained (typically, a number of samples in the initial "burn-in" period will be discarded).

The work in [341] implements MCMC inference for conditional random fields using UDFs coded in the procedural extension of SQL. The implementation requires a good deal of database expertise as it employs a number of advanced SQL features for efficiency, e.g., sequences for expressing iterations, and OLAP window functions for passing state across iterations.

If we are willing to go a step further to extend SQL and database internals, support for MCMC can be made much more declarative. This approach is taken by *SimSQL* [63]. *SimSQL* supports "stochastic" tables, whose entries may be random variables. Conceptually, when querying stochastic tables, *SimSQL* samples the random variables and generates many possible (deterministic) database instances; the collection of query results over these database instances gives an empirical distribution for the query result over the stochastic tables. To generate random samples, *SimSQL* lets users define "VG (variable generation)" functions. VG functions can be parameterized with input tables, so one stochastic database can be used to parameterize the generation of another. This abstraction is perfectly suited to MCMC algorithms, and makes the variable dependencies in the sampling procedure very clear. Finally, *SimSQL* supports "versioning" of stochastic tables. To specify a Markov chain, we simply define a stochastic table in terms of its "older" versions. The desired samples for analysis can also be conveniently selected by version using SQL.

Of course, *SimSQL*'s extensions to database systems go much deeper than syntax. To evaluate a query involving stochastic tables, it would be impractical if we fully instantiate each sample database instance and evaluate the query on this instance independently from other instances.

Hence, *SimSQL* and its precursor *MCDB* [158] employ a host of optimizations tailored toward Monte Carlo iterations. For example, they use a "tuple bundle" to group together multiple realizations of the same tuple across different database instances, allowing a query to be processed over multiple database instances simultaneously. Moreover, they delay realization of the random variables as long as possible during query evaluation—e.g., right before their values are needed for output or computation. Finally, sampling and analysis can be optimized jointly—e.g., pushing down query operators below instantiation of samples; pushing query conditions into the sampling process was considered in [341]. ∎

From the above example, we see that database systems are capable of implementing sampling-based methods commonly used in ML, although efficient implementation requires either considerable knowledge of advanced database system features [341] or extensions [63] that go beyond what traditional database extensibility features (UDTs, UDFs, and UDAs) offer. Nonetheless, there remains a strong case for SQL-style declarative specification of sampling-based algorithms, as it enables new automatic, database-style optimizations; we will return to such optimizations further in subsequent chapters.

2.4   DISCUSSION

So far, we have seen a number of examples of implementing ML algorithms within database systems in this chapter.

- SQL supports a good chunk of linear algebra, and immediately brings the convenience and scalability of database systems to some ML workloads. However, not all linear algebra operations (e.g., matrix inverse) are easy to express in SQL. Also, achieving higher efficiency requires native support of non-relational operations. UDTs and UDFs offer one mechanism for extending database systems with some such smarts, but a full-fledged solution will need new storage, execution, and optimization techniques that work with more appropriate abstractions for ML workloads (Chapters 4–6).

- UDAs can be a good fit for some iterative ML algorithms (e.g., SGD and k-means clustering), and automatically enable a number of optimizations by database systems. On the other hand, going beyond the confines of UDAs would open up even more optimization opportunities—e.g., as we will see later (Chapters 5 and 7) with *parameter servers* for SGD.

- Sampling-based ML algorithms such as MCMC can also be implemented inside database systems. However, truly declarative support for such algorithms (e.g., as offered by *SimSQL* [63]) requires extensive changes to database systems, from language to internals. As with other scenarios, there is always the alternative of using UDFs to code ML algorithms in procedural extensions of SQL or other languages, but at the cost of optimizability of computation inside such UDFs.

We also take this opportunity to compare, along several dimensions, various approaches toward doing ML with database systems.

- **How is the database system used for backend processing?**

  - In *AIDA* [105], the database system primarily handles the preprocessing of relational data into matrices. For executing linear algebra operations, *AIDA* does not use UDFs, but instead relies on an embedded Python interpreter that shares the same address space with the database system to minimize burden on the client. Similarly, in *NAnA* [225], the database system primarily handles data retrieval. Iterative optimization algorithms used by ML are executed by FPGA accelerators that directly access data in the database buffer pool pages.

  - Some systems, such as *RIOT* [381, 385], *MAD* [81], and *SimSQL* [221], rely heavily on SQL query optimization and execution for their ML workloads. They prefer relatively simple UDFs and leave more execution planning to the database system.

  - Other systems, such as *Bismarck* [115], *MADlib* [141], and *GLADE* [74, 296], rely more on UDAs and driver UDFs, which exert tighter control over execution and leave less freedom for the database system to optimize.

  - Yet other systems, such as *Oracle Data Mining* and *Microsoft SQL Server Analysis Services*, utilize wrapper UDFs and/or SQL language extensions for invoking, from SQL, custom implementations of ML algorithms. Such implementations do not necessarily rely on the database system for the bulk of their processing. Nonetheless, they often exploit opportunities of moving processing closer to data, analogous to *AIDA*.

- **Is the database system extended or changed?**

  - Some systems, such as *RIOT* [381, 385], *MAD* [81], *MADlib* [141], *Bismarck* [115], *GLADE* [74, 296], and *AIDA* [105], are built on top of a database system, using its standard extension mechanisms without modifying its internals. Many such systems expect users to work directly with the underlying database system, but some of them (e.g., *RIOT* and *AIDA*) employ a middleware layer that provides a more seamless interface with the host programming language (e.g., R and Python, respectively) as well as extra optimizations (e.g., what computation can be pushed inside the database system). Also related to the latter is the line of work on *learning over joins*, discussed in detail in Chapter 3.

  - Another approach has been to build new database systems with better support for ML tasks. Examples include *MCDB* [158] and *SimSQL* [63, 221] in this chapter, as well as a number of systems discussed in Chapter 3 under *deep ML/database integration*. These systems have the freedom to change databases interfaces and internals in ways not possible with standard extension mechanisms.

- Yet another approach is building a "database-inspired" system for ML on top of an alternative backend, such as *Hadoop* or *Spark* for cluster computing. We call these systems "database-inspired" because they aim at supporting declarative specification and automatic optimization, reminiscent of database systems. Examples include *SystemML* [54, 55, 123, 150] and *Cumulon* [149, 151–153] (discussed in more details in Chapters 4–7). In fact, *SimQL* [63] is also built on top of *Hadoop*, although its feature set makes it much more like a database system than the others.

- **Is SQL or the database system used as the frontend?**

  - Some systems let users specify ML tasks directly in SQL and/or its extensions, e.g., *MADlib* [141], *SimSQL* [63, 221], *NAnA* [225], *Oracle Data Mining*, and *Microsoft SQL Server Analysis Services*. As we have seen in this chapter, not all computations in ML can be naturally expressed by SQL, but one can always fall back to black-box UDFs. A potential appeal of SQL is that if we further extend it to support other tasks in the ML lifecycle beyond learning, e.g., as *Oracle Data Mining* and *Microsoft SQL Server Analysis Services* have done, then users would have the convenience of a single, end-to-end platform for data management and analysis.

  - Other systems choose to support ML tasks expressed in languages more familiar and/or natural to ML developers and users, even though database or database-inspired systems are still used for processing. Some example systems include *RIOT* [381, 385], *AIDA* [105], *SystemML* [54, 55, 123, 150], and *Cumulon* [149, 151–153], where the language of linear algebra makes many ML workloads easier to express and optimize than in SQL. Another example is *BUDS* [118], a declarative language for Bayesian ML; it supports a richer set of data types beyond linear algebra, and has an implementation on top of *SimSQL* [63].

As mentioned in some discussion above and at the beginning of this chapter, there are opportunities for database systems to help with a variety of tasks in the complete "source-build-deploy" lifecycle of ML. While this chapter has focused primarily on using database systems to implement algorithms for learning models from data, Chapter 8 will discuss how other tasks in the ML lifecycle can benefit from data management in general.

2.5   SUMMARY

In this chapter, we examined a number of ways of leveraging a database systems for ML, ranging from writing linear algebra in SQL, to using database extension mechanisms such has UDFs, to modifying database internals to support ML. In closing, we note that research on ML through database systems is deeply rooted in database extensibility research. Over the years, the database research community has worked on a number of topics that are particularly relevant. *Array databases*, surveyed in [295], are a natural starting point for the implementation of vectors, matrices, and tensors. Recent examples of such systems include *SciDB* [321] and *SciQL* [382].

Integration of data mining and statistical data processing into database systems has also been studied extensively in the past two decades. For example, the idea for model lifecycle management using SQL has appeared in [244]; the use of UDAs as a general mechanism for implementing data mining algorithms can be seen in [343, 344]. In the context of sensor data management, where much of data processing involves stochastic models, *MauveDB* [102] is a system that represents model prediction results as database views and allows them to be queried and updated as raw input data changes. There are numerous other examples, such as Gupta and Sarawagi [130] for Conditional Random Fields used by information extraction, *BayesStore* [342] and Kanagal et al. [168] for probabilistic graphical models, *Lahar* [207, 287] for Hidden Markov Models, and *Staccato* [203] for stochastic automata used by optical character recognition, just to name a few.

Recently, there has also been work on new database extensibility mechanisms. For example, going beyond traditional UDFs, to perform advanced analytics in *HyPer*, a main-memory relational database system, users can use a new SQL iteration construct, or invoke specialized operators for ML algorithms that can accept anonymous functions as input parameters to further customize their behavior [263]. Finally, a key challenge for ML/database integration is the extensibility of the database optimizer. Simply adding new language features, function libraries, and/or operators is not enough. We must teach the database system how to optimize not only each feature, function, or operator independently, but also in conjunction with others; the optimizer needs to be able to estimate relevant properties of intermediate result, such as size and sparsity. Optimizer extensibility is classic topic in database extensibility research [127, 166, 268]; recent work [290] has examined how to extend an optimizer to handle user-defined operators in addition to relational ones.

CHAPTER 3

Multi-Table ML and Deep Systems Integration

Building on the body of work on using UDFs and UDAs to integrate ML algorithms with relational database management systems (RDBMSs), a few lines of research expanded such integration along various dimensions. The first set focuses on making ML algorithm implementations more aware of the underlying data model of RDBMSs: the multi-table relational model. The second set focuses on deeper systems modifications to RDBMSs that are tailored toward ML workloads or creating new systems designed for specific ML workloads. In this chapter, we dive into both of these sets of systems that deepened the integration of ML with relational data management.

In the first set is a recent line of work on **learning over joins**, which exploit common database dependencies present in multi-table datasets, e.g., key-foreign key dependencies (KFKDs) and multi-valued dependencies (MVDs) [281], to accelerate ML algorithms over such data. The basic idea is that since joins in such datasets typically introduce a large amount of redundancy in the data, which in turn introduces redundancy in the computations of many ML algorithms, learning "over" joins rather than constructing the join output could reduce runtimes. Also in the first set are systems that are tailored toward supporting and scaling multi-relational ML models known as **statistical relational learning** (SRL) models that are custom-designed for databases with MVDs [122]. Unlike regular ML models such as neural networks or decision trees, SRL models do not make the *IID assumption*, which requires every entity in the (training) dataset to be represented by a single example. Since joins involving MVDs can cause examples to get replicated, they might violate the IID assumption, which would make regular ML models statistically biased.

In the second set are two lines of work. The first focuses on modifying the actual system internals of RDBMSs to specifically accelerate linear algebra operations, which are central to many ML algorithms. The modifications range from better support for different matrix datatypes to modifying scheduling decisions for query execution. The second line of work focuses on data type-specific systems that were custom designed for data manipulation and ML operations over such data.

3.1   LEARNING OVER JOINS

Let us start with an example for learning over joins of multi-table data. We also use this (simplified) example to introduce key notation used in this section. Figure 3.1 illustrates the example and notation.

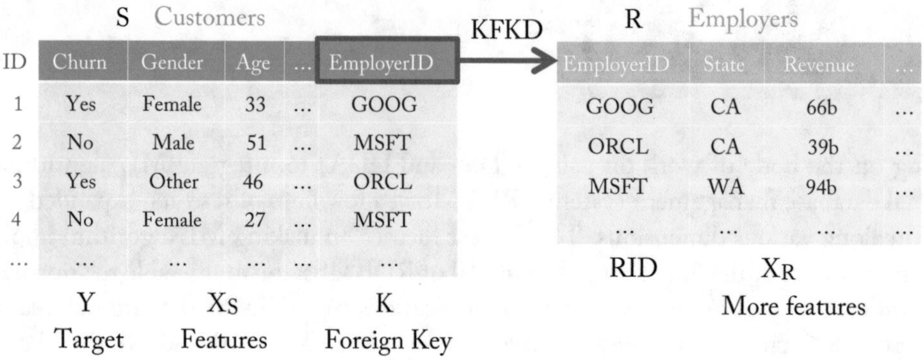

Figure 3.1: Illustration of a two-table dataset with a Key-Foreign Key Dependency (KFKD). The join brings in more features from **R** to help the ML classifier predict Y in **S**.

Example 3.1   ML over Joins (from [201])   Consider a data scientist at an insurance company using ML classifiers on their customers dataset to predict who might churn, i.e., cancel their policy and move to a competitor. She builds a logistic regression classifier using the customers table (simplified for exposition sake): Customers (ID, Churn, Gender, Age, ..., EmployerID). EmployerID is the ID of the customer's employer, a foreign key that refers to a separate table about organizations that potentially employ the customers: Employers (EmployerID, State, Revenue, ...). She decides to join these two tables to bring in the features about employers because she has a hunch that customers employed by rich corporations in rich states are unlikely to churn. Note that this is a key-foreign key (KFK) join, since each customer has only one employer but many customers might have the same employer. Examples such as this are ubiquitous in ML-based data analytics and arise in diverse domains, including retail (joining sales with store data), Web security (joining login events with profile data), recommendation systems (joining ratings with user and product data), bioinformatics (analyzing gene-chemical interactions), and more. ∎

   To ground further technical discussion with concrete terminology and notation, we consider the simplest scenario of a two-table KFK join. The main table, akin to the "fact table" in OLAP, is denoted **S**, as shown in the illustration in Figure 3.1. The foreign table, akin to a "dimension table," is denoted **R**. The general schemas of these tables are as follows: $\mathbf{S}(\underline{ID}, Y, X_S, K)$ and $\mathbf{R}(\underline{RID}, X_R)$. Here, Y is the target (class label for classification), X_S is the set of features (interchangeably considered a feature vector) in **S**, *RID* is the key of the foreign table **R**, K is the foreign key in **S** that refers to *RID*, and X_R is the set of features in **R**. In the above example, Y is Churn, X_S is {Age, Income}, X_R is {Country, Revenue}, and K is EmployerID. The notation for the output of the equi-join-project query is $\mathbf{T}(\underline{ID}, Y, X) \leftarrow \pi(\mathbf{S} \bowtie_{K=RID} \mathbf{R})$, wherein $X = [X_S, X_R]$ is the *concatenation* of the base tables' feature vectors that is eventually used for training ML models. In general, there could be more foreign tables, e.g., another table with neighborhood information joined on the zipcode of the customer, representing star and snowflake schemas that are common in OLAP. Even more generally, the database dependencies connecting multiple tables may be more general multi-valued dependencies or join dependencies. For the latter case with more general non-KFK key joins, specialized ML methods called SRL methods are common [122]. We will discuss SRL in the next section.

Joins of multiple tables can blow up the data in size, even by orders of magnitude. Thus, if users are forced to materialize **T**, storage space and memory will be wasted. Even worse, the join introduces *redundancy* in **T** caused by repetitions of the feature vectors from **R** for every record in **S** that refers to the same *RID*. Thus, ML computations over **T** could have redundancy, which wastes runtime. Even if materialization is avoided and the join is performed on the fly, such computational redundancy remains and could waste runtime. The central idea of the recent line of work on "learning over joins" is to avoid materialization of the join output and instead, "push ML through joins," inspired by selection and aggregation push downs in relational query optimization [66, 281, 365]. It involves *rewriting* the ML algorithm's computations to operate directly over the base tables, typically in a way that does not affect ML accuracy.

We categorize systems for learning over joins into three main groups based on their scope and/or system environment: specific ML algorithms on general data systems, custom libraries for specific ML algorithms, and generalized learning over joins.

Specific ML Algorithms over Joins on Data Systems: The idea of "factorized learning" on database systems was introduced by [201] for fully pushing the computations of generalized linear models such as logistic regression solved using gradient descent through joins in RDBMSs and parallel dataflow systems. They observed that the core computations for such models involved inner products of the model's hyperplane **w** and feature vectors: $\mathbf{w}^\top \mathbf{x}$. In the two-table join setting, this inner product decomposes as follows:

$$\mathbf{w}^\top \mathbf{x} = \mathbf{w}_{|\mathbf{R}}^\top \mathbf{x}_{|\mathbf{R}} + \mathbf{w}_{|\mathbf{R}}^\top \mathbf{x}_{|\mathbf{S}}.$$

In the above, $\mathbf{w}_{|\mathbf{R}}$ is the sub-vector containing only the features from **R** (the other terms are similarly defined). Thus, given two large tables, one could do one sequential pass over **R** to pre-compute the partial inner products, store it in an in-memory associative array, and do one pass over **S** to look up into this array to finish the respective full inner products. For some models, a second pass over **R** would be needed to finish one iteration, with these passes repeated for each iteration. Overall, [201] showed that this obviates the need to join the tables physically.

In a similar vein, the tool F [302] focused specifically on linear regression models solved using a variant of gradient descent that computes the Gramian matrix over the features. They showed how to push this matrix's computation through joins fully to the base tables. But they also expanded the idea to apply to more general types of joins. This tool was integrated with "factorized databases" that represent relational datasets in losslessly compressed decomposed forms based on the distributivity of relational cross products over unions. *F-IVM* is a higher-order incremental view maintenance engine for maintaining such regression models when the base tables change [250]. It expresses such models, as well as other analytics tasks over normalized data as views on joins with group-by aggregate queries over relations that maps keys, representing tuples, to payloads, which represents the values to process. This unified abstraction enables *F-IVM* to handle maintenance for matrix chain multiplication and certain conjunctive queries as well by reducing the task to maintaining a tree of simpler views.

Finally, *TensorDB* [183] focused specifically on tensor decomposition algorithms over joins of multiple tables in the RDBMS context. They introduced a new "tensor-relational algebra" framework to rewrite the computations of that algorithm.

Custom Libraries for ML over Joins: It is common for ML analytics to be performed in purely in-memory toolkits that are not associated with data systems. A couple of such ML libraries also offer ML over joins even if they do not recognize the join operations explicitly. In particular, *libFM* [289] is a tool for compressed execution of so-called "factorization machines," a popular ML algorithm for regression and recommendation tasks, solved using coordinate descent. They introduce a new file abstraction called a "block-structured dataset" that explicitly encodes known patterns of bulk repetitions in the dataset, which could be the result of joins of multiple tables. It reduces redundancy in computations by running the ML algorithm over this file abstraction. *Santoku* [199] is an R library that offers factorized execution of a few simple ML models, including logistic regression. It includes an abstraction built on top of `data.frames` in R to retain base tables as individual dataframes under the covers. The ML algorithms are rewritten to operate over this abstraction instead of forcing users to join all tables, say, using the *merge* function in R.

Generalized ML over Joins: All the systems and libraries discussed so far focus on specific ML algorithms or a small class of ML algorithms (like generalized linear models). This creates a daunting development overhead for ML engineers or data scientists to figure out how to rewrite other ML algorithms, e.g., k-means clustering, to push them through joins. To mitigate this overhead, *Morpheus* [70] introduced the idea of generalized factorized learning. It is a formal framework to push any ML computations expressible in the formal language of *linear algebra* through joins. Since many ML algorithms can be expressed as compositions of matrix operations such as matrix-vector multiplications, matrix-matrix multiplications, etc. [123], by introducing rewrite rules for pushing a large set of basic and derived matrix operations through joins, Morpheus can "automate" factorized learning to an extent. Similar to *Santoku*, *Morpheus* introduced a new multi-matrix abstraction that represents a join using a sparse indicator matrix and which is applicable to any linear algebra setting, including in-memory tools like R and Python NumPy. For instance, consider our running two-table join example. The feature matrix in **S** is $\mathbf{X_S}$; the same in **R** is $\mathbf{X_R}$. The KFKD is represented by a matrix **K** of size $|S| \times |R|$, wherein the (i, j) entry is 1 if the ith record of **S** refers to the jth record of **R**. Given this abstraction, the *Morpheus* rewrite rule for a bulk left matrix multiplication **XW** (**W** is the model matrix or vector), which is a ubiquitous operation in ML, is as follows:

$$\mathbf{XW} \rightarrow \mathbf{X_S W_{|S}} + \mathbf{K}(\mathbf{X_R W_{|R}}).$$

In the above, $\mathbf{W_{|R}}$ is the row-wise slice of **W** corresponding to the features in **R** only (similarly for **S**). The multiplication within the parentheses represent partial inner product computations, while the subsequent multiplication with **K** stands in for the join, except without introducing computational redundancy. Similarly, the *Morpheus* rewrite rule for right matrix multiplication **WX**, which also arises in many ML algorithms, is as follows:

$$\mathbf{WX} \rightarrow [\mathbf{WX_S}, \ (\mathbf{WK})\mathbf{X_R}].$$

In the above, the pre-multiplication of **W** with K is essentially a set of group-by aggregates that ensure the multiplication with $\mathbf{X_R}$ does not have redundancy introduced by joins. The comma indicates a column-wise concatenation of the two matrices. *Morpheus* integrated about a dozen such linear algebra operations with the new multi-matrix abstraction and created rewrite rules for them. The rewrite rules are also easily extensible to transposed matrix operations, multi-table joins, and more general join schemas. Invoking these rewrites when needed in a linear algebra-based ML algorithm automates the push down of the computations through joins. This approach was shown to work efficiently for a variety of ML algorithms, including those studied for the original factorized learning techniques and in *FDB* (linear models) and other ML algorithms such as k-means clustering and non-negative matrix factorization. *MorpheusFI* extended this framework to enable pairwise feature interactions, a non-linear pre-processing operation popularly used to boost the accuracy of linear models, but still executed on top of a linear algebra system [211]. It introduced new write rules for linear algebra operations that avoid the double redundancy caused by the interplay of joins and feature interactions. This approach was shown to be often faster than both *Morpheus* with feature interactions being materialized (but not joins) and stochastic gradient descent-based training on the fully materialized datasets.

On a different axis of generalization, [180] took the idea of fusing in-database ML and relational query expressions for feature engineering further using *sparse tensors* as a unifying abstraction. This integration allows them to represent both numeric features and one-hot encoded categorical features inside a database and express a suite of models over such data using queries, including linear regression models, polynomial regression, factorization machines, and principal component analysis (PCA). Join dependencies present in the feature engineering queries are exploited as in F to push down computations. In addition, they also exploit functional dependencies present in the data to reduce the computations needed for estimating model parameters. Finally, they exploit the mechanism of functional aggregate queries [181] to reduce the time and space complexity of computing gradients when one-hot encoded categorical features are involved, thus making their approach even faster than materialization-based training.

3.2 STATISTICAL RELATIONAL LEARNING AND NON-IID MODELS

As alluded to briefly in the last section, multi-table datasets can have more general database dependencies such as embedded multi-valued dependencies. In such cases, standard ML models that make the so-called "independently-and-identically distributed" (IID) assumption cannot be used directly [122]. The IID assumption states that all examples in the training dataset are independent and identically distributed samples from some underlying (hidden) data distribution. To see why general joins could violate the IID assumption, consider performing a general join between two tables that causes records to get duplicated—a record corresponding to one training example might now get repeated multiple times in the join output. This alters the data distribution and biases the ML model.

One solution to the above issue is to do some "feature engineering," which is the process of converting the raw data into "flat" feature vectors for IID ML models. This could involve, say, group by aggregates of the variables in some of the joined tables (e.g., averages, standard deviations, modes, etc.). This process converts general joins into key-key joins or the snowflake joins described in the previous section. But such flattening loses information because the granularity of the features becomes coarser. SRL is a family of ML models that do not make this IID assumption and avoid the need to flatten the data. Instead, they learn directly over general multi-table datasets logically and exploit the structure information during learning. Note that SRL is an ML modeling issue—a logical decision—that is orthogonal to factorized learning, which is a physical execution decision.

A powerful aspect of SRL compared to IID models is that SRL enables "collective inference" that allows us to predict multiple correlated variables simultaneously with one model. In contrast, with IID models, one would have to redo feature engineering from scratch for each variable and build separate models. SRL is common for datasets with complex join schemas, especially in healthcare applications [122]. There are various SRL models in the ML literature such as Markov Logic Network (MLN) [292], Probabilistic Soft Logic (PSL) [121], etc.; explaining them all is beyond the scope of this book. We pick MLN as a representative SRL model and explain it with an example. We then discuss the data management issues that arise when using MLNs at scale.

Example 3.2 Example for MLN (from [251]) Figure 3.1 illustrates a multi-table schema, a database instance, and an example MLN. The database instance is a collection of facts or "evidence," which is akin to the training dataset for regular IID ML models. Note that the prediction task has many variables to predict, as indicated with a "?," for many tuples in the instance. These examples are similar to the prediction set on which IID ML models are asked to make predictions. An SRL model's inference process assigns values to all the "?" collectively. Note that the variables to predict are correlated in complex ways. An MLN is a first-order logic program consisting of a set of *rules* and associated *weights*. Each rule captures some domain knowledge about the data and application. A rule with a positive (resp. negative) weight is expected to be true (resp. false) on examples in the evidence and prediction set. Rules with positive (resp. negative) infinity weight are called "hard" rules that should always be true (resp. false) on all examples, both in the evidence and in the variables. The MLN's weights are learned from training data *a priori* (to be explained shortly). ∎

Database Schema	Training Data/Evidence	Markov Logic Program	
Paper (PaperID, URL)	Paper("P1", "...")	Weight	Rule
Wrote (Author, PaperID)	Paper("P2", "...")	5	Area (p, c1), Area (p, c2) => c1 = c2
Area (Paper, Category)	Wrote ("Joe", "P1")	1	Wrote (a, p1), Wrote(a, p2), Area (p1, a) => Area (p2, a)
Refers (PaperID, PaperID)	Wrote ("Joe", "P2")	2	Area (p1, a), Refers (p1, p2) => Area (p2, a)
	Wrote ("Jane", "P2")	+ ∞	Paper (p, u) => ∃x . Wrote (a, p)
To Predict	Area ("P1", "Databases")	-1	Area (p, "Networking")
Area ("P3", ?)	Area ("P2", "ML")	...	...
Wrote (?, "P3")	Refers ("P3", "P1")		
...	...		

Figure 3.2: Illustration of a database schema, dataset instance ("evidence"), and a Markov Logic Network (MLN) program. Since SRL performs "collective inference," it can be used to predict many variables simultaneously.

MLN inference assigns values from a discrete known set to all missing entries. This inference problem is known to be NP-Complete [292]. Thus, MLN inference in practice uses a sampling procedure such as Gibbs sampling [375]. Inference involves two steps in cycles: *grounding* and *search*. Grounding essentially assigns one set of chosen values to the missing entries (called a "possible world") and evaluates all rules in the MLN to compute a cost function. Crucially, this process could involve several joins of the base tables. Search essentially changes the set of chosen values with the aim of decreasing the cost function value. This process proceeds for many iterations until convergence. Training an MLN is an outer loop that involves repeated MLN inference based on a similar loss function, albeit over the training set.

In-RDBMS and Scalable SRL Systems: Since inference in MLNs involves repeated joins of tables, *Tuffy* [251] exploits an RDBMS for executing those ML computations using the advanced join processing capabilities of the RDBMS (e.g., hash joins) instead of a simple nested loops join performed in prior MLN tools. This boosts the efficiency of the grounding step of MLN inference. However, since the search process involving so-called "random walks" over the set of variables, doing it naively in an RDBMS could lead to too many random accesses.

Thus, *Tuffy* introduced a hybrid architecture that performed search in memory and grounding with the RDBMS's execution engine. *Felix* [252] is a successor to *Tuffy* that expands upon the observation that specialized operator implementations (e.g., for joins) can be exploited for MLN inference. It identified chunks of MLNs that can be compiled into simpler ML models (e.g., logistic regression) and invokes specialized operator implementations for processing those chunks more efficiently than general-purpose inference. It introduced a compiler and rules to automatically decompose an MLN into such chunks.

Finally, *Elementary* [375] is a successor to both *Tuffy* and *Felix* that takes scalable Gibbs sampling-based inference all the way to build a custom from-scratch ML system. It focuses on MLNs and evidence that are so large that the compiled intermediate representation, which is the so-called "factor graph," does not fit in single-node memory. Thus, *Elementary* created a data model for such factor graphs that arise in MLN inference and introduced materialization optimizations, page layout optimizations, and buffer cache replacement tweaks tailored to the access pattern of Gibbs sampling. All these database-inspired optimizations helped *Elementary* improve both the scalability and throughput of Gibbs sampling and MLN inference. *Elementary* was used as a core part of the larger *DeepDive* system that extended MLNs to enable more complex collective inference [377]. Finally, an incremental version of *DeepDive* modified the sampling process of factor graph-based inference to take advantage of previously computed results to improve efficiency when new evidence is added [313].

Other Data Management Issues in Non-IID ML: Apart from scalability and performance of SRL techniques, other aspects of the close relationship between relational databases and multi-table non-IID ML models have also been explored. *ERACER* [231] modeled a relational database using a probabilistic graphical model called a relational dependency network (RDN), inspired by Bayesian networks, to help unify many data cleaning and missing value imputation tasks on relational databases. With some approximations to factorize the joint distribution across variables, RDNs can model the data cleaning and repair tasks as statistical inference queries that require iterative processing. Interestingly, these inference queries of RDNs are amenable to an in-RDBMS implementation using regular SQL combined with a few user-defined functions and aggregates, as discussed in Chapter 2.

A potential usability issue with SRL is the need for specifying the domain-specific rules in the first place. A line of work on non-IID ML has focused on learning such rules themselves from the relational database. The most prominent among them is inductive logic programming (ILP). First-order inductive learner (FOIL) is a popular ILP technique [240, 277]. The basic idea is to specify a template for the kinds of rules one wants to learn using, say, syntactic constraints for Horn clauses in Datalog. Then, given a training dataset and a set of target predicates, a (typically greedy) search heuristic learns a set of rules that entail the given data with some coverage-related scoring function as the optimization objective. *QuickFOIL* [372] is an in-RDBMS implementation of a new FOIL-inspired greedy heuristic for ILP. Essentially, *QuickFOIL* recognizes that the search performs a large number of joins and aggregate queries. By recasting this process to a "query-generator" approach and fusing related queries that share parts of the data, *QuickFOIL* improves runtime performance, while the customized search process also helps improve accuracy.

Finally, an issue with common ILP techniques is that the rules they learn are too tied to the specific representation of the database schema. So, even if the schema representation is modified slightly without losing information, one could get a different model, which could affect usability. To mitigate this issue, *Castor* [267] introduced the notion of "schema-independence" for ILP, which requires the rules learned to be semantically equivalent (based on logical inference) for content-preserving schema transformations over the database. It showed that many popular ILP techniques are not schema-independent and presented a new ILP technique that is by enforcing new constraints over the sets of rules explored during the search. Ensuring this property also helped *Castor* improve accuracy.

3.3   DEEPER INTEGRATION AND SPECIALIZED DBMSS

ML-related Operators inside RDBMSs: So far, we have seen how to integrate linear algebra and ML techniques into RDBMSs and dataflow systems without having to modify their internals, say, using UDFs. But UDFs could introduce high overhead and are also hard to use as a programming interface. Thus, there has also been some work on deeper integration of linear algebra and ML workloads that requires modifying the internals of an RDBMS. This involves supporting data types such as matrices as first-class citizens alongside relations and/or altering the query processing stack to improve the efficiency ML-oriented workloads.

SLACID [177] introduced primitives for mutable sparse matrices in a column-oriented in-memory DBMS that are optimized for both read-only and read-write workloads. It organizes the data storage to separate a static main data structure for read operations, while using an incremental delta index to handle updates. Primitive linear algebra operations such as matrix-vector multiplications, as well as point lookups are implemented on these data layout to ensure efficient processing within the DBMS environment. Recent work also extended the SAP HANA RDBMS to improve the throughput of multi-threaded execution for complex stored procedures that may invoke linear algebra libraries or ML routines [355]. Since naively handling multi-threaded execution of application logic can interfere with the DBMS workload scheduling and waste resources, it integrated *OpenMP* for shared memory programming within the DBMS task scheduler. This reduces the overhead of leveraging efficient ML code within the RDBMS stack.

Finally, *MauveDB* [102] introduced the concept of a "model-based view" to RDBMSs to more deeply integrate ML models into relational data processing. Analogous to views in SQL, such views are defined by probabilistic models for regression and imputation tasks, with the main application being handling missing values in noisy sensor datasets. *MauveDB* supports various materialization strategies to maintain the model-based view data efficiently when the underlying data is updated, since updates are common in such applications. This functionality was integrated with the query processing stack of an RDBMS, and it was accessible in SQL with extensions for handling such views.

Data Type-specific ML Systems: RDBMSs and parallel dataflow systems such as *Spark* were designed mainly for processing structured (relational) data and semi-structured data (XML or JSON). However, modern data-driven applications also need to process large amounts of other data types, including unstructured data types [2]. Since ML can be applied to virtually any type of data, several systems build custom processing stacks for ML workloads over specific non-relational data types. We categorize such systems based on the data type they target and discuss a few prominent examples.

- **Array-oriented:** Large multidimensional arrays are a common form of data in many scientific data processing applications. *SciDB* [320] and *TileDB* [260] are DBMSs built from scratch for this data model. Their storage layer manages block-partitioned arrays, and they support both read and write operations on such arrays. It supports a new query language called Array Query Language (AQL) that is inspired by SQL syntax. *SciDB* also support APIs in other environments, including R. *SciDB* offers a few in-built linear algebra operators to perform feature extraction and simple regression tasks. Compared to *SciDB*, *TileDB* optimizes further for storage of sparse arrays as well. Both of these systems employ numerous array-specific optimization techniques, which we will discuss further in subsequent chapters.

- **Time Series-oriented:** Multi-variate time series datasets have become ubiquitous thanks to various monitoring applications, e.g., in IoT. A common ML application on time series data is "forecasting," which involves predicting the future values of the monitored variables. *Fa* [106] and F^2DB [117] are time series-oriented analytics systems that elevate forecasting applications to a declarative level and optimize the model building process for such data. *Fa* includes a few simple time series data transformations, model selection from among a fixed of statistical ML models, and feature subset selection as part of its plan space for building a forecasting model. F^2DB integrates forecasting model building queries with an RDBMS. It supports materialization, caching, and reuse of forecasting models, as well as sampling of the time series data within the DBMS to automatically optimize a forecasting query.

- **Text-oriented:** Many RDBMSs support text processing, including with inverted indexes, while systems such as *Hadoop* were originally invented to deal with large corpora of Web text documents. However, most database systems offer almost no native support for ML over text data. *TextDB* [348] is a recent project that aims to mitigate this gap by creating a DBMS that can store, index, and support analytics over large amounts of text. It uses

Lucene as the underlying storage and indexed retrieval engine. It supports an SQL-like query language and aims to support a roster of text analysis operators, including an integration with the Stanford CoreNLP toolkit [227] for ML-oriented analytics over text data.

- **Graph-oriented:** Graphs are an increasingly prevalent data type, especially in social media and Web applications. Naturally, graph processing and analytics systems have been intensively studied in the last several years. While the full scope of graph systems is beyond the scope of this book, we discuss a key example of a graph-oriented ML system and refer the interested reader to other surveys and texts on this topic [363, 364]. *GraphLab* [218] is a system that offers a graph-oriented abstraction for expressing graph-parallel ML algorithms such as matrix completion for recommendation systems, as well as other non-ML graph analysis techniques. The abstraction requires users to "think like a vertex" and write so-called "vertex programs" that perform node-local computations on the graph being processed. Under the covers, *GraphLab* automates the parallel execution on a cluster, including with potentially asynchronous processing, in a fault tolerant manner.

- **Multimedia-oriented:** Multimedia DBMSs have received much attention in the past, with a primary focus being the so-called "content-based" queries that enable users to query semantic content of images and video (e.g., what objects are in a picture) [322]. Once again, such systems are beyond the scope of this book. But in the last few years, the popularity of deep convolutional neural networks (CNNs) for more accurate computer vision has led to renewed interest in multimedia querying systems that use CNNs. Optasia [219] is a video querying system that offers efficient vision-oriented modules for stitching together video processing pipelines, including various image processing, feature extraction, and object identification modules. It offers a declarative language for composing such pipelines and presents RDBMS-inspired query optimization techniques and parallel execution to reduce latency and resource costs.

BlazeIt [169] supports an SQL-like language for spatiotemporal queries such as for selecting and aggregating semantic content (e.g., vehicle occurrences in traffic videos). Under the covers, it trains numerous CNNs over a set of labeled videos to extract semantic information relevant to a given query over other archived videos and exploits approximate query processing techniques such as sampling, control variates to reduce errors, and spatial and temporal filtering to improve runtime performance. Focus [147] also targets deep CNN-based object recognition queries over post-hoc video. It introduces new video ingestion schemes that employ a smaller pre-trained CNN to create an approximate index of object occurrences, which it employs to reduce query latency. Finally, VideoStorm [137] aims to enable live video querying at scale in a near real time manner. It introduces tradeoffs such as reducing the quality of the video queried to reduce resource costs and also supports lags for some queries, which enables it to reassign resources and optimize scheduling in an online manner.

3.4   SUMMARY

Normalized or multi-table databases are perhaps the best example to show why decoupling ML training from data pre-processing could raise resource requirements for managing intermediate data. As shown by several recent lines of work, integrating ML computations with data pre-processing computations that exploit the knowledge of the schema of the database can yield significant efficiency and usability benefits regardless of the system environment: RDBMS, in-memory ML tools, etc. Taking this integration further, some database vendors and open source projects are modifying the kernel of the RDBMS itself to be more amenable to ML computations.

However, it remains an open challenge as to how one can fully abstract data preparation steps that precede ML training to automatically avoid costly intermediate data materialization. A complicating factor is that while RDBMSs and parallel dataflow systems may offer rich support for data transformations, they may no longer be the preferred execution environment for ML training for a majority of ML users. Thus, an impactful avenue for further research could be hybrid execution environments that combine the capabilities of linear algebra, relational algebra, and other data processing steps to reduce the grunt work of manual data materialization and movement, while still retaining the full power of popular ML frameworks.

CHAPTER 4

Rewrites and Optimization

Similar to optimizing compilers for programming languages and high-performance computing (HPC), or query optimization in database systems, many ML systems apply a broad range of rewrites and optimization techniques to improve the efficiency of ML programs. In this chapter, we first categorize existing systems according to their optimization scope, survey important classes of logical and physical rewrites, and also discuss means of adapting execution plans during runtime.

Comparison to Query Optimization: In contrast to generic programming language compilers, most ML systems provide domain-specific languages with abstract types for matrices or tensors as well as linear algebra and other ML operations. This focus on linear algebra programs preserves the semantics of individual operations, which—together with relaxed guarantees for round-off errors—greatly simplifies rewrites such operator reordering and the selection of physical operators. Such an operator-centric view renders the optimization of ML programs very similar to traditional query optimization. However, major differences include the focus on linear algebra operations, data flow plans in the form of directed acyclic graphs (DAGs) instead of trees, conditional control flow of loops and branches, as well as the handling of sparse and dense inputs.

Impact of Rewrites on Result Correctness: Since linear algebra operators in ML systems primarily rely on floating point operations, these rewrites and optimization techniques might affect the result correctness due to round-off errors. This includes errors induced by partial aggregation for data-parallel computation in the context of multi-threaded or distributed operations, issues of numerical stability due to operator reordering, and the handling of special values such as NaN and INF in the context of sparse linear algebra operations. In most real-world scenarios, moderate round-off errors are acceptable due to the inherently approximate nature of ML algorithms. Additionally, ML systems typically provide different optimization levels that allow disabling rewrites and data-parallel computation if needed. For example, in *SystemML* [54], users can disable rewrites and force single-threaded, single-node operations. In the following sections, we disregard such round-off errors.

4.1 OPTIMIZATION SCOPE

One of the most differentiating aspects of ML systems with regard to rewrites and optimization is their optimization scope in terms of the compilation granularity (i.e., the (sub)program subject to optimization), and the time when compilation and optimization take place. At a high level, we distinguish the following major categories:

1. **Interpretation:** single operation at-a-time;

2. **Lazy expression compilation/evaluation:** single operator-graph at-a-time, triggered on implicit or explicit actions; and

3. **Program compilation:** entire program including control flow;

whose advantages and disadvantages we shall discuss in the remainder of this section.

Example 4.1 Linear Regression Conjugate Gradient   As a basis for a detailed discussion, we first introduce our running example of an algorithm for linear regression via a conjugate gradient method as used in [39, 111, 123, 366]. This algorithm was derived from [253, Algorithm 5.2], with the difference of not materializing the $m \times m$ matrix $\mathbf{A} = \mathbf{X}^\top \mathbf{X}$ to ensure scalability to large numbers of features.

```
 1:  X = read($X); # n x m matrix
 2:  y = read($Y); # n x 1 vector
 3:  maxi = 50; lambda = 0.001;
 4:  intercept = $icpt; ...
 5:  r = -(t(X) %*% y);
 6:  norm_r2 = sum(r * r); p = -r;
 7:  w = matrix(0, ncol(X), 1); i = 0;
 8:  while(i<maxi & norm_r2>norm_r2_trgt) {
 9:     q = (t(X) %*% X %*% p) + lambda*p;
10:     alpha = norm_r2 / sum(p * q);
11:     w = w + alpha * p;
12:     old_norm_r2 = norm_r2;
13:     r = r + alpha * q;
14:     norm_r2 = sum(r * r);
15:     beta = norm_r2 / old_norm_r2;
16:     p = -r + beta * p; i = i + 1;
17: }
18: write(w, $B, format="text");
```

This example script uses *SystemML*'s R-like syntax, where %*% is a matrix multiplication, t(X) is the transpose of $\mathbf{X}$, and other operations such as +, * are element-wise addition and multiplication. The model w is initialized via the matrix constructor as a zero matrix of ncol(X) rows and one column. ∎

#1 Interpretation: The basic interpretation of ML programs provides the smallest optimization scope of a single operation at a time, which does not require compilation. Instead of modifying the parser and compiler of existing languages such as R, operations on relevant data types can simply be overridden to inject the necessary optimization rules. This simplicity comes with a major drawback though. Operations are optimized in isolation, which renders techniques such as operator reordering, operator fusion, and common subexpression elimination inapplicable. Examples for this optimization scope are *R*, *Julia* [47], and *PyTorch* [264], as well as *Morpheus* [70], which use eager execution but apply operator selection for type-specific code selection as well as factorized learning, respectively. Overall, interpretation is mostly applied in ML systems for local (i.e., single-node) computation and without the aim for program-wide optimizations.

#2 Lazy Expression Compilation: A second very common approach is lazy expression evaluation with an optimization scope of entire expressions, i.e., DAGs of operations. The basic idea is to collect operations—on dedicated abstract data types—during interpretation into a DAG of operations and lazily trigger optimization and execution on actions that need to produce the results. This approach is often used for domain-specific languages (DSLs) that are embedded in host languages because it does not require modifications of the host language compiler. Given the widespread use of lazy expression evaluation, we need to distinguish the types (a) with and without support for control structures, (b) with dynamic and static graphs, and (c) with implicit and explicit actions. Examples without control structures and implicit/explicit actions are *Mahout Samsara* [301] and *RIOT* [381]. Here, DAGs are built while interpreting—and thus, potentially unrolling—the control flow, and operations such as full aggregations (e.g., sum(p * q) in Example 4.1) or collect (materializing an intermediate as local matrix in the driver) trigger evaluation. Other systems also allow control structures in the operation graph to represent loops, branches, and temporal dependencies for operations with side effects. Examples are *Thenao* [45], *OptiML* [325], *Emma* [30], *TensorFlow* [22], *DyNet* [245], and *Weld* [257], where for example *TensorFlow* relies on static graphs with multiple returns which require explicit actions via session.run(...). Overall, lazy expression evaluation allows for a non-invasive integration into a host language, while providing a moderately large optimization scope which is a great fit for embedded DSLs.

#3 Program Compilation: Finally, there are also numerous ML systems whose compiler and runtime is built from scratch. With the control over the own compilation chain, these systems often aim at program compilation with an optimization scope of the entire ML program to maximize the optimization potential. The global optimization scope allows for rewrites involving control flow such as loop vectorization, branch removal, and the merge of sequences of basic blocks, as well as global data flow rewrites such as caching, partitioning, and compression before loops. For instance, in Example 4.1, we can inject compression and caching directives[1] for

---

[1]While *SystemML* handles data flow properties via automatic rewrites, *Samsara* also allows for caching but—because of the expression compilation scope—requires the user to specify these caching directives manually.

X before the loop to avoid I/O per iteration. However, despite the global scope, most systems follow a hybrid approach—where certain rewrites are still limited to individual operator DAGs of unconditional basic blocks—in order to reduce the compilation overhead. In comparison to lazy expression evaluation—where expressions are optimized for each evaluation—full program compilation before execution can also significantly reduce the compilation overhead in the presence of loops and functions over small data. Example systems include *SystemML* [55, 123], *Cumulon* [149], *Tupleware* [89], *Emma*'s `parallelize` construct [30], and function compilation in *Julia* [47]. Overall, full program compilation allows for advanced rewrites of the entire program which requires a custom compiler but can provide performance benefits on very small or very large data.

Optimization Objective: Related to the used optimization scope is also the optimization objective. The most common objective is to minimize execution time, subject to memory constraints. However, more advanced optimizers also aim at multi-objective optimization but usually linearize this problem via additional constraints. Examples are: (1) minimizing monetary cost subject to time constraints in *Cumulon* [149]; (2) minimizing time subject to accuracy constraints in *BlinkML* [262]; and (3) maximizing accuracy subject to time constraints in AutoML-tools like *TuPAQ* [317].

4.2   LOGICAL REWRITES AND PLANNING

An optimization scope of DAGs of operations or entire ML programs allows for optimization via rewrites and planning in general. ML programs exhibit ubiquitous optimization opportunities that are addressed via traditional programming language (PL) rewrites, advanced rewrites such as loop vectorization, algebraic simplification rewrites, as well as dedicated techniques for incremental computation and optimizing chains of matrix multiplications. In this section, we focus on logical rewrites that are independent of the underlying physical execution plans, while physical rewrites are subsequently discussed in Section 4.3.

Example 4.2   Linear Regression Direct Solve   To aid the discussion, we introduce another example algorithm for linear regression via a (simplified) direct solve method that computes the normal equations in a closed form and solves this linear system. If the user requests a model with intercept (`icpt`), we simply append a column of ones to **X** via `cbind` and otherwise proceed equivalently.

```
1:  X = read($X); # n x m matrix
2:  y = read($Y); # n x 1 vector
3:  lambda = 0.001;
4:  if( $icpt == 1 )
5:     X = cbind(X, matrix(1, nrow(X), 1));
6:  I = matrix(1, ncol(X), 1);
```

```
 7:   A = t(X) %*% X + diag(I) * lambda;
 8:   b = t(X) %*% y;
 9:   beta = solve(A, b);
10:   write(beta, $B);
```

This algorithm is typically applied for up to few thousands of features in matrix $\mathbf{X}$ because its compute workload grows with $\mathcal{O}(n \cdot m^2 + m^3)$. For the common case of tall and skinny matrices (i.e., $n \gg m$), the algorithm is dominated by the costs for $\mathbf{X}^\top \mathbf{X}$ with $\mathcal{O}(n \cdot m^2)$, not the call to solve with $\mathcal{O}(m^3)$. In systems with program compilation scope like *SystemML*, this script is parsed into a hierarchy of statement blocks, where the control flow such as loops and branches delineates individual blocks and computation graphs are constructed for each block. In the above example, this results in graphs for lines 1–3, 4–5 (if block), 4 (predicate), 5, and 6–10. In contrast, in systems with expression compilation scope like *Samsara*, $\mathbf{X}^\top \mathbf{X}$ and $\mathbf{X}^\top \mathbf{y}$ are optimized independently if the results are collected into local matrices.   ∎

Traditional Programming Language (PL) Rewrites: Several ML systems apply PL rewrites such as (1) common subexpression elimination (CSE), (2) constant folding, (3) branch removal, and (4) merge of block sequences. Examples are *OptiML* [325], *SystemML* [54], *TensorFlow* [22], and *MatFast* [367]. First, common subexpression elimination is usually done by consolidating leaf nodes (inputs and literals) and merging equivalent operations (same inputs and operation types) in a bottom-up pass through the graph [54]. Certain operations such as rand without seed or print are handled in an operation-specific manner to prevent invalid elimination. Second, constant folding aims to replace sub-DAGs of operations over literals with the resulting literal. An elegant approach to constant folding is the compilation and evaluation of runtime instructions because this ensures consistent runtime behavior [25, 54]. Third, after constant folding, we can remove branches with literal predicates. In the above example, the if block (line 4–5) is either completely removed (if $icpt==0) or replaced with the basic block of line 5 (if $icpt==1). Fourth, after branch removal or function inlining we might end up with sequences of basic blocks, which can be merged into single blocks. In our Example 4.2, the entire program is merged into a single block and thus computation graph.

Loop Vectorization: An advanced PL rewrite—that is already domain-specific as it targets array operations—is loop vectorization. This rewrite requires an optimization scope of entire ML programs or at least the dedicated handling of loops. The basic idea is to identify loops that—often due to the lack of experience with vectorized operations (as shown, for example, by custom scripts for HMM inference [221, Figure 8])—emulate array operations, and replace these loops via vectorized (i.e., element-wise) array operations as follows:

```
1:  for( i in a:b )              -->  X[a:b,1] = Y[a:b,2] + t(Z[1,a:b]);
2:      X[i,1] = Y[i,2] + Z[1,i];
```

At a high level, we simply substitute—for cases where result correctness can be guaranteed— the index variable i with its range a:b [31] along with additional compensations (here, t(Z[1,a:b])) to ensure alignment for element-wise matrix operations. This technique can be applied repeatedly to nested loops. For special cases, where the index ranges match the matrix dimensions, subsequent simplification rewrites then also eliminate unnecessary left and right indexing operations. Besides instruction overhead, loop vectorization also avoids unnecessary copy-on-write, that is, copying **X** on performing even a single cell update like X[i,1].

Update In-place: For scripts with fine-grained updates in loops that cannot be vectorized, copy-on-write still poses performance challenges. In general, systems such as *R*, *SystemML* [55], and *PyTorch* [264] all use copy-on-write[2] to ensure result correctness despite by-reference variable assignments. For example, Y=X; X[1,]=tmp would otherwise not just modify the first row of **X** but also **Y**. However, most systems with copy-on-write semantics employ techniques for automatic update-in-place if possible. As an example, consider the following script for computing cumulative sums, although built-in support for cumulative aggregates is readily available in *R*, *MATLAB*, *Julia*, *NumPy*, and *SystemML* [56]:

```
1:  B = A; csums = matrix(0,1,ncol(A));
2:  for( i in 1:nrow(A) ) {
3:     csums = csums + A[i,];
4:     B[i,] = csums;
5:  }
```

This loop qualifies for updating **B** in-place but different systems use different conceptual approaches. First, *R* employs reference counting and update in-place if the reference count is one, which works great even for cases where it cannot be inferred at script level. Here, the first iteration creates a copy of **B** because the reference count is two (for **A** and **B**), but subsequent iterations are performed in-place of the already copied **B**. *PyTorch* provides user-level, in-place operations and similarly employs version counting for raising errors when these operations are executed on invalid aliasing or auto differentiation. In contrast, *SystemML* uses rewrites to annotate entire loops with update-in-place variables. Such variables like **B** are then copied—and potentially pinned into memory—on entry of these loops. The compile-time decision allows for taking the entire program context into account.

Incremental Computation: Apart from offline training, there are many use cases that could benefit from incremental computations. Widely used techniques include (1) warm start offline learning, where a previously trained model is used as the starting point for an iterative ML algorithm, and (2) online learning, where new observations are used to approximately adapt the current model [87]. Other work aims to perform exact incremental computation. For example,

---

[2]In contrast, *Julia* [47] uses by-reference assignments and update-in-place by default and thus, requires an explicit B=copy(A) if this is not desired.

MauveDB [102] and *LINVIEW* [248] keep state of small intermediates and generate incremental linear algebra programs. For the program in Example 4.2, we would keep **A** and **b** to incrementally adapt the betas $\boldsymbol{\beta}'$ for additional data $\Delta\mathbf{X}$ and $\Delta\mathbf{y}$ via

$$
\begin{aligned}
\mathbf{A}' &= \mathbf{A} + \Delta\mathbf{X}^\top\Delta\mathbf{X} \\
\mathbf{b}' &= \mathbf{b} + \Delta\mathbf{X}^\top\Delta\mathbf{y} \\
\boldsymbol{\beta}' &= \text{solve}(\mathbf{A}', \ \mathbf{b}'),
\end{aligned}
\tag{4.1}
$$

which is very beneficial for the common case of $n \gg m$ and $n \gg n_\Delta$ because it reduces the update costs from $\mathcal{O}(n \cdot m^2 + m^3)$, to $\mathcal{O}(n_\Delta \cdot m^2 + m^3)$. Similar approaches were recently also applied to factorized learning (see Section 3.1) [249], and to the generation of occlusion-based explanations for convolutional neural networks in *Krypton* [242]. Furthermore, for iterative linear algebra programs, often only deltas are propagated over iterations. For example, *LINVIEW* [248] maintains a dedicated delta matrix in factored form—i.e., as a product of two low-rank factors—and incremental iterations [113] use delta sets for incremental fixpoint computations such as connected components.

Size Propagation: There are two types of rewrites, static and dynamic, where dynamic rewrites require size information of matrix dimensions and sparsity for cost comparisons and validity constraints. For this purpose and other techniques such as selection of execution or operator types, it is important to propagate sizes from the inputs through the entire ML program. There are two important aspects. First, propagating sizes through an unconditional DAG of operations is used for the optimization scope of expression compilation and as a basic primitive for program compilation. Except for data-dependent operations, computed size expressions, or UDFs, matrix dimensions can often be inferred exactly based on the operation semantics. Example systems that propagate dimensions are *SystemML* and *TensorFlow*. Estimating sparsity is more challenging. *SystemML* uses worst- and average-case estimates for matrix multiplications, and other operations [54]. *SpMachO* [178] relies on the same average-case estimate for matrix multiplications but introduced a density map of variable granularity—where sparsity estimates are derived as aggregates of cell estimates—to account for skew. Other work for estimating the number of non-zeros of matrix products uses hashing and sampling [33], systematic sampling [367], layered graphs of non-zeros [80], and boolean matrix multiplication as employed in *NVIDIA cuSPARSE* and *Intel MKL* [216]. Second, intra- and inter-procedural analysis (IPA) propagates these sizes over the entire ML program including conditional control flow and complex function call graphs. Due to worst-case estimates in *SystemML*, IPA propagates sizes only into functions (or over conditional control flow) if all paths result in equivalent dimensions and/or sparsity [54]. Note that size propagation is done in a best-effort manner to keep the compilation costs low. Similar to adaptive query processing [101], runtime adaptation—as described in Section 4.5— then corrects initial unknowns or changing sizes, which is very important in practice.

Example 4.3   DAG and Program-Level Size Propagation   Figure 4.1 shows example size propagation techniques using the ML script introduced in Example 4.1. First, Figure 4.1a shows the logical plan after rewrites for the main expression of the algorithm's inner loop (line 9). Given the input dimensions and sparsity of $\mathbf{X}$ (10M $\times$ 1K, sparsity 0.2) and $\mathbf{p}$, we propagate this size information bottom-up through the DAG by computing the output sizes of each operation based on the given input sizes and operation semantics; if this is not possible we assign -1 to indicate unknowns. With this approach, we now can propagate sizes through unconditional DAGs. However, for an entire ML program, we additionally need to propagate sizes in awareness of conditional control flow. For example, Figure 4.1b shows the skeleton of our example script. Since the `while` body is executed zero or many times, we need to ensure that sizes propagated into the loop body are in fact constant. Similarly, we have to ensure that sizes propagated into DAGs after the loop are independent from how often we execute the while body. In our example, $\mathbf{X}$ and $\mathbf{y}$ are read-only while $\mathbf{w}, \mathbf{r}, \mathbf{p}$ are updated and have constant dimensions but unknown sparsity. If the reconciliation step fails, partial unknowns per variable have to be propagated into the while loop to revert incorrect propagation. ∎

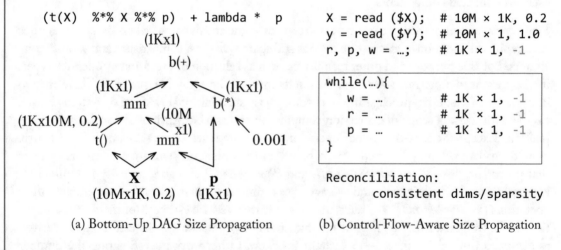

(a) Bottom-Up DAG Size Propagation   (b) Control-Flow-Aware Size Propagation

Figure 4.1: Examples of sparsity-exploiting fused operators.

Algebraic Simplification Rewrites: As already mentioned, in general, there are static and dynamic rewrites, which also applies to algebraic simplification rewrites. Such simplifications aim to replace known expression patterns with expressions that are more efficient or exhibit better numerical stability. Systems that apply static—i.e., size-independent—rewrites include *Theano* [45], *OptiML* [325], *SystemML* [54], and *TensorFlow XLA* [125]. Examples for static rewrites are $\mathbf{X} - \mathbf{Y} \cdot \mathbf{X} \rightarrow (1 - \mathbf{Y}) \cdot \mathbf{X}$ to avoid unnecessary matrix-matrix element-wise operations, $\text{sum}(\mathbf{X}^\top) \rightarrow \text{sum}(\mathbf{X})$ and $\text{sum}(\lambda \cdot \mathbf{X}) \rightarrow \lambda \cdot \text{sum}(\mathbf{X})$ to avoid unnecessary intermediates and operations, $\text{colSums}(\mathbf{X}^\top) \rightarrow \text{rowSums}(\mathbf{X})^\top$ for aggregation pushdown, and $\text{trace}(\mathbf{XY}) \rightarrow \text{sum}(\mathbf{X} \cdot \mathbf{Y}^\top)$ for better asymptotic behavior. Furthermore, *SystemML* also applies dynamic—i.e., size-dependent—rewrites. Examples are $sum(\mathbf{X}^2) \to \mathbf{X}^\top \mathbf{X}$ iff $ncol(\mathbf{X}) = 1$ (e.g., Example 4.1, lines 10 and 14), $sum(\mathbf{X} + \mathbf{Y}) \to sum(\mathbf{X}) + sum(\mathbf{Y})$ iff $dims(\mathbf{X}) = dims(\mathbf{Y})$, and $\mathbf{X}^\top \mathbf{y} \to (\mathbf{y}^\top \mathbf{X})^\top$ (e.g., Example 4.1 line 5, and Example 4.2 line 8), which all use sizes for validity constraints and cost comparisons, respectively. Although many of these rewrites are very simple, they often yield cascading effects where rewrites enable other rewrites, and larger expressions are significantly simplified by repeated application of a library of such basic rewrites.

Example 4.4   Optimized Linear Regression Direct Solve   After applying traditional PL rewrites, size propagation, and simplification rewrites, the linear regression script from Example 4.2—invoked with `icpt=0`—would look like this:

```
1:  X = read($X); # n x m matrix
2:  A = t(X) %*% X + diag(matrix(0.001, ncol(X), 1));
3:  b = t(t(read($Y)) %*% X);
4:  beta = solve(A, b);
5:  write(beta, $B);
```

The rewrites *constant folding* and *branch removal* eliminated the unnecessary if-statement block, and the rewrite *block sequence merge* collapsed the entire program into a single statement block. Furthermore, *constant propagation* replaced the read-only variable `lambda` with the literal 0.001. Simplification rewrites then pushed the multiplication into the diag operation, where it was further fused into the constant matrix creation. Also, $\mathbf{X}^\top \mathbf{y}$ was rewritten to $(\mathbf{y}^\top \mathbf{X})^\top$ to avoid the expensive transposition of $\mathbf{X}$ and leverage metadata vector transpositions.   ∎

Matrix Multiplication Chain Optimization: Another dynamic rewrite is optimization of matrix multiplication chains, which uses size information for cost comparisons. Given a matrix multiplication chain of n matrices $\mathbf{M}_1, \mathbf{M}_2, \ldots, \mathbf{M}_n$ (associative), find the optimal parenthesization of the product $\mathbf{M}_1 \mathbf{M}_2 \ldots \mathbf{M}_n$. For example, consider line 9 of Example 4.1 and $\mathbf{X}$ to be a 10M × 1K matrix. Computing $(\mathbf{X}^\top \mathbf{X})\mathbf{p}$ would require $\approx 20\,\text{TFLOP}$, whereas $\mathbf{X}^\top (\mathbf{X}\mathbf{p})$ would only require $40\,\text{GFLOP}$. A naïve search space evaluation is known to follow the Catalan numbers with $\Omega(4^n / n^{3/2})$. However, dynamic programming (DP) applies due to optimal substructure and overlapping subproblems, resulting in the textbook DP algorithm which requires $\Theta(n^3)$ time and $\Theta(n^2)$ space complexity [85]. This DP algorithm uses a *cost matrix* to compute and memoize the optimal costs for subproblems in a bottom-up fashion starting from single matrices to longer product chains. The algorithm keeps track of selection decisions in an *optimal split matrix*, which is finally recursively read out to yield the optimal parenthesization. Example systems that leverage this algorithm are *SystemML* [54], *RIOT* [381], and *SpMachO* [178], were the latter two extend this algorithm with I/O costs and sparsity of intermediates, respectively. Similarly, Cohen used this algorithm in an extended form for sparse matrix multiplication chains as well [80]. However, the best-known DP algorithm requires only a time complexity of $\mathcal{O}(n \log n)$ [148] but it is rarely implemented due to its complexity and rather moderate lengths of matrix multiplication chains in practice, at least unless additional operations such as element-wise addition and multiplication are considered. Other systems like *GigaTensor* manually optimized matrix multiplication chains for specific algorithms under expected size differences [171]. Finally, note that matrix multiplication chain optimization is only a special case of the sum-product optimization problem [99] and the even more general functional aggregate query (FAQ) framework [181], which has already been used for in-database ML [180] as well.

Open Research Questions: Most ML systems address the tradeoff between optimization benefits and compilation overhead with a combination of heuristics and cost-based decisions, which lacks a principled approach. Hence, there are plenty of open research questions. This includes matrix multiplication chain optimization for DAGs of operations, the combination with other operations such as transpose, element-wise multiplication and addition, and more broadly the holistic optimization under consideration of other rewrites, physical operators, and interesting data flow properties. As cost-based optimizers get more sophisticated, we would also benefit from better sparsity estimation for expressions of matrix multiplications and other operations to accurately reflect their costs, without the need for large and costly synopsis [80, 178, 216] or step-wise evaluation [367].

4.3   PHYSICAL REWRITES AND OPERATORS

So far, we discussed logical rewrites and optimizations that are independent of the physical runtime plans. A second major class of rewrites and optimizations are physical optimizations, which include data flow rewrites, execution type and physical operator selection, operator-specific physical rewrites, as well as fused operators to avoid intermediates, redundant scans, or to exploit sparsity across operations.

Data Flow Rewrites: For large-scale machine learning, data flow properties can significantly impact performance by avoiding redundant read and unnecessary data shuffling. Accordingly, many distributed ML systems use data flow rewrites to influence these data flow properties. Important rewrites include distributed caching, partitioning, compression, and rewrites related to joins and aggregations.

- **Distributed Caching:** Frameworks like *Spark* [370] with distributed caching require the user to decide upon the caching of intermediates, which is a tradeoff between redundant computation and memory consumption and thus, potential evictions from memory. Interestingly, existing systems use very different heuristics. *Emma* aggressively caches all intermediates that are consumed multiple times [30], whereas *SystemML* more conservatively caches only large matrices after initial read (after text to binary conversion) and variables that are used read-only in loops [55]. Yet other systems like *Mahout Samsara* expose caching at script level, which lets the user control caching manually [301].

- **Partitioning:** Many frameworks keep track of partitioning (e.g., hash partitioning imposed by previous shuffle operations or explicit partitioning) for more efficient joins as used in binary operators. Accordingly, systems like *Emma* [30], *SystemML* [55], and *Mahout Samsara* [301] provide dedicated partitioning-exploiting operators that avoid key changes to preserve and exploit this partitioning. Furthermore, *SystemML* explicitly injects partitioning before loops if this avoids data shuffling per iteration [55]. Systems like *DMac* [366], *Kasen* [380], and *SystemML* [58] even perform plan-specific data partitioning in the scope of a single operation DAG and `parfor` body program, respectively.

- **Other Data Flow Rewrites:** Other rewrites include compression (as discussed in Section 6.2), joins, and aggregation types. For example, *SystemML* injects directives for lossless compression before read-only loops if the data is known to exceed aggregate memory [111]. *Emma* applies *Exists Unnesting*, where filters with broadcasts are rewritten to joins [30], which is similar to Query-Data joins in streaming systems [65]. *Emma* further performs *Fold-Group Fusion* to automatically rewrite `groupByKey` to `reduceByKey`, which allows for local pre-aggregation that can avoid unnecessary data shuffling.

Operator Selection: Similar to the selection of physical operators like hash or nested loop joins in database systems, another important optimization is operator selection for operations such as matrix multiplications and other operations. This entails two major steps: (1) the selection of execution types in terms of execution backends; and (2) the selection of backend-specific physical operators.

- **Execution Type Selection:** The selection of execution types includes decisions on local vs. distributed and CPU vs. GPU operations. For example, *SystemML* selects local operators whenever their worst-case memory estimates fit into the driver memory budget and otherwise falls back to distributed operations [54]. This heuristic works very well for data-intensive ML algorithms because it generally avoids unnecessary overheads of distributed operations. Other systems such as *Spark MLlib* [368] and *Mahout Samsara* [301] also provide local and distributed operations but require the user to perform execution type selection manually. For the decision between CPU and GPU operations, *SystemML* again relies on memory estimates, heuristics, and manual configurations. Similarly, other systems such as *Theano* [45] and *TensorFlow* [22] allow the manual placement of operations onto devices. However, there is also recent work on learning the CPU/GPU placement in *TensorFlow* automatically [238].

- **Physical Operator Selection:** After execution type selection, we can then select backend-specific physical operators based on data and cluster characteristics (e.g., data size/shape, memory budgets, and degree of parallelism), matrix and operation properties (e.g., diagonal or symmetric matrices, and sparse-safeness), and data flow properties (e.g., co-partitioning, and data locality). Table 4.1 provides an overview of important classes of operators, where most systems exhibit a selection preference from local and special operators to shuffle-based operators. For instance in Example 4.2, *SystemML* and *Samsara* compile the expression $\mathbf{X}^\top\mathbf{X}$ to special `tsmm` (transpose-self mm, which is similar to a BLAS `dsyrk`), or AtA operators if certain constraints are met. With the commonly used blocked or tiled matrix representations [123, 149, 320, 368], this includes a blocksize constraint to ensure that entire rows are accessible despite distributed data-parallel computation. Note that the broadcast-based, co-partitioning-based, and shuffle-based operators are very similar to data-parallel broadcast joins, improved repartition joins, and repartition joins [53]. Finally, after physical operator selection, often additional physical rewrites are applied that are dependent on the chosen operator. For example, if we have chosen a broadcast-based `mapmm` for a matrix-vector multiplication such as $\mathbf{Xp}$, we decide upon the need for aggregation that is only required for multiple column blocks.

Table 4.1: Classes of physical matrix multiplication operators

Class Name	Example Operators
Local Operators	*SystemML*: `mm`, `tsmm`, `mmchain`;
	Samsara/Mllib: local linalg
Special Operators	*SystemML*: `tsmm`, `tsmm2`, `mapmmchain`, `pmm`; *Samsara* `AtA`
Broad-Based Operators	*SystemML*: `mapmm`, `mapmmchain`
Co-Partitioning-Based Operators	*SystemML*: `zipmm`; *Emma/Samsara*: `OpAtB`
Shuffle-Based Operators	*SystemML*: `cpmm`, `rmm`; *Samsara*: `OpAB`

Example 4.5 Execution Plan for Example 4.2   Armed with the basics of logical and physical rewrites as well as execution type and operator selection, we can now have again a closer look at the core of Example 4.2: $\mathbf{X}^\top\mathbf{X} + \mathrm{diag}(\mathbf{I}) \cdot \lambda$ and $\mathbf{X}^\top\mathbf{y}$. Assume driver and executor memory budgets of 20 GB and 100 GB as well as $\mathbf{X}$ to be a dense 10M × 1K matrix in double precision with block size 2K. After constant folding, branch removal, and merge of block sequence, the entire program is represented as a single block—as shown in Example 4.4—and thus, a single operation DAG. Subsequently, we rewrite $\mathrm{diag}(\mathbf{I}) \cdot \lambda$ to $\mathrm{diag}(\lambda)$ which pushed λ into diag() and subsequently fuses the constant multiply into the matrix constructor. Figure 4.2a shows the resulting logical plan after rewrites. Given that the size of $\mathbf{X}$ (80 GB) exceeds the driver budget, we then inject a caching directive after the initial read to avoid unnecessary read on the second access of $\mathbf{X}$. Furthermore, we select the special `tsmm` operator for $\mathbf{X}^\top\mathbf{X}$ because its blocksize constraint (i.e., $1K \leq 2K$ to ensure accessibility of entire rows) is met as well as the broad-cast-based operator `mapmm` for $\mathbf{X}^\top\mathbf{y}$ because $\mathbf{y}$ (of size 80 MB) easily fits into the broadcast budget. Finally, `mapmm` allows applying an additional rewrite from $\mathbf{X}^\top\mathbf{y}$ into $(\mathbf{y}^\top\mathbf{X})^\top$ to avoid the transposition of $\mathbf{X}$. Figure 4.2b shows the physical plan, which also includes the selected

execution types (CP for control program, i.e., local operations, and SP for *Spark*, i.e., distributed data-parallel operations). Furthermore, we set the `mapmm` aggregation type—based on the output size of $1K \times 1$—to `singleblock`, which allows runtime operations with reduce-all instead of reduce-by-key characteristics. ∎

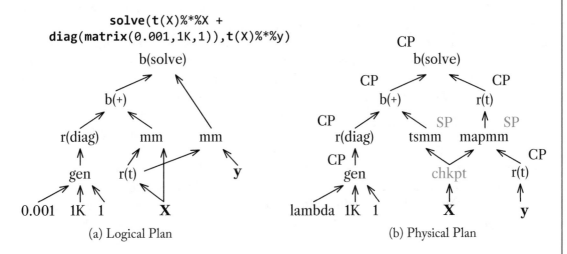

Figure 4.2: Examples of logical and physical plans.

Fused Operators: Besides basic rewrites and operator selection, there is also ubiquitous potential for fused operators in terms of composite operators for chains of operations. These fused operators aim to avoid unnecessary scans of inputs, eliminate materialized intermediates, and exploit sparsity across operations. For example, consider the `mmchain` operator in *SystemML* [39, 54], which can be applied to the core expression $\mathbf{X}^\top(\mathbf{Xp})$ in Example 4.1. Without fusion, this expression requires two passes over $\mathbf{X}$ and creates a vector intermediate of size $\text{nrow}(\mathbf{X})$, which needs to be collected and broadcast from the driver. A key observation, however, is that this intermediate is produced and consumed in a row-aligned manner. The `mmchain` operator exploits this characteristics by computing a scalar intermediate for each row and immediately scanning the same row again to perform the second multiplication. For the common case of tall-and-skinny matrices, individual rows fit into L1 or L2 cache such that $\mathbf{X}$ is read just once from main memory. Other fused operators reduce materialized intermediates whose allocation and write are often much more expensive than the actual computation. Examples in *SystemML* are ternary aggregates $\text{sum}(\mathbf{X} \cdot \mathbf{Y} \cdot \mathbf{Z})$, sample proportion $\mathbf{X} \cdot (1 - \mathbf{X})$, sigmoid $1/(1 + \exp(-\mathbf{X}))$, and axpy $\mathbf{X} + s \cdot \mathbf{Y}$. Similarly, *MatFast* provides compound operators to fold multiple element-wise operations into a single operator [367].

Sparsity-exploiting, Fused Operators: Furthermore, there are two common approaches for sparsity exploitation: pattern-specific fused operators and more generic masked operators, where the latter is similar to worst-case optimal joins via semijoin reductions [247]. Both leverage a sparse driver **S**—that is, a sparse matrix together with a sparse-safe operation such as multiply— to avoid dense intermediates and unnecessary computation via selective computation only for non-zero entries in **S**. Figure 4.3 shows examples for these two approaches. *SystemML's* fused `wsloss` operator [55] in Figure 4.3a is commonly used in matrix factorization algorithms to compute the weighted squared loss only over non-zero entries. The sparse indicator matrix **W** (often with **W** = (**X** ≠ 0)) along with the multiply operator allows performing this computation only for non-zeros in **W** and **X** without materializing the huge dense intermediate **UV**$^\top$. Based on the same concept, *GigaTensor* [171] provides a similar fused operator for the more complex expression **S**(**U** ⊗ **V**), where ⊗ is the Khatri-Rao product (i.e., column-wise Kronecker product). In contrast, *Cumulon's* generic `MaskMul` operator [149] in Figure 4.3b requires the materialization of a sparse mask **M** derived from **O**. This filter is passed to the ternary `MaskMul` operator, which only performs necessary computation according to the given mask. Such masked operators still require the materialization of sparse intermediates but are more broadly applicable if masked physical operators exist for all operations. Despite the high-performance impact of fused operators, they are fundamentally limited to patterns of few basic operators and incur large development effort. Hence, there is a trend toward automatic operator fusion as we shall discuss in Section 4.4.

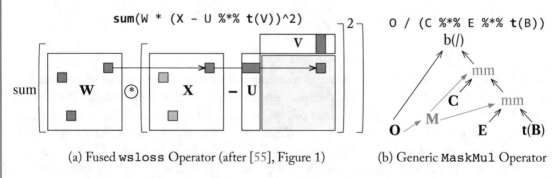

(a) Fused `wsloss` Operator (after [55], Figure 1)   (b) Generic `MaskMul` Operator

Figure 4.3: Examples of sparsity-exploiting, fused operators.

Operator Scheduling: An often overlooked but important compilation step is the scheduling of DAG operations for execution. All existing techniques follow a dependency-based approach to ensure correctness but differ in terms of the ordering of operations and their execution. First, *operator ordering* linearized the DAG into an evaluation order. Systems like *SystemML* [123] and *TensorFlow* [22] basically employ a queue-based approach where a processed node decrements dependency counts of consumers and nodes are placed into a ready queue whenever their dependency count is zero. *SystemML* originally performed a strict topological sort of operations that resulted in a breadth-first-search (BFS) exploration. BFS simplified the consolidation of multiple operations into a minimal set of distributed jobs, potentially with multiple outputs. However, since BFS often leads to larger memory requirements for all live intermediates per DAG level, *SystemML* on Spark later switched to a depth-first-search (DFS) exploration that—depending on the DAG structure—can reduce the number of live intermediates and thus memory requirements, and improve temporal locality. Second, *operation execution* can be sequential or parallel. For example, *SystemML* eventually generates a list of instructions that are executed sequentially, while *TensorFlow* places ready operators directly into a queue and executes them in an undefined order [22]. In this setting, *TensorFlow* prevents device over-provisioning by using a common thread pool for concurrent and multi-threaded operations. While sequential operation execution simplifies the compilation with regard to memory budgets and multi-threaded operations, for mini-batch algorithms, this can lead to low resource utilization due to synchronization barriers per operation. Therefore, the chosen operator scheduling technique often reflects a system's primary application area. Loosely related to operator scheduling are also automatic decisions on operator placement as shown in a *TensorFlow* prototype [238], and automatic decisions on recomputation to reduce peak memory consumption as used in *SuperNeurons* [345] and MXNet [72, 345].

Open Research Questions: Most ML systems apply physical optimizations such as data flow rewrites in a heuristic manner. An interesting research direction is global data flow optimization over the conditional control flow, where data flow properties can be viewed as interesting properties and optimized jointly with other rewrites and physical operator selection. Additionally, automatic operator fusion for sparsity exploiting operators is challenging and received—despite its impact on asymptotic behavior—only little attention in the literature so far. Finally, memory-constrained scoring scenarios on edge devices would benefit from resource-constrained operator scheduling that takes the memory constraints into account.

4.4   AUTOMATIC OPERATOR FUSION

Opportunities for fused operators—in terms of fused chains of basic operators—are ubiquitous in ML programs. Benefits originate from avoiding unnecessary scans and materialized intermediates, as well as exploiting sparsity across operations. Given the high-performance impact and limitations of hand-coded fused operators, automatic fusion and code generation has received a lot of attention in the recent literature on database systems (e.g., query compilation), high-performance computing (e.g., loop fusion), and ML systems (e.g., operator fusion) [57]. While loop fusion requires an inter-loop dependency graph with fine-grained analysis of loop-carried dependencies, for operator fusion the dependencies are implicitly given by the data flow graph and operation semantics. From a compilation perspective, operator fusion only applies to the optimization scopes of lazy expression compilation and program compilation as defined in Section 4.1 because the goal is to merge sub-DAGs of operations into composite operations. Major challenges include fusion for sparse and compressed data, local and distributed operations, as well as optimizing fusion plans for complex DAGs of operations.

Example 4.6 Operator Fusion Assume the following expression of element-wise vector operations: $\mathbf{R} = (\mathbf{A} + s \cdot \mathbf{B}) \cdot \mathbf{C}$, which creates three vector intermediates, whose allocation and write is much more expensive than performing the actual multiply and add operations. Each vector operation can be viewed as a loop over its input cells. Operator fusion aims to merge the chain of operations into a single loop to improve temporal locality and avoid the two vector intermediates `tmp1` and `tmp2`.

```
for( i in 1:n )              -->  for( i in 1:n )
   tmp1[i,1] = s* B[i,1];          R[i,1] = (A[i,i] + s*B[i,1]) * C[i,1];
for( i in 1:n )
   tmp2[i,1] = A[i,1] + tmp1[i,1];
for( i in 1:n )
   R[i,1] = tmp2[i,1] * C[i,1];
```

For large vectors that do not fit into the last-level cache, these operations are memory-bandwidth bound. Since operator fusion reduces five reads and three writes to three reads and one write, performance is significantly improved. However, the memory requirements are slightly increased from 2+1 to 3+1 matrices, because all three inputs need to be pinned into main memory at the same time. ∎

Basic Approaches: There are two major approaches for fused operators in the literature: loop fusion and templates. First, loop fusion aims to generate code for the actual loop structures including data access to dense and/or sparse inputs, and potentially multiple outputs. This is a very generic approach but faces challenges regarding access to sparse input data, cache blocking, multi-threading, and the integration with data-parallel frameworks such as Spark. Second, the use of templates aims at a hybrid approach of hand-coded template skeletons combined with generated custom operator body code. Different template skeletons are provided for different accesses patterns (e.g., cell- or row-wise), which allows the dedicated handling of sparse or compressed inputs (especially for fused operators with multiple sparse inputs), cache blocking and multi-threading. The generated code then only deals with a single cell or row at-a-time, resulting in lean yet very efficient code. Table 4.2 provides an overview of current ML systems with operator fusion techniques. Note that other recent libraries like *NVIDIA TensorRT* [255] and *Intel Nervana Graph* [185] are subsumed by *TensorFlow XLA* as they plug into the *XLA* architecture as accelerators. Apart from the basic approach, important classification aspects are the support for sparse inputs and outputs, support for distributed operations, and the optimization strategy to find fusion plans in DAGs of linear algebra programs.

Specific Fusion Techniques: Many of the above systems further provide novel techniques covering individual aspects of efficient fusion plans.

Table 4.2: Overview of ML systems with operator fusion techniques

System	Year	Approach	Sparse	Distributed	Optimization
BTO [44]	2009	Loop Fusion	No	No	k-Greedy Cost-Based
Tupleware [89, 90]	2015	Loop Fusion	No	Yes	Heuristic
Kasen [380]	2016	Templates	(Yes)	Yes	Greedy Cost-Based
SystemML [57, 110]	2017	Templates	Yes	Yes	Exact Cost-Based
Weld [256, 257]	2017	Templates	(Yes)	Yes	Heuristic
Taco [184]	2017	Loop Fusion	Yes	No	Manual
Julia [47]	2017	Loop Fusion	Yes	No	Manual
TensorFlow [125]	2017	Loop Fusion	No	No	Manual
Tensor Comprehensions [338]	2018	Loop Fusion	No	No	Evolutionary Cost-Based
TVM [71, 73]	2018	Loop Fusion	No	No	ML-/Cost-Based

- **Micro Optimizations:** Similar to tiling for loop fusion, *Tupleware* [89] may chose a hybrid execution strategy for tile-at-a-time execution (to balance locality and vectorization), and it performs micro optimizations such as predication (replace control with data dependencies) and result allocation techniques.

- **Cross-Library Optimizations:** By providing a generic intermediate representation (IR) based on parallel loops and builders, *Weld* [256, 257] allows for cross-library optimization and code generation with the optimization scope of lazy expression evaluation.

- **Sparsity Exploitation:** As discussed in Section 4.3, exploiting sparsity across chains of operations can help avoid huge unnecessary intermediates and computation. *SystemML-SPOOF* [57, 110] provides means to automatically compile such sparsity-exploiting operators via `Outer` and `Cell` templates.

- **Iteration Schedules:** Fused operators with multiple dense/sparse inputs pose the problem of defining an iteration schedule. *Taco* [184] constructs iteration schedules according to recursively defined tensor storage formats with a focus on heterogeneous sparse formats. *TVM* considers loop transformations, thread binding, locality, memory scopes, latency hiding, and HW-aware tensorization [73]. Other work mapped this problem to the problem of join ordering [230].

Optimizing Operator Fusion Plans: Optimizing fusion plans for DAGs of linear algebra operations is challenging but important to tradeoff redundant computation vs. materialization if intermediates are consumed multiple times, and to enable sparsity-exploiting operators. Given that the problem of loop fusion is known to be NP-complete [94, 176], most systems use greedy algorithms [44, 338, 380], static or ML-based heuristics [73, 89, 256], or even manual declaration [47, 125, 184] to ensure moderate compilation overhead despite the exponential search space. However, recent work in *SystemML* [57] introduced a simple algorithm for the exact cost-based optimization of fusion plans with negligible optimization overhead. The key ideas are: (1) to explore all valid partial fusion plans; (2) partition these partial fusion plans into connected components that can be optimized independently; (3) restrict the search to interesting materialization points per partition; and (4) apply structural and cost-based pruning techniques, which work very well in practice.

Open Research Questions: Major open research questions center around algorithms for the optimization of fusion plans, especially with regard to DAG-structured execution plans, sparsity exploitation, optimality guarantees, heterogeneous hardware (such as FPGAs and ASICs in *TVM* [71, 73]), the interaction with logical and physical rewrites, and combinations thereof.

4.5   RUNTIME ADAPTATION

Many rewrites and optimization techniques—such as dynamic rewrites and execution type selection—rely on propagated size information in terms of matrix dimensions and sparsity for cost comparisons and validity constraints. Since this size information is also used in hard-constraints (e.g., memory estimates subject budgets), size propagation is usually done conservatively, meaning that sizes are only propagated if they can be guaranteed for all code paths. In practice, this often leads to unknowns during the initial compilation of complex ML algorithms, which in turn leads to very conservative fallback plans such as distributed operations with shuffle-based operators. Runtime adaptation techniques address this challenge by modifying runtime plans according to the size of intermediates during runtime.

Sources of Unknowns: Before we discuss common approaches to runtime adaptation it is important to understand the sources of these unknowns. We generally distinguish the following classes of sources.

- **Conditional Control Flow:** Control flow such as branches or loops with an unknown number of iterations can cause unknown sizes if different code paths result in different sizes of variables. Other sources include complex function call graphs, where functions are called with different sizes, as well as UDFs that render the size information of outputs and all intermediates derived from them as unknown.

- **Data-Dependent Operators:** There are also many data-dependent operators such as `aggregate` (grouping with aggregation), `table` (contingency tables), or `removeEmpty` (removal of empty rows or columns), where the data values affect the output dimensions. Similarly, computed index ranges and computed size expressions for `rand`, `seq`, or `matrix` (i.e., reshape or constructor) also render the output dimensions unknown. Furthermore, the propagation of sparsity is data-dependent for most operations, except reorg operations such as transpose, reshape, or order, which exactly preserve the sparsity.

- **Changing Dimensions/Sparsity:** Finally, there are several ML algorithms (e.g., for feature selection) that systematically change dimensions and sparsity in loops but due to a large or unknown number of iterations these loops cannot be unrolled such that the changed intermediates become unknown.

Some of these challenges can be addressed with better sparsity estimators, size propagation, and PL rewrites, while other fundamentally require runtime adaptation.

Basic Approaches: Overall, we differentiate two basic approaches to runtime adaptation that are directly influenced by the optimization scope, as discussed in Section 4.1. First, systems with interpretation or lazy expression compilation inherently adapt to changing sizes as expression are compiled—with an unconditional scope of a single operation or DAG of operations—for each evaluation of this expression. However, data-dependent operators in expressions still cause unknowns for remaining operations. Second, systems with the optimization scope of program compilation have to deal with all sources of unknowns. Therefore, existing work, for example in *SystemML*, aims for runtime adaptation via dynamic recompilation [54]. The basic idea is to mark DAGs with unknowns during initial compilation, and recompile runtime plans of marked DAGs during runtime according to the exact sizes of intermediates. Other systems that employ similar techniques are: (1) *SciDB* that repeatedly optimizes sub-plans, executes these sub-plans, and collects size information from local nodes [320]; as well as (2) *MatFast* that greedily selects operations of matrix multiplication chains via sampling, executes the first operations, and repeats with exactly known sparsity information [367]. However, note that a too fine-grained—e.g., single- or few-operation granularity—can negatively impact performance especially for lazily evaluated, distributed operations because it requires materialization or redundant evaluation of intermediates. In the following, we discuss dynamic recompilation in more detail.

Compile-Time Decisions on Recompilation: For simplicity and validity of generated plans, the granularity of recompilation are DAGs of operations, because the transition between basic blocks anyway requires to produce and bind the DAG outputs to logical variable names. This necessitates two compile-time decisions on recompilation: where to split DAGs to create necessary recompilation points, and if a DAG should be marked for recompilation. First, *SystemML* uses the original DAG structure (delineated by control flow) as a starting point but also splits DAGs after data-dependent operators and UDFs with unknown output sizes. Multiple data-dependent operations can be handled via a single split if there are no data dependencies between them. Second, if a DAG contains at least one operation for which a distributed execution type is chosen due to unknown dimensions or sparsity, the entire DAG is marked for dynamic recompilation during operator selection. This turned out to be a good heuristic because the latency of distributed operations easily hides the recompilation overheads (which is less than a millisecond for average DAGs of 100s of operators), while the benefits can be huge if unnecessary distributed operations can be avoided. Additionally, functions are marked as recompile-once—i.e., for re-compiling the function body on function entry with the sizes of the passed arguments—if they contain DAGs that require recompilation within loops.

Recompilation During Runtime: For recompilation during runtime, the DAGs from initial compilation are kept available for individual program blocks. Before executing the instructions of a block, we then check if the DAG is marked for recompilation. In this case, we create a deep copy of the DAG to perform non-reversible rewrites that are potentially enabled by known sizes. To avoid thread contention in task-parallel programs—as described in Section 5.2—each worker of a parallel `parfor` loop gets a separate copy of DAGs that require recompilation. Subsequently, the exact sizes of live variables are put into the leaf nodes of the DAG and propagated—with the same approach as described in Section 4.2—recursively bottom-up through the DAG. After size propagation, we apply again logical rewrites and operator selection to produce a temporary list of runtime instructions that are executed and subsequently discarded. With additional techniques for size propagation, this primitive for DAG recompilation is also used to recompile (1) entire functions on entry, (2) the body of `parfor` loops before optimization [58], and (3) what-if plans during resource optimization [150].

Open Research Questions: Runtime adaptation is important for generating efficient execution plans for complex ML algorithms but it is a trade-off between compilation overhead and the benefit from better size estimates. Interesting research directions include more sophisticated techniques for learning and reusing previous optimization decisions—as done for learning optimizers [318] and plan caching in database systems—to avoid unnecessary re-optimization, especially in the context of mini-batch algorithms where this overhead can be significant.

4.6   SUMMARY

This chapter surveyed common compilation techniques—in terms of rewrites and other compiler optimizations—of ML systems. Starting from different optimization scopes and objectives, we discussed size propagation and logical rewrites, physical rewrites and operators, as well as advanced techniques such as operator fusion and runtime adaptation. Many of these techniques have counterparts in query compilation and optimization, but DAGs of linear algebra operations and conditional control flow create additional challenges. Interestingly, the optimization of stored procedures in database systems also receives increasing attention (e.g., *SQLScript* [50], *Froid* [280], and *GraalVM* [60]) and shares many of these challenges. We, therefore, believe that these challenges such as cardinality estimation, size propagation, and holistic optimization constitute interesting directions for data management research. In the words of Pat Selinger: *"It's a never-ending quest for an increasingly better model and repertoire of optimization and execution techniques"* [353].

CHAPTER 5

Execution Strategies

So far, we primarily discussed compilation techniques in terms of rewrites and optimizations. A second major aspect of ML systems—but especially of large-scale ML systems—is the underlying execution strategy. Generally, there are three categories.

- **Data-parallel Execution:** (run the same operation over data partitions in parallel) for batch algorithms, or hybrid batch/mini-batch algorithms;

- **Task-parallel Execution:** (run different tasks such as iterations in parallel) for custom parallelization of independent subtasks; and

- **Parameter Servers:**[1] (compute partial or full model updates over data partitions, with periodic model synchronization) for mini-batch algorithms.

There are also hybrid approaches, which combine forms of these execution strategies. In this chapter, we provide an overview of these execution strategies, classify existing ML systems accordingly, and discuss interesting runtime techniques, including special runtime optimizers. Finally, in the context of deep learning, there is a trend toward exploiting accelerators such as GPUs, FPGAs, and custom ASICs for training and scoring, which is another specific hybrid execution strategy.

Classification of Existing Systems: Many systems provide multiple execution strategies, which usually target the system's primary application use cases. Table 5.1 summarizes the main system categories and their execution strategies. Numerical computing frameworks like *R*, *MATLAB*, and *Julia* focus primarily on general-purpose numerical computing and, thus, provide low-level means of thread-level and distributed task parallelism. For example, parallel for loops can be realized in *R* with the packages doMC and doSNOW [103], in *MATLAB* with the parallel computing toolbox [311], and *Julia* with @parallel and @distributed. Batch ML systems primarily focus on data- and task-parallel large-scale ML for training and scoring. An example is *SystemML* which automatically compiles local or distributed data-parallel operations and provides parfor loops for local or distributed task parallelism. In contrast, mini-batch-centric systems—as often used for deep learning—like *TensorFlow* do not need distributed data-parallel operations but primarily focus on a parameter server architecture for data- and model-parallelism, very good accelerator support, and local task parallelism for concurrent operations

---

[1]Parameter server architectures are often separated into model- and data-parallel execution but we use model parallelism synonymous with parameter servers to differentiate them from purely data-parallel strategies.

and parallel loops (e.g., `tf.while_loop` with `parallel_iterations`). The boundaries between these categories are fluent, because for example parallel for loops can emulate data-parallel operations and synchronous parameter servers. However, this classification allows for a high-level comparison of existing systems with regard to their primary focus.

Table 5.1: Categories of ML systems with different execution strategies (TLP/Dist.)

Category	Examples	Data-Par	Task-Par	Param-Serv	Accelerators
Numerical Computing	*R, Julia*		✓/ ✓		
Batch ML	*SystemML*	✓/ ✓	✓/ ✓	(✓/ ✓)	(GPUs)
Mini-Batch ML	*TensorFlow*		✓/	✓/ ✓	ASICs/GPUs

5.1 DATA-PARALLEL EXECUTION

Probably the most common approach to large-scale ML is a data-parallel execution strategy, leveraging existing data-parallel frameworks such as *MapReduce* [97], *Spark* [370], or *Flink* [29] for fault-tolerant computation on commodity hardware. The basic approach is to run an operation over partitions of the data—in local or distributed environments—in parallel, which might also involve global grouping and aggregation. For multi-threaded (i.e., local) operations, this execution strategy is rather straightforward, disregarding efficient cache-conscious operations, due to direct access to subsets of the data. Therefore, in this section, we primarily focus on distributed data-parallel execution using distributed collections of key-value data, and only briefly discuss the exploitation of multi-threading and single instruction multiple data (SIMD) parallelism.

Data Representations: One of the most important aspects of data-parallel ML is the underlying data representation of matrices and more general tensors. In general, matrices are logically partitioned into blocks and represented as collections of block indexes and block values. Blocks might have fixed or variable logical size, which in turn leads to variable or fixed physical block sizes in the presence of sparsity; most systems rely on fixed logical sizes as it simplifies global index reconstruction and join processing [55, 320]. Regarding the concrete logical partitioning and data representation, there are three predominant approaches with different tradeoffs.

- **Block-Partitioned Matrices:** Blocked (also known as tiled or chunked) matrices are partitioned into fixed-size squared (e.g., 1K × 1K) or rectangular blocks. Squared blocks provide the unique advantages of: (1) guaranteeing input and output alignment in binary and ternary operations independent of the join dimensions; and (2) allowing block-local transpose operations without shuffle. Additional advantages of blocks in general are (3) amortizing processing and storage overheads; (4) bounding memory requirements even in the presence of millions or billions of features; and (5) allowing for cache-conscious blocked operations. At the same time, converting row-wise text files or *Spark* datasets into blocked representations requires shuffling in case of unaligned physical partitions and rows might be split up into different blocks, potentially residing on different nodes. Example systems with blocked matrix representations are *RIOT* [381], *PEGASUS* [172], *SystemML* [55, 123], *SciDB* [320], *Cumulon* [149], *Distributed R* [222, 339], *DMac* [366], *Spark MLlib*'s block matrices [368], *Gilbert* [293], *MatFast* [367], and *SimSQL* [221]. Finally, *FlexiFaCT* also uses squared block representations for tensor and tensor-matrix factorizations [46].

- **Row-/Column Partitioned Matrices:** A second very common representation are row- (and less common column-) partitioned matrices. These row-partitioned matrices are simple collections of row indexes and rows. The major benefits are a seamless conversion (without shuffling) from row-wise text files and datasets, and guaranteed local access to entire rows, which also allows row aggregates such as rowSums without shuffling. However, in languages like Java or Scala this representation causes additional storage overhead due to object and array headers per row, which can be significant in case of few features or ultra-sparse matrices. Furthermore, operations like $\mathbf{X}^\top \mathbf{X}$ become very inefficient in the presence of many features as row-wise access does not allow for cache blocking and thus, very cache-unfriendly behavior. For example, with a matrix of 2K features, each row outer product flushes the entire L3 cache and thus, causes cache thrashing across threads. A special case of row-partitioned matrices are *Spark MLlib*'s LabeledPoint, which represents entire rows and their label. Example systems with row-partitioned matrices are *Spark MLlib* [234], *Mahout Samsara* [301], *Emma* [30], *SimSQL* [221], and many UDF-centric systems such as *Bismarck* [115], *Tupleware* [89], and *Hyper* [263]. Obviously, systems with support for rectangular blocks such as *Distributed R* [222, 339] can also enforce row- or column partitioned matrices.

- **Algorithm-Specific Partitioning:** Additionally, there are also operation- and algorithm-centric data representations. This includes, for example, heterogeneous block partitioning for matrix inversion [357], redundant matrix storage with complementary row and column partitioning for matrix factorization [95, 226], as well as joint data-and-model partitioning for independent updates in *DSGD* [120] and *Fugue* [198]. Although the pre-processing costs are often easily amortized for such expensive operations or algorithms, any specific data representations might not allow for data reuse across algorithms anymore.

Example 5.1   Various Operations with Squared Blocks   Squared block-partitioned matrices are probably the most versatile distributed matrix representation. For example, Figure 5.1 shows common linear algebra operations with different requirements and how they exploit squared blocking. First, element-wise multiplication requires a join over matrix cells. Fixed-size blocking allows for a one-to-one join over block indexes and produces an equivalently blocked output.

Second, matrix transposition flips row and column indexes. Squared blocking allows for a block-local transpose reorganization without the need for data shuffling. Third, matrix multiplications require a join over the common dimension, i.e., column indexes of the left and row indexes of the right input. Squared blocking again ensures alignment, which would be impossible with rectangular blocks, and equivalent output blocking, which is important for composing complex distributed programs. ∎

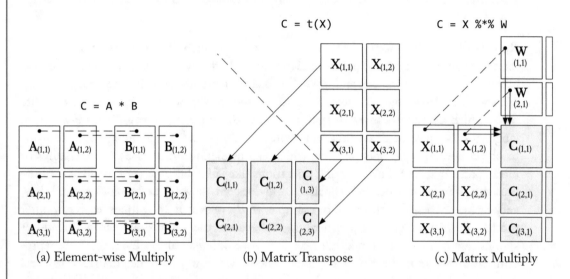

(a) Element-wise Multiply   (b) Matrix Transpose   (c) Matrix Multiply

Figure 5.1: Example data-parallel operations.

Sparse Block Representations: Representing a matrix as a collection of index-block pairs further allows to encode blocks independently as dense or sparse blocks in order to account for skew of non-zero entries. Probably the most common sparse representations are compressed sparse rows (CSR), compressed sparse columns (CSC), and coordinate format (COO) [157, 254, 297], which all encode non-zero values as index-value pairs or triples in row- or column-major representation. For example, a 3×3 matrix with the non-zeros .7, .1, .2, .4, .3 at positions $(0, 0)$, $(0, 2)$, $(1, 0)$, $(1, 1)$, and $(2, 1)$, would be represented in CSR with an array for row pointers (offsets) $[0, 2, 4, 5]$ and two arrays for column index and values $[0, 2, 0, 1, 1]$ and $[.7, .1, .2, .4, .3]$. In contrast, the COO format, simply stores—sometimes sorted—triples of (row-index, column-index, value), which is advantageous for ultra-sparse matrices where the CSR row offsets would dominate the storage requirements. There are also numerous hybrid formats such as hybrid (HYB), which combines ELLPACK (ELL) and COO [43] and SLACID, which combines CSR and COO [177] that aim to combine advantages of the individual formats. ML Systems often support a subset of common schemes. For example *SystemML* uses CSR, MCSR (modified CSR with row-local allocation for more flexibility on incremental updates, *SystemML*'s default), and

COO and selects formats for intermediates according to data and operation characteristics [55], while *TensorFlow* only supports COO because it easily generalized to tensors of (e.g., quadruples for a 3D-tensor), and it allows the internal storage as a (d+1)-column dense block [22].

Physical Partitioning: The distributed collection of indexes and values is then physically organized in partitions, where each partition is stored and processed locally on a single node [222]. This partitioning is important because it is the granularity for caching and processing. When reading from persistent storage such as HDFS, the underlying block storage (with its block size configuration) determines the initial partitioning. Typical sizes are 128 MB partitions, but if the underlying storage is compressed (e.g., in Parquet) the in-memory partition may be significantly larger. For block- or row-partitioned matrices, these physical partitions then hold multiple key-value pairs (e.g., 16 dense blocks for *SystemML*'s default $1K \times 1K$ squared blocks), which implies that the data representation influences the maximum number of partitions—and thus, the maximum degree of parallelism—as well as the minimum size of physical partitions. Furthermore, data-parallel frameworks such as Spark and other systems allow custom partitioning functions for data shuffling, which can be used to co-partition matrices and avoid data transfer [368]. Commonly used partitioning functions are hash-partitioning [55, 221, 222], round-robin-partitioning [221], or 2D-block-partitioning [95]. This partitioning is created either explicitly via `repartition` transformations, or implicitly on each shuffle-based operation (e.g., when converting a row-wise input into a blocked representation).

Partitioning-Preserving Operations: As mentioned before, data-parallel frameworks such as *Spark* [370] exploit any existing data partitioning for reducing data transfer on joins (e.g., on binary operations such as matrix multiplications and element-wise operations). For example, consider a simple hash partitioning, where key-value pairs are assigned to partitions with `hash(key)%#partitions`. Given two inputs with hash partitioning and an equal number of partitions, allows for an efficient 1-1 join of partitions with equal IDs instead of a repartition (i.e., shuffle-based) join. Hence, it is crucial for performance to preserve this partitioning. A data-parallel operation is implicitly partitioning-preserving if keys remain unchanged and the distributed computing framework can recognize that. Examples are `filter` and `mapValues`, but also explicit declaration on `mapPartitions`. Partitioning is also important for mini-batch algorithms over large-scale data as used in deep learning. Typical batching approaches are coarse-grained batching or queues, which allow to overlap indexed batch access and computation of the previous batch. Both scenarios can benefit from partitioning. Data-parallel frameworks usually perform a full scan for block lookups, which is unproblematic for in-memory datasets because filtering blocks only touches keys which are—for squared $1K \times 1K$ dense blocks—10^6 times smaller than the overall datasize. However, for out-of-core datasets—i.e., datasets that do not fit in aggregate cluster memory—entire partitions are read and deserialized, which causes unnecessary overhead. In contrast, existing hash partitioning allows for computing relevant partition

IDs for given block indexes and direct partition access via `lookup` or `PartitionPruningRDDs`, which avoids the unnecessary I/O.

Multi-threading and SIMD: For efficient block operations—on local or blocked matrices—many frameworks also employ data-parallel SIMD intrinsics and multi-threading. Frameworks in native programming languages primarily focus on SIMD to exploit the increasing width of SIMD registers, and thus, the available compute bandwidth and more efficient memory access. Multi-threading is additionally applied by creating one or more tasks of row- or column-ranges per thread together with (reused) thread pools for load balancing. For memory-bandwidth-bound ML workloads, multi-threaded operations quickly saturate peak memory bandwidth, independent of the use of SIMD. However, for mini-batch algorithms, where intermediates might fit in the cache hierarchy and, of course, compute-intensive operations, SIMD is essential. For this reason, *Spark MLlib*'s block matrices [368] and *SystemML* [259]—which both rely on the Java virtual machine's (JVM's) auto vectorization capabilities that are currently very limited regarding packed SIMD instructions—use Java native interface (JNI) to call basic linear algebra subprograms (BLAS) and custom operations.

Open Research Questions: Most data-parallel frameworks—except traditional array databases—support only matrices. It is an interesting open question how to support efficient data-parallel operations over tensors, especially with regard to distributed blocked representations as well as sparse tensor formats and operations. Other challenges include operations over inputs of different data types, and the handling of heterogeneous and nested tensors.

5.2   TASK-PARALLEL EXECUTION

While large-scale ML systems primarily focus on data-parallel computation, there are also numerous use cases for task-parallel computation such as cross validation (CV), ensemble learning (EL), hyper-parameter tuning, and special partitionable ML algorithms. For example, algorithms like Random Forest are very naturally expressed in a task-parallel manner to learn many decision tress in parallel. While these use cases are often embarrassingly parallel, they exhibit other challenges such as the optimization of hybrid data- and task-parallel computations (as discussed in Section 5.4), data partitioning and locality in distributed environments, as well as the integration with schedulers of data-parallel frameworks to share cluster resources.

Taxonomy of Task-Parallelism: Language constructs such as *MATLAB*'s `parfor` [311], *SystemML*'s `parfor` [58], or *R*'s parallel `foreach` [103] provide parallel for loops, which allow a wide variety of task-parallel computations. To provide an overview of relevant problems, we use a taxonomy of task-parallel ML algorithms [58]. Table 5.2 shows the two data- and model-oriented dimensions. The data-oriented dimension distinguishes three main classes. First, disjoint data means that iterations access non-overlapping subsets of the input data. An example are univariate statistics, which compute summary statistics per column. Second, overlapping data refers to overlapping subsets of the data as used for model selection, where each iteration builds a model over a subset of features, or k-fold cross validation, where each iteration builds a model over k-1 partitions. Third, all data consumes the entire dataset per iteration. This is often the case for hyper-parameter tuning or ensemble learning, which allow optimizations such as caching and shared scans.

Table 5.2: Taxonomy of task-parallel M algorithms with examples

	Single Model	Multiple Models
Disjoint Data	DSGD [120], Data Generation	Univariate Statistics, Independent Models
Overlapping Data	Cascade SVM [129], ALS-DS, EM	Bivariate Statistics, Meta Learning, CV
All Data	Multi-Class/-Label (1-vs-rest), EL	Meta Learning, EL

Example 5.2   Task-Parallel Hyper Parameter Tuning   As an example of hyper-parameter tuning, consider a scenario of systematically evaluating the model accuracy with different regularization parameters $\lambda \in (10^{-1}, 10^{-2}, 10^{-3}, 10^{-4})$ for our linear regression script from Example 4.1.

```
1:  lambda = 10^(-seq(1,4));
2:  R = matrix(0, nrow(lambda), 2);
3:  parfor(i in 1:nrow(lambda)) {
4:    beta = linregCG(X, y, as.scalar(lambda[i,]));
5:    R2 = evalLinreg(Xval, yval, beta);
6:    R[i,] = list(lambda[i,], R2);
7:  }
```

In detail, we first create a vector of the different lambda values. For each such value, we then train and evaluate a linear regression model, where we use the coefficient of determination R^2 to validate the goodness of fit over a hold-out validation set. Due to the absence of loop-carried dependencies, we use a `parfor` loop to indicate the potential for task parallelism. Since we train and evaluate the models over the same inputs $\mathbf{X}$, $\mathbf{y}$, $\mathbf{X}_{val}$, and $\mathbf{y}_{val}$, there is substantial potential for reusing intermediates and scan sharing across parallel iterations.   ■

Physical Operators: Executing a task-parallel subprogram such as `parfor(i in 1:N){...}`, entails the steps of: (1) task partitioning for grouping iterations into tasks (e.g., via fixed size partitioning, or factoring [154]); (2) optional data partitioning for efficient distributed data access and execution; (3) parallel execution of tasks; and (4) result aggregation to merge the individual results of all parallel tasks. Similar to the selection of physical operators described in Section 4.3, state-of-the-art systems provide different physical operators for each of these steps, depending on data, cluster, and program characteristics [58]. For example, common physical operators for parallel execution include the following.

- **Local parfor**: A local `parfor` operator runs in the driver process with multi-threaded workers to execute the individual parfor tasks. There are two major uses cases. First, for small data and moderate compute workload—where all body operations are also scheduled to local operations—this strategy avoids unnecessary latency and data transfer for distributed execution. Second, for very large, non-partitionable input data, the body operations are scheduled to distributed data-parallel operations. Having such data-parallel operations in the `parfor` body requires a local `parfor` driver because nested resilient distributed dataset (RDD) operations (RDD operations spawn out of tasks of an RDD operation) are not supported by *Spark* (or *MapReduce*) as nested parallelism on a fully occupied cluster might cause cluster deadlocks. A multi-threaded driver with data-parallel operations leads to concurrent data-parallel jobs, potentially inter-mixed with local operations. The available degree of parallelism is distributed top-down over potentially nested `parfor` loops to multi-threaded operations.

- **Remote parfor**: Complementary to the local `parfor` operator, the remote `parfor` operator runs the entire `parfor` loop as a single distributed job. This operator is applicable if the memory estimates of body operations—potentially over partitioned inputs, as discussed later—fit into the memory budget of remote workers. For example, in *SystemML* such a remote `parfor` operator translates to a single map-side MR or Spark job, sharing cluster resources with other data-parallel jobs. Read-only input matrices are read once and reused across executor tasks. The primary use cases for this strategy are loops with a very large number of iterations, loops with expensive iterations (e.g., compute-intensive operations, or iterative algorithms), and partitionable problems over large datasets.

- **Remote DP parfor**: Special cases of partitionable workloads are addressed with fused operators that combine data partitioning and execution to avoid materializing individual partitions in HDFS, which can be problematic for large numbers of files. Specifically, if the `parfor` body is guaranteed to access disjoint data of a single partitioned input, where each partition is accessed exactly once, a remote DP `parfor` operator can be used to execute the entire `parfor` loop in a data-parallel manner via map-side partitioning, shuffling, and reduce-side execution. An example are univariate statistics—which compute various summary statistics per column—over a dataset that is too large for broadcasting to all executors. Here, the fused operator partitions the major input in blocked representation column-wise, and executes the body program for each column.

In *SystemML*, these operators are selected—as part of a larger rewrite set—by a dedicated `parfor` optimizer, which is triggered on each execution of a top-level (i.e., potentially nested) `parfor` loop because this ensures that the number of iterations as well as input and output data characteristics are known.

Partitioning and Data Locality: Apart from purely task-parallel problems, `parfor` is also used to execute—potentially complex—subprograms over independent partitions of the data. At the surface this is similar to emulating data-parallel operations. However, in contrast to data-parallel execution strategies as described in Section 5.1, these subprograms dictate the access to entire partitions and thus, affect the physical partitioning. The challenge is to automatically identify the access patterns of indexing operations in the `parfor` body and partition the inputs if it is valid and beneficial. Examples are row-, column-, or block-partitioning [58, 149]. For efficient distributed operations over partitioned inputs, it is further necessary to explicitly map `parfor` iterations, or `parfor` tasks in terms of groups of iterations, to accessed partitions in order to leverage data locality on data-parallel execution frameworks [58]. Furthermore, if the partitioned matrix is used read-only in a surrounding iterative algorithm, this partitioning can be reused to amortize the partitioning costs across multiple `parfor` instances.

Example 5.3   Batch Partitioning for DL Scoring   Consider an example scenario of prediction, where we have a trained CNN model and want to classify a large number of images. Since the classification of individual images is independent, this is naturally expressed in a task-parallel manner, either row-wise (per image) or batch-wise (batch of images), where the latter allows for better exploitation of the underlying HW. Here, Ni is the number of images (i.e., nrow(X)), Nc is the number of classes, and B=100 is the batch size.

```
# a) row-wise CNN prediction        # b) batch-wise CNN prediction
Prob = matrix(0, Ni, Nc)            Prob = matrix(0, Ni, Nc)
parfor( i in 1:Ni ) {               parfor( i in 1:ceil(Ni/B) ) {
   Xb = X[i,];                         Xb = X[((i-1)*B+1):min(i*B,Ni),];
   Prob[i,] = ... # CNN scoring        out = ... # CNN scoring
}                                       Prob[((i-1)*B+1):min(i*B,Ni),] = out;
                                    }
```

Since X is large and CNN scoring is compute-intensive, we aim to compile a remote `parfor` for distributed computation, with appropriate partitioning of X. For the row-wise formulation (a), this requires row partitioning to reconstruct entire rows, from the underlying blocked representation. Similarly, the batch-wise formulation (b) requires block partitioning into batches of 100 rows. In contrast to data-parallel operations, the CNN scoring is a complex, user-defined linear algebra program.   ∎

Integration with Data-Parallel Systems: Systems that aim to support both data- and task-parallel computation, typically map task-parallel constructs like `parfor` to data-parallel primitives such as map or reduce tasks in *MapReduce* and `flatMapToPair` or `foreach` on *Spark*

[55, 58]. This integration allows sharing the underlying distributed computation framework, as well as cluster resources including the reuse of cached data. Other work similarly allows general OpenMP applications and provides a custom OpenMP backend that maps tasks to the database scheduler in order to enable prioritization of concurrent transactional or analytical workloads [355]. Furthermore, this hybrid task- and data-parallel execution also allows for additional optimizations, which will be discussed in Section 5.4

5.3 PARAMETER SERVERS (MODEL-PARALLEL EXECUTION)

For mini-batch algorithms—as commonly used for deep neural networks (DNNs) and general-purpose optimizers like SGD—as well as complex models like latent dirichlet allocation (LDA), the predominant parallelization strategy is the *parameter server* architecture [24, 96]. The existing literature often distinguishes between data- and model-parallel parameter servers [96, 359, 360]. However, to separate these execution strategies from data-parallel execution introduced in Section 5.1, we use model-parallel execution as a general term for parameter servers. In this section, we give an overview of design choices for the deployment of these parameter servers, covering their architecture and update strategies, as well as their impact on the tradeoff between statistical and hardware efficiency.[2]

Data-Parallel Parameter Servers: The general parameter server (PS) architecture consists of N workers (sometimes clustered into worker groups [210]), M parameter servers, and an optional coordinator. Figure 5.2a shows the architecture of a data-parallel parameter server. In this architecture, each worker holds a disjoint partition of the input data (or overlapping but differently randomized partitions), and a replica of all model parameters. While processing a batch, each worker performs an entire forward and backward pass of the given training function to compute parameter gradients (ΔW in Figure 5.2a), which are then sent back to the central parameter server to apply it to the global model. There are different optimizers such as SGD, SGD-Nesterov, SGD-momentum, RMSprop, Adam, and Adagrad, but their model updates are commonly basic element-wise operations. Before processing the next batch, each worker fetches the current model from the parameter server. This communication is often implemented via *push* (update the global model) and *pull*/fetch (obtain the global model from the PS) primitives [96, 210]. The most fine-grained (and common) update frequency is once per batch, but there are also scenarios that allow other regimes of multiple batches [96], an entire epoch [273], or based on the size of sparse updates [161]. However, communicating full model updates per batch often constitutes prohibitive communication and aggregation overhead. This challenge is tackled via optimizations such as pre-fetching [91, 159], range-based push and pull

---

[2]Statistical efficiency is a well-defined term for algorithm efficiency in terms of the number of accessed data points to achieve a certain accuracy. Clearly, increasing the independence of distributed computation increases the hardware efficiency, but decreases the statistical efficiency due additional staleness of model replicas. However, this tradeoff is nonlinear because too small batches also increase the variance per batch, which can be counter-productive in terms of statistical efficiency.

(communicate only subset of the model) [159, 210], and residual accumulation as used in 1-bit stochastic gradient descent (communicate partial gradients quantized to 1 bit but remember local quantization error) [305]. Example systems that support data-parallel parameter servers include all major deep learning frameworks such as *TensorFlow* [23], *MXNet* [72], *PyTorch* [264], and *CNTK* [304].

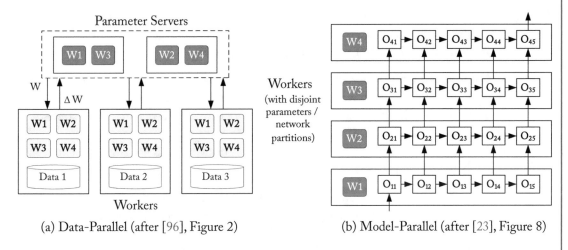

(a) Data-Parallel (after [96], Figure 2)   (b) Model-Parallel (after [23], Figure 8)

Figure 5.2: Data- and model-parallel parameter server architectures.

Model-Parallel Parameter Servers: In contrast to the general PS architecture (which still requires each worker to hold the entire model), model-parallel parameter servers address the challenge of very deep or wide networks, where the entire model (i.e., the weight matrices/tensors for all layers) does not fit into a single node or device. In this architecture, shown in Figure 5.2b, each worker is responsible for a disjoint partition of the overall learning network or model, and only holds the weights or data required for these partitions. Thus, each worker acts simultaneously as worker and parameter server. However, network edges (i.e., data dependencies) that cross partition boundaries require the exchange of intermediate results. For example in Figure 5.2b, we have a chain of four workers with five dependencies between adjacent workers. Apart from distributed model storage, this architecture also offers parallelization opportunities for independent network partitions (e.g., parallel lanes in a large network architecture) and pipeline parallelism. This is similar to query plan partitioning in distributed data stream management systems [163]. As an example for pipeline parallelism, consider again Figure 5.2b: the computation of O_{12} in worker 1 can be overlapped with transferring the intermediate from O_{11} to O_{21} and computing O_{21}. For sufficiently deep pipelines of operators, this approach can fully utilize all workers. Due to the dependence on the network architecture—which can be very narrow for deep networks—and often larger communication overhead, this model-parallel architecture is, however, more common in multi-device than multi-node setups. In contrast to data-parallel parameter servers, this model-parallel architecture does not affect the statistical efficiency. Hence, in practice both data- and model-parallel parameter servers are sometimes combined to effectively leverage large clusters of machines [96]. In contrast, *Petuum's* model-parallelism [359] uses so-called *scheduling functions* to select independent or weakly correlated parameters for parallel processing, which also offers the flexibility of combining data- and model-parallel computation.

Update Strategies: In the context of data-parallel parameter servers, one of the most important design choices is the used update strategy, which offer different tradeoffs between statistical and hardware efficiency. Major categories include the following.

- **Synchronous (BSP):** Basic synchronous parameter servers use a global barrier to wait for parameter gradients from all workers and redistribute the model after aggregation. While this ensure that each worker gets the current model for the next batch, this strategy is prone to stragglers because all workers are blocked until the slowest worker finishes. In this setting, the batch size per worker is sometimes derived via B/N from the batch size and number of workers [126].

- **Asynchronous (ASP):** Since optimizers such as SGD are robust to additional noise introduced by asynchronous updates, asynchronous parameter servers update and redistribute the global parameters without blocking individual workers. While this approach overcomes the problem of stragglers, it decreases the statistical efficiency because workers use stale parameters.

- **Synchronous with Backup Workers [67]:** More recently, a hybrid approach that combines the strength of both strategies, synchronous with backup workers, has been introduced [22, 67]. In this approach, there are N+b workers and the parameter server blocks until updates from N workers have been received.

- **Stale-Synchronous [144] (SSP):** Similar to backup workers, the stale-synchronous regime [144, 159, 359] uses weak synchronization barriers but via a maximum staleness constraint of s clocks between the fastest and slowest worker. If this constraint is violated, the faster workers are forced to wait; otherwise, workers can use locally cached versions to reduce communication.

- **Hogwild! [288]:** For multi-threaded environments and sparse optimization problems (i.e., where each model update affect only a small subset of parameters), *Hogwild!* optimistically updates the shared model without any locking. This approach avoids thread contention while achieving near optimal convergence rates because conflicts are very unlikely for sparse model updates. Similar techniques can also be applied in the context of asynchronous parameter servers for aggregating concurrently arriving model updates.

- **Decentralized [213]:** Despite the general parameter server architecture of M physical parameter servers, the global parameter server can be viewed as a central coordinator, which might become a scalability bottleneck for large numbers of workers. Therefore, recent work explored an alternative architecture where workers only communicate updates to their local peers in a given network topology [213]. This approach has the potential to reduce communication and aggregation overheads, while still being able to globally converge over time. Systems with a similar decentralized architecture include *Ako* with peer-to-peer exchange of partial gradient updates [349], and *FlexRR*, with peer-to-peer re-assignment of work [138].

Data Partitioning Schemes: Furthermore, there are a number of common data partitioning schemes, which all can be realized via linear algebra operations. This enables the reuse of local and distributed data-parallel operations to ensure robustness for large training data sets.

- **Disjoint Contiguous:** Each worker receives a contiguous partition of rows from the feature and label matrices, which can be realized via right indexing
  `Xp = X[id*blocksize+1:(id+1)*blocksize,].`

- **Disjoint Round Robin:** Rows of **X** are distributed to workers round robin, which can be realized with a selection matrix multiply per worker
  `Xp = removeEmpty(diag(seq(1,nrow(X))%%k)==id), margin=rows) %*% X.`

- **Disjoint Random:** In this scheme, each worker receives a random non-overlapping selection of rows. This can be implemented by creating a random permutation matrix **P** (e.g., with `table(seq(1,nrow(X)), sample(nrow(X),nrow(X),FALSE))`) and subsequent permutation matrix multiply per worker
  `Xp = P[id*blocksize+1:(id+1)*blocksize,] %*% X.`

- **Overlap Reshuffle:** Here, every worker receives the full data set but in a different randomly reshuffled order. For each worker we create a new random permutation matrix **P**$_i$ and reshuffle the entire dataset with `Xp = Pi %*% X`.

Fault Tolerance: Training deep neural networks can take hours to weeks. This time scale together with distributed data- or model-parallel computation requires fault tolerance to mitigate failures and preemption [22]. However, in contrast to fault tolerance via lineage or materialization in *Spark* and *Hadoop* (as explained in more detail in Section 7.2), weaker schemes are sufficient for mini-batch algorithms that are able to tolerate the loss of individual batches or partitions [22, 243]. Common techniques include user-defined checkpointing primitives such as `save`/`restore` and custom checkpoint retention schemes in *TensorFlow* [22], replication of parameters between parameter servers for hot failover [210], and loss function approximation for lost partitions [243].

Federated ML: Distributed parameter servers still require data consolidation in a dedicated cluster infrastructure. In contrast, federated ML [187] aims at equipping edge and end-user devices (such as IoT and mobile devices) with necessary ML training capabilities to ensure *data* *privacy* by refraining from data consolidation. Major challenges are the data communication overhead (limited communication, massively distributed, unbalanced data), processing performance and capabilities of the end devices (unreliable or offline compute nodes), training and validation without direct access to labeled or raw data, and data privacy [187, 232]. Similar to data-parallel parameter servers, in Federated ML, each device acts as a worker that computes local updates, and sends gradient or model updates to a central group of parameter servers that aggregate and redistribute the global model. Due to the massive scale and limited communication, a major focus is on reducing the communication overhead. Apart from different update strategies and frequencies, lossless and lossy compression, sparsification, and residual accumulation, additional specialized techniques have been proposed in this context. First, random client sampling per iteration [187, 232] ensures a moderate number of workers, and copes with unbalanced data and unreliable nodes. Second, structured and sketched updates [188] perform systematic sparsification of updates, where structured updates learn from a restricted space (low-rank or random selection), while sketched updates learn a full update and subsample or quantize afterward. Similarly, deep gradient compression only sends sparse gradients [214]— i.e., values that are larger than a threshold, with residual accumulation—but combines that with momentum correction, gradient clipping, momentum factor masking, and warm-up taining.

Open Research Questions: The diversity and complexity of applied techniques for reducing the communication overhead and staleness is rapidly increasing. This trend together with the complex accuracy-runtime tradeoff, renders it increasingly difficult to find good configurations (e.g., number of workers/servers, or quantization/sparsification techniques). Similarly, it has been shown that the maximum useful batch size varies significantly, and is strongly optimizer- and data-dependent [309]. Accordingly, we believe that the online tuning of configurations and communication patterns during runtime poses an interesting direction for future work.

5.4   HYBRID EXECUTION STRATEGIES

Apart from purely data-, task-, or model-parallel execution, there are various use cases that necessitate hybrid execution strategies. Example use cases are ensemble learning, cross validation, or hyper-parameter tuning over large datasets, which allow for task-parallel training of different configurations, while requiring distributed data-parallel jobs accessing the feature matrix **X**. The most common hybrid strategies are (1) task- and data-parallel, as well as (2) model- and data-parallel execution.

Batching: Many iterative ML algorithms for classification, regression, and clustering rely on matrix-vector multiplications over the feature matrix **X** to converge to an optimal model. These matrix-vector multiplications are not compute- but memory-bandwidth-bound due to a low operational intensity of only two floating point operations per matrix entry read from main memory.[3] A common technique to address this bottleneck in the context of task-parallel training over a shared input matrix is scan sharing via batching. Instead of performing multiple independent matrix-vector multiplications $\mathbf{Xv}_1$, $\mathbf{Xv}_2$, and $\mathbf{Xv}_n$, the idea is to concatenate $\mathbf{v}_1$, $\mathbf{v}_2$, and $\mathbf{v}_n$ to $\mathbf{V}$ and perform a single matrix-matrix multiplication $\mathbf{XV}$ which requires a single pass over the feature matrix. Example systems that apply batching are *Columbus* [373] and *TuPAQ* [317]. This static batching often improves performance by better utilization of the compute bandwidth. However, this approach is limited to scenarios with a homogenous ML algorithm—without data-dependent control flow—and a fixed number of iterations. Instead, recent work introduced on-the-fly batching for dynamic computation graphs (like *PyTorch*) via lazy evaluation, padding and masking [246].

Example 5.4 Batching of Matrix-Vector Multiplications Assume we have a $1M \times 1K$ dense matrix in double precision (of size 8 GB), and we want to compute 8 matrix-vector multiplications. Further assume a node with two Xeon E5-2440, 2×32 GB/s memory bandwidth and 2×115.2 GFLOP/s compute bandwidth. The expected improvement of batching is then computed—under the assumptions of reaching peak performance, and no cache reuse across concurrent scans—as follows:

$$\begin{aligned}
T(8MV) &= 8 \cdot \max(8\,\text{GB}/64\,\text{GB/s}, 2\,\text{GFLOP}/230.4\,\text{GFLOP/s}) \\
&= 8 \cdot \max(0.125\,\text{s}, 0.009\,\text{s}) = 1\,\text{s} \\
T(M8V) &= \max(8\,\text{GB}/64\,\text{GB/s}, 8 \cdot 2\,\text{GFLOP}/230.4\,\text{GFLOP/s}) \\
&= \max(0.125\,\text{s}, 0.069\,\text{s}) = 0.125\,\text{s}.
\end{aligned} \tag{5.1}$$

In this scenario, we get an ideal improvement of 8x but we see that the read and compute times almost reach a break-even point. This characteristic is the underlying reason why systems such as *TuPAQ* [317] use a heuristic batch size of 10 to tradeoff the performance benefit from batching and the potential accuracy benefit from searching models sequentially. ■

Runtime Piggybacking: In order to allow scan sharing for convergence-based ML algorithms—i.e., with an unknown number of iterations—runtime piggybacking moves these batching decisions to the runtime level. For examples, *SystemML's* parfor optimizer [58] automatically enables runtime piggybacking without the need for script changes. The basic idea is a *wait-merge-submit-return* loop. When enabled, distributed jobs from concurrent parfor tasks are intercepted, put into a queue, merged into a smaller or equal number of jobs, and submitted concurrently on the cluster. Finally, the results are distributed back to the waiting client jobs. In this execution strategy, the block-level operations remain unchanged but read blocks of a shared input are reused with better temporal locality. Choosing a good waiting strategy is crucial for performance to maximize sharing potential without negatively affecting the client latency. The basic time-based waiting strategy simply triggers the merge and submission periodically every

---

[3] A hardware-specific roofline analysis is a great tool for visualizing this characteristic [352].

Δt. However, this constant period introduces unnecessary latency for small datasets, and misses sharing potential for large datasets. The utilization-based strategy overcomes these problems via a time-decayed utilization threshold: if the current cluster utilization exceeds this threshold, we keep collecting jobs until the next check interval. Intuitively, if the cluster is already utilized, submitted jobs would anyway wait for free slots; hence, we wait longer to increase sharing potential. Since this threshold is monotonically decreasing with time, there is no danger of starvation.

Fine-grained Data-Parallelism: In addition to the previously discussed scan sharing techniques, there are even more use cases that leverage hybrid execution strategies with fine-grained data parallelism. For example, consider a simple task parallel program [58] of `parfor(i in 1:n) R[i,] = linregDS(X, y, ...)`. If n is less than the number of threads, we can assign the remaining parallelism to multi-threaded data-parallel operations of the body program in order to fully utilize the underlying hardware. Another example is model-parallel training with parameter servers. At a coarse-grained level, we partition the data set across workers, where each worker runs local iterations. Operations within each worker then again may leverage multi-threaded data-parallel CPU or GPU operations. *SystemML* optimizes these decisions during compilation and recompilation, while *TensorFlow* uses common thread pools to dynamically assign threads.

5.5 ACCELERATORS (GPUS, FPGAS, ASICS)

The success of deep learning architectures—with their high computation and energy demands—was largely enabled by significant hardware advancements over the last couple of years, especially for GPUs but also CPUs. This includes wider SIMD registers, increasing degree of parallelism, and specialized instructions such as fused multiply-add. Increasing data and model sizes, however, pose challenges for general-purpose devices regarding training time, scoring latency, and energy demand. These challenges are increasingly tackled via different means of hardware specialization, often broadly termed—albeit imprecise—"accelerators." In this section, we give a general overview of the spectrum of these accelerators, and discuss in more detail aspects related to data management, including specific data types, the increasing importance of efficient data transfer, and the exploitation of sparsity.

A Spectrum of Accelerators: The landscape of existing accelerators ranges from general-purpose devices to chips for specific deep learning applications such as vision. The design and use of these accelerators makes a conscious tradeoff between performance and energy consumption vs. flexibility with regard to diverse and future (and thus unknown) workloads. In the following, we review the most popular categories and give examples of devices and systems.

- **Graphics Processing Units (GPUs):** Over the last decade, GPUs have been widely deployed as accelerators for a number of workloads ranging from high-performance computing (leveraging the high compute capabilities) to query processing (leveraging its high memory bandwidth). These GPUs are now also extensively used for deep learning training and scoring [279]. However, recent architectures such as NVIDIA Volta show a trend toward specialization by providing dedicated "tensor cores" which are dedicated instructions for 4x4 half-precision matrix multiply (i.e., 64 half-precision fused multiply-add) [93].

- **Field-Programmable Gate Arrays (FPGAs):** For more hardware specialization according to application needs, other systems leverage customizable hardware such as FPGAs. Examples are Microsoft's *Catapult* [64], which uses servers of dual Xeon CPUs with a PCIe-attached FPGA for prefiltering neural networks and compression, as well as its successor Microsoft's *Brainwave* [78], which uses neural processing units (NPUs) for dense matrix-vector multiplication and other specialized instructions on the FPGA. Related to ML in DB systems, *DAnA* [225] focuses specifically on compilation aspects, efficient data transfer of DB data pages, and a multi-threaded FPGA execution engine.

- **Application-Specific Integrated Circuit (ASICs):** Additional improvements regarding performance and power/energy consumption are often achieved via specialization in the form of custom ASICs. The spectrum of chips ranges from general DL accelerators (with HW support for matrix multiply, convolution, and activation functions) to custom chips for applications such as vision and image processing. Examples of general-purpose ASICs include Google's tensor processing units (TPUs) [165], NVIDIA's deep learning accelerator [93], which is—besides other accelerators like a programmable vision accelerator—part of NVIDIA's Xavier SoC, and Intel's Nervana neural network processors (NNP) [283]. An example of a more specialized chip is the Cadence Tensilica Vision Processor [109], which provides custom instructions for image processing and CNN operations.

Other Technologies: Parallel to the above mainstream development, several projects explored alternative architectures such as *neuromorphic computing* and *analog computing*. For example, the DARPA SyNAPSE program supported the development of the IBM TrueNorth ultra-low-power architecture of neurosynaptic cores [37, 271] and the HP memristor chip for computational storage [182]. These technologies are often referred to as spiking neural networks. We refer the interested reader for more details to a recent survey on neuromorphic computing [303]. The common use of lossy compression such as ultra-low precision and quantization—which we will discuss in Section 6.2—further spurred a renewed interest in analog computing [361]. However, there has been criticism regarding cost, scalability, and noise compared to digital computing.

Data Transfer and Types: With increasing compute capabilities of accelerators in terms of their peak compute bandwidth, even many deep learning scoring applications are rendered memory bandwidth bound [165]. Furthermore, despite emerging link and memory technologies, most accelerator devices have very limited on-device memory, which causes repeated data transfer over PCIe for training (e.g., in a model-parallel manner, as shown in Section 5.3). Similarly, scoring requires transferring the input data stream to the accelerator device. Currently, the most common approaches are compression techniques as discussed in Section 6.2. These include low- and ultra-low-precision storage and operations, quantization, and sparsification. However, because these lossy compression techniques affect accuracy, often heterogeneous data types are used (e.g., ultra-low precision for weights but higher precision for accumulators). Some libraries even use (1) custom data types (e.g., Intel's Flexpoint [189]) with different allocation of exponent and mantissa bits to satisfy special scaling requirements, or (2) use dedicated scaling techniques of intermediates at algorithm level to ensure certain value ranges. For this reason, many accelerators like Google's TPUs have dedicated support for mixed precision operations built in [165]. However, the global, i.e., program-wide, tradeoffs of performance, memory requirements, and the impact on algorithm convergence could be best addressed at ML systems level with full context knowledge and control of the ML program.

Sparsity Exploitation: Most accelerators focus on dense operations only, which is wasteful both in terms data transfer and computation. There are existing libraries such as cuSPARSE for sparse BLAS operations on GPUs but these libraries have—even for simple expressions— substantial room for improvement [39]. The high peak performance of existing accelerators, however, mitigates this shortcoming by pushing the break-even point of dense and sparse operations. Nevertheless, it is important to understand that dense operations over sparse inputs have a worse *asymptotic* behavior and thus exhibit increasing overhead with increasing sparsity. The key problem are irregular structures [93]—in terms of sparsity skew across rows and columns— which makes it hard to achieve high utilization in a massively parallel system and even harder to construct custom hardware. Multiple vendors and research projects aim to address this challenge in the future [93, 165]. For example, the NVIDIA DLA ASIC defers weight decompression just before instruction execution [93], while SCNN works on sparse weights and activations [261]. Complementary software techniques include the clustering of rows by non-zeros with partial padding [38], which is possible for a subset of operations such as matrix-vector multiply but faces challenges for mini-batch algorithms with small numbers of rows per batch.

Open Research Questions: Increasing HW specialization reduces flexibility and often relies on vendor-provided libraries for full exploitation near peak performance. This creates major challenges for ML systems. First, calling predefined kernels for well-defined operations by itself is simple, but deciding when this is beneficial, especially with data transfer, potential format conversions, and memory management is a non-trivial task. These decisions need good performance and memory models, which often require reverse engineering due to the lack of white-box specifications of the underlying HW and internals of these vendor-provided libraries [175]. Second, automatic operator fusion via code generation, as described in Section 4.4, is even more challenging because it requires well-defined instruction sets and a deep understanding of the underlying accelerator. The *TVM* project [71, 73] aims at a compilation stack for FPGA and ASICs by leveraging tensor instructions of the underlying accelerators and an ML-based construction of a cost-model from few exploration runs. However, these instructions are still constantly evolving. Therefore, until now, this problem is primarily addressed via vendor-provided accelerator backends for popular ML systems such as *TensorFlow's XLA* and thus, limited to single-device targets (e.g., *Intel's Nervana Graph* [185] or *NVIDIA TensorRT* [255]).

5.6   SUMMARY

In this chapter, we gave an overview of the major execution strategies of ML systems: namely data-parallel for batch algorithms, task-parallel for independent sub problems, and parameter-servers for data- or model-parallel mini-batch algorithms. We also surveyed hybrid strategies for combining these execution models, as well as means of hardware specialization in the form of accelerators. However, most ML systems still primarily focus on subsets of these execution strategies. Given the diversity of algorithms, statistical tests, and model management workloads, further work on seamlessly combining these execution strategies could significantly improve user productivity, performance, as well as deployment agility and robustness. This includes different runtime abstractions, broader support for distributed tensor operations, and automatic tuning of runtime configurations and techniques that affect performance as well as accuracy.

CHAPTER 6

Data Access Methods

Apart from physical rewrites like caching or partitioning, and data representations discussed so far, there are several existing techniques for efficient data access in ML systems. These techniques bear strong similarity with corresponding data access methods in database systems, with the difference of focusing on dense and sparse matrices or tensors, as well as specific access patterns of ML workloads. In this chapter, we survey existing techniques for caching and buffer pool management (what to keep in memory), compression and data types (how to represent the data), Non-Uniform Memory Access (NUMA)-aware partitioning and replication (where to place the data), index structures (how to access the data), as well as side effects between these techniques.

6.1 CACHING AND BUFFER POOL MANAGEMENT

Especially for iterative ML algorithms, caching and buffer pool management is crucial for performance. In this section, we provide an overview of strategies for distributed caching, graceful eviction of local intermediates, as well as dedicated out-of-core operations. Interestingly, caching and buffer management in ML systems follows an approach similar to anti-caching in modern memory-centric database systems [98], where the primary storage is the deserialized in-memory representation, which is gracefully serialized and evicted to local or remote storage on demand.

Distributed Caching: Probably the most common form of caching is distributed caching in data-parallel frameworks such as *Spark* [370]. Decisions on cached intermediates and their storage level can be made manually, or automatically as described in Section 4.3. A very commonly used storage format for distributed matrices—but also implicitly for all broadcasts—is MEMORY_AND_DISK that stores the matrix in deserialized blocked representation, with LRU eviction[1] to local storage at the granularity of physical partitions [55]. For iterative ML algorithms—that are often memory-bandwidth bound—this is beneficial for performance as it avoids deserialization per iteration. Eviction to local storage also avoids unnecessary recomputation or text-to-binary conversion, which involves expensive data shuffling. However, there are scenarios of sparse and ultra-sparse matrices with row-oriented sparse block formats, where deserialized caching can cause unnecessary evictions due to the storage overhead of object and array headers per block or row. In *SystemML*, these scenarios are addressed by (1) converting sparse matrix blocks into the read-optimized CSR format on caching, and (2) storing large ultra-sparse ma-

---

[1]Spark uses recursive inspection and sampling for larger arrays to estimate the size of deserialized objects.

trices in serialized form with `MEMORY_AND_DISK_SER`. Additional techniques include the use of lightweight general-purpose compression such as Snappy or LZ4, which we will discuss in Section 6.2.

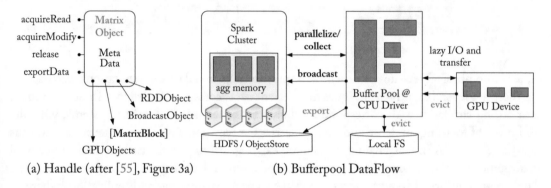

(a) Handle (after [55], Figure 3a)   (b) Bufferpool DataFlow

Figure 6.1: Example multi-level buffer pool (device memory, FS, HDFS).

Multi-Level Buffer Pools: Systems with multiple backends such as local and distributed operations, or CPU and GPU operations often provide a buffer pool for intermediate variables along with automatic memory management for evictions to handle cases where all live variables do not fit into available memory. Similar to traditional buffer pools in databases systems, such a buffer pool provides primitives for pinning and unpinning matrices. This abstraction enables, for instance, an in-memory CPU operation to explicitly pin its inputs to prevent evictions, while the operator is running. In this context, we classify existing techniques according to the granularity of memory management. *SystemML*, for example, pins entire matrices [55], whereas systems like *Elementary* [375], *RIOT* [381], and *ARCHIE* [104], work at the level of individual pages. For example, Figure 6.1 shows key primitives of *SystemML*'s buffer pool, which enables lazy I/O and data transfer (i.e., data transfer on the first operation that requires the data), lazy Spark-RDD and GPU-kernel evaluation (e.g., job scheduling on RDD actions[2]), as well as graceful evictions from GPU and CPU memory. First, pinning a matrix into memory—via `acquireRead`—can trigger pending RDD operations (e.g., collect the output of lazy RDD transformations), or wait for asynchronous GPU kernels. Second, data is only read from persistent storage (e.g., HDFS or S3) or transferred between devices (e.g., CPU to GPU memory) if an operation actually pins it into GPU or CPU memory, respectively. For dense GPU operations, a similar strategy is used to preallocate and pin the output, while sparse outputs generally require incremental allocation. Finally, the buffer pool is also responsible for (1) creating RDDs and broadcast variables for distributed operations, and (2) exporting dirty matrices—that have been modified or only exist in memory—to persistent storage on request. Example scenarios that require an export are explicit

---

[2]Spark's RDDs provide two kinds of operations: transformations and actions, where only actions such as `reduce` or `collect` trigger the evaluation.

persistent writes or operations that expect their inputs in persistent storage (e.g., MapReduce jobs). Other multi-level buffer pools as used in *ARCHIE* detect access patterns, and perform pre-fetching and data movement between disk and SSDs [104].

GPU Memory Management: In the context of training deep neural networks and other applications, scarce GPU memory resources can become a major limitation. This challenge is commonly addressed with the following four techniques.

- **Live Variable Analysis:** First, systems like *SystemML* [55], *TensorFlow* [22], *MXNet* [72], and *SuperNeurons* [345] all rely on live variable analysis to remove intermediates that are no longer needed from GPU memory. However, as mentioned in Section 4.3, we are not aware of a single system that performs operator scheduling with the aim of minimizing peak memory consumption.

- **GPU-CPU Eviction:** Second, *SystemML* [259], *SuperNeurons* [345], and *GeePS* [92] evict data from GPU to CPU memory under memory pressure, while *TensorFlow* evicts long-lived objects. This is part of the overall buffer pool management and thus, relies on pinning (also called locks) to guard currently used tensors against eviction. *SuperNeurons* and *GeePS* further asynchronously move data between CPU and GPU based on predicated access patterns.

- **Recompuation:** Third, *MXNet* and *SuperNeurons* also recompute inexpensive operations [345]. Activations from the forward pass are dropped to reduce memory consumption, and recomputed during the backward pass when most other intermediates are already freed. In contrast to *MXNet*, *SuperNeurons* decides on recomputation in a cost-based manner.

- **Reuse of Allocations:** Fourth, *SystemML* and *SuperNeurons* reuse allocated matrices and tensors via data-size-specific free lists. However, this only works for dense tensors and can cause—without dedicated handling—memory fragmentation. In contrast, *faimGraph* [354] supports dynamic graphs by GPU-local memory management based on queuing structures (index, vertex, page queues).

Out-of-Core Operations: Apart from large-scale ML systems that usually fall back to distributed operations over blocked matrix representations for large matrices, there is also substantial existing work on out-of-core[3] linear algebra operations [331]. This includes basic matrix multiplications, expensive factorization operations, and algorithm-level approaches. Often these out-of-core algorithms are combined with custom data partitioning or index structures [331, 383], which we will discuss in detail in Section 6.4. Common evaluation metrics in this context are the number and total size of transfers from secondary storage. For example, the lower bound of element and block I/Os for matrix multiplication is known to be $O(n^3/\sqrt{M})$

---

[3]Out-of-core operations generally refer to operations that do not require the entire input in memory but use a small in-memory working set, as well as read and evict data as needed.

[331] or $O(lmn/(B\sqrt{M}))$ [381], where B is the block size and M is the available main memory. Important operations such as sparse matrix-vector multiplication for very large numbers of features—where the dense vector does not fit into available memory—have been addressed by the dot-product operator [276]. The basic idea is to reduce reads of range-partitioned vector pages by reordering sparse vectors according to their non-zero structure and batching of page requests. Furthermore, an example of an algorithm-level approach is *Elementary* for Gibbs sampling with out-of-core factor graphs [375], where the authors evaluate materialization and co-clustering strategies, as well as page layouts and eviction policies.

Open Research Questions: For multi-backend systems, buffer pool management is challenging because it includes a broad-range of related concerns like (1) distributed caching and maintaining parallelized/broadcast variables (which are potentially used in lazily evaluated operations and also subject to eviction), (2) transfers between HDFS, local FS storage, and CPU/GPU device memory, as well as (3) graceful evictions across the different storage levels. An interesting direction is a unified memory management for all these aspects, which could exploit the known program structure and operations to improve memory efficiency, pre-fetching, and avoid unnecessary evictions. Major challenges originate from conditional control flow, lazy evaluation, and sparse matrix representations.

6.2   COMPRESSION

Similar to compression and query processing over compressed data in database systems [21, 128, 282, 350], existing work in ML systems addresses the problem of storing graphs, matrices, and tensors in compressed form and performing linear algebra operations directly over the compressed representation. The major motivation is to reduce I/O costs from disk and memory, reduce computation costs, and reduce resource requirements for memory, power, and CPU time, which translate to monetary costs in cloud environments. ML workloads are amenable to online compression because the initial compression overhead can be amortized over repeated data access. In general, we distinguish lossless and lossy compression techniques, which both have compelling use cases, determined by the optimization objective as discussed in Section 4.1.

Lossless General-Purpose Compression: Lossless compression techniques aim to improve I/O costs while guaranteeing result correctness, which allows for their transparent—i.e., invisible—application. Similar to page-wise compression in database systems, a baseline solution is the use of general-purpose compression techniques, but these require block-wise decompression for each operation. Example systems that leverage general-purpose compression techniques are array DBMS like *SciDB* [320] and storage manager like *TileDB* [260]. Unfortunately, heavyweight techniques like *Gzip* often suffer from slow decompression, while lightweight methods like *Snappy* or *LZ4* achieve only modest compression ratios [111]. Scientific data formats such as *NetCDF* and *HDF5* also support compression at chunk granularity, where the user can control the tradeoff between decompression speed and compression ratio by specifying the chunk size, the deflation level and optionally enable byte interlacing [332]. *PStore* combines such general-purpose techniques with specific byte-wise and floating point schemes for compressing scientific simulation datasets [48]. Similarly, data-parallel frameworks such as Spark also provide storage levels and configurations for compressing RDDs, broadcast variables, and shuffled data[4] with lightweight techniques such as *Snappy* or *LZ4* [370].

Lossless Matrix Compression: In contrast to lossless general-purpose compression techniques, lossless matrix compression further aims at supporting dedicated techniques for sparse and dense matrices, and performing operations directly over the compressed representation to avoid blockwise decompression. This is especially important for iterative ML algorithms that make many passes over a read-only feature matrix. Apart from well-known sparse representations such as CSR, CSC, and COO [297], more recent work applies forms of dictionary coding to also compress values or groups of values [111, 190, 208]. These value-based approaches to matrix compression can be classified into the following two major categories.

- **Homogeneous Compression:** For scientific data like images and videos—where the individual values come from a common domain—it is often beneficial to share a single dictionary of distinct values across all columns. For example, Kourtis et al. introduced compression techniques for sparse matrix formats, where they applied run-length encoding of column index deltas [174, 190] and dictionary encoding [174], with a value dictionary that is shared across all columns. Such a shared dictionary in turn leads to a homogeneous code-size for all values. Tuple-Oriented Coding (TOC) [208] also uses a shared dictionary but additionally exploits common sub-sequences of values via a prefix tree, and compresses the dictionary itself with bit packing in order to properly support mini-batch algorithms.

- **Heterogeneous Compression:** Homogeneous compression might miss compression opportunities if the data characteristics such as cardinality, sparsity, or sortedness varies significantly among features. Such a skew is very common for enterprise data. Compressed Linear Algebra (CLA) [111, 112] addresses this challenge via *column–wise* compression and heterogeneous encoding formats such as dictionary, run-length,[5] and offset-list encoding, as well as fallbacks for incompressible columns. Additionally, CLA also applies column co-coding to exploit column correlations. Each encoded column group has a separate dictionary and thus code size, which is determined by its number of distinct values. All these decisions are strongly data-dependent. Therefore, CLA computes compression plans based on a small sample of data. Similarly, *Sprintz*—a lossless compression scheme for time series data, which can be viewed as a stream of matrix blocks—uses *column–wise* delta coding or predictive filtering, zig-zag coding, bit packing, and huffman coding, but

---

[4]Spark compresses by default all broadcast variables and shuffled data with lightweight techniques. In that context, *Spark's* default compression codec was *Snappy* in Spark 1.x, but it changed to *LZ4* in *Spark* 2.x.

[5]Run-length encoding is also used by other systems such as *SciDB*, see `https://www.paradigm4.com/technology/multidimensional-array-clustering/`

with very small blocks for low memory requirements, and vectorization for low latency [52].

Column co-coding—as used in CLA—is also similar to existing lossless techniques for graph compression, which can be seen as a special case of Boolean matrix compression. Existing techniques use so-called compressor nodes [224], virtual nodes [61], or hyper nodes [114] to compress common edges to neighboring sub-graphs. Inspired by related techniques for graph sparsification [298] and graph summarization [217], an interesting direction is the use of locality-sensitive hashing such as minhash for more efficient column co-coding decisions.

Lossy Compression: Compared to lossless compression, lossy compression techniques have even more potential for improvements but these techniques require careful manual application due to their impact on model accuracy. However, there are numerous ML algorithms that can tolerate a loss in accuracy because these algorithms are approximate in nature, and additional noise can even improve the generalization of the trained model. In the context of deep learning, common techniques include: (1) mantissa truncation or quantization for remote data transfers [23, 305] (in parameter servers as described in Section 5.3); (2) sparsification [134, 214] (reduce non-zero values); and (3) low-precision floating- or fixed-point storage and arithmetic [86, 131], which is also called quantization (reduce value domain) [388]. Recent work focuses on dynamic quantization schemes [135], where value boundaries are trained in a data-driven manner. Similarly, *ZipML* [378] and *SketchML* [160] use dynamic quantization schemes to prevent quantization bias on skewed data distributions, but *SketchML* additionally uses delta coding and bit packing for lossless key compression on sparse gradient updates. With lossy compression, the models are often carefully crafted, for example, with different precision for multiply and accumulator units [86]. In the context of factorized learning (see Section 3.1), the *Hamlet* project [202] explored decision rules for safely avoiding KFK joins for significant runtime improvements with moderate impact on accuracy. Here, the foreign key can be viewed as a lossy compressed representation of the joined features. Finally, some projects also investigated lossy compression in the context of other ML-lifecycle tasks. For example, *PStore* [48] explored lossy compression for disk I/O reductions in scientific computation, and *MISTIQUE* [335] uses lossy quantization together with de-duplication for the efficient creation and storage of intermediates in model diagnosis scenarios. Overall, the tradeoff space for lossy compression is very large, but it requires a good understanding of how lossy compression impacts the accuracy of the given ML algorithm or analysis workload, which is often data-dependent and thus, hard to estimate and decide upfront.

Sampling: Other lossy compression techniques, are related to sampling or approximate query processing in general. For example, approximate gradient decent [274] and matrix factorization via random projections [134, 310, 328], sample subsets of the input data and compute the gradient or factorization on the "compressed" input. Furthermore, Kaoudi et al. used sampling to estimate the number of iterations until convergence as a basis for selecting a gradient decent optimizer (e.g., batch vs. min-batch) in *ML4all* [173]. Model training over downsampled data is also a frequently used technique for model initialization before working with the entire dataset. For example, *Columbus* used samples and CoreSets in feature-selection workloads [373]. In contrast, *BlinkML* allows the specification of different approximation contracts [262], and trains—locally or in an distributed manner—an approximate classification or regression model that satisfies the given constraints with probabilistic guarantees. This is enabled by deriving—via the central-limit theorem—the smallest feasible sample size from an initial sample run.

Open Research Questions: Due to the major focus on homogenous image or text data, and the existing tooling for homogeneous tensors, many lossy compression techniques like quantization are applied in a homogeneous way. For structured data—with a mix of numerical and categorical, i.e., one-hot-encoded, features—this is, however, unnecessarily wasteful and and results in a poor compromise between quality and compression. Hence, heterogeneous quantification and sparsification schemes are a promising direction for future work. Challenges include efficient matrix-matrix operations and automatic operator fusion over heterogeneously compressed matrices, as well as efficient compression for ultra-sparse matrices with many features. Similarly, freeing the user from these low-level decisions on selecting compression and sampling schemes (i.e., providing data independence) is challenging but would significantly simplify typical experimentation workflows.

6.3   NUMA-AWARE PARTITIONING AND REPLICATION

Multi-processor systems predominately exhibit a NUMA architecture, where CPU-cores have local caches (e.g., L1 and L2 on Intel processors), CPU-sockets—which act as NUMA nodes—have an additional last-level cache, locally attached main memory, and other sockets are accessible through an interconnect topology. Therefore, accessing data at different levels of this hierarchy exhibits very different latency and bandwidth characteristics. Thus, data placement has a major impact on performance for memory-bandwidth-bound ML workloads. NUMA-aware operations such as dense and sparse matrix multiply have been studied extensively in the HPC literature [351]. In this context, a common approach is to partition the feature matrix across NUMA nodes and bind processes or threads with `numactl` or `openmp` to individual nodes. This is also applicable to large-scale ML on Spark—which does not support NUMA aware scheduling—by creating and binding an executor per NUMA node. Furthermore, there is also recent work on making container schedulers such as *Kubernetes* NUMA-aware [323]. Apart from these broadly applicable techniques, ML systems explored the tradeoffs of NUMA-aware model and data replication as well as NUMA-aware index structures.

NUMA-Aware Model and Data Replication: *DimmWitted* [376] investigated model and data replication tradeoffs in NUMA architectures for the general-purpose algorithms SGD (stochastic gradient decent) and SCD (stochastic coordinate decent). In this setup, different replication strategies exhibit different hardware (time per iteration) and statistical efficiency (iterations to convergence), which both contribute to the end-to-end runtime. Alternative model replication strategies include `PerCore` (core-local model with update per epoch), `PerNode` (NUMA-node-local model with update per epoch), and `PerMachine` (direct *Hogwild!* [288] updates). In contrast to the mutable model, the data is immutable in SGD and SCD. Hence, data replication strategies include basic disjoint partitioning and full replication with random reshuffling. These partitions are then accessed in a row- or column-wise manner. Similar trade-offs also apply to distributed database systems like *Impala* [51]. Overall, the choice of these methods are heavily algorithm-, data-, and architecture-dependent and hence require automatic optimization.

NUMA-Aware Index Structures: A major problem with disjoint data partitioning, is skew of sparse matrices and tensors. The Adaptive Tile Matrix (AT Matrix) format [179]—which we will discuss in Section 6.4—addresses skew via a two-level blocking into variable-sized tiles and squared basic blocks, where tiles can be represented in either dense or sparse formats. Partitioning is then done via a quad-tree recursion, subject to constraints of minimum and maximum tile sizes. For NUMA-aware matrix multiplications, all AT matrices are then horizontally partitioned into tile rows and distributed round-robin across NUMA nodes. Each NUMA node is assigned a worker team and the authors use *SAP HANA*'s NUMA-aware task scheduling framework [272] to pin these tasks to CPU cores. This way the system handles NUMA-aware data placement and heterogeneous tile representations, while leveraging existing basic linear algebra subprograms (BLAS) routines—for which most HW vendors provide well-optimized library implementations—to effect the individual basic block operations.

Open Research Questions: Despite the exploration of NUMA-aware operations and optimizers like SGD, it remains an open question how to integrate these techniques into an ML system and automatically optimize the data placement of inputs and intermediates for arbitrary linear algebra programs. Even more challenging is the full integration of NUMA-aware operations with buffer pool management, sparse and compressed matrices, as well as heterogeneous HW accelerators.

6.4   INDEX STRUCTURES

In the context of ML systems, index structures are primarily used—especially in single-node settings—for efficient data storage, out-of-core operations, and data placement. Overall, these index structures often combine database indexing techniques with hierarchical block storage with the aim of supporting efficient scans, range indexing, as well as block-wise linear algebra operations such as matrix-multiply. To this end, these index structures are also related to data partitioning strategies. In this section, we first discuss common techniques shared by many index structures, and subsequently, we give an overview of three concrete indexes along with how they instantiate the common techniques.

Common Techniques: The goal of supporting efficient linear algebra operations over indexed matrices, or arrays often results in an index design centered around the following two key techniques.

- **Multi-Level Blocking:** Most matrix index structures consist of a multi-level access hierarchy and leaf blocks that are individually encoded in traditional dense or sparse matrix formats, as described in Section 5.1. Such a design is well suited for data partitioning in NUMA topologies as well as direct access of blocks on disk for blocked out-of-core operations or range indexing (e.g., accessing consecutive rows or columns). At the same time, existing operations (e.g., native BLAS libraries) can be used to perform block-wise operations such as matrix multiply very efficiently.

- **Storage and Iterator Linearization:** A second major characteristic is how the logical matrix is linearized for physical storage and scan-based operations (i.e., operations that read the entire matrix). The spectrum of index structures ranges from a single static linearization function for both storage and scans to user-defined linearization functions for storage and each individual operation. Examples are row-major, column-major, and Z-order. In combination with multi-level blocking, some systems further allow to specify linearization functions per level (e.g., row-major tile order, column-major cell order per tile).

Example 6.1 Indexed Matrix Storage   For a sake of clear terminology, Figure 6.2a shows an example of an indexed matrix. This matrix is stored—with single-level blocking—in blocks of 4×4 cells. Within each block (i.e., page), cells are stored in row-major order. Similarly, the sequence of blocks is also ordered in a row-major layout. Users can now issue range queries, for which only relevant blocks have to be retrieved from disk. For instance, Figure 6.2b shows a range query of rows 4 through 9 and columns 3 through 5 (both inclusive). Such queries return an iterator of values or key-value pairs, where the order of cells is derived from the storage layout by default. However, custom iterator orders are possible. For instance, in our example, we have a column-wise retrieval order, which can be useful for binary operations with inputs in different storage layouts. ∎

LAB-Tree [383]: The Linearized Array B-tree (which was proposed as a disk-based index structure in the context of the *RIOT* system [381]) uses a B-tree over a user-defined linearization function of cell indexes, along with a specified default "zero"-value, which is not stored in sparse leaf blocks. Users can then perform key lookups, scans via a user-defined linearization function, and range indexing (e.g., for block-wise matrix multiply) for both reads and writes. Additionally, the LAB-tree provides dedicated leaf-splitting strategies to improve space utilization as well as update batching via an indexed buffer—similar to common write stores or delta indexes for read-optimized column stores [197, 319]—and related flushing policies.

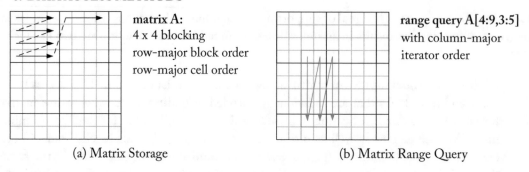

matrix A:
4 x 4 blocking
row-major block order
row-major cell order

range query A[4:9,3:5]
with column-major
iterator order

(a) Matrix Storage   (b) Matrix Range Query

Figure 6.2: Indexed matrix storage and data access.

TileDB Storage Manager [260]: The *TileDB* storage manager maps the cell order to fixed-sized two-dimensional space tiles, which can be sparse or dense. These tiles are linearized in row- or column-major order and cells within each tile are stored either row- or column-major. Individual cells are either primitive or vector types, which allows storing 3D arrays. Additionally, users can specify a capacity to group non-empty space tiles into data tiles, which are the unit for compression and storage. The storage manager then supports concurrent read and write operations. Similar but more advanced than the LAB-Tree update batching, updates are collected into so-called fragments (dense or sparse) of overlapping index ranges, which ensure sequential writes and isolation in a parallel environment, while reads take all fragments (except partial, i.e., currently written, fragments) into account. On user request, fragments can be consolidated via a simple read-write operation.

AT MATRIX [179]: Furthermore, the AT Matrix (which was proposed as a NUMA-aware in-memory index structure) uses a Quad-tree over a Z-order of basic 1K × 1K blocks. Basic blocks are grouped into homogeneous dense or sparse tiles (with minimum and maximum size constraints) consisting of one or many blocks. Both dense and sparse blocks use a row-major layout, with sparse blocks being encoded in CSR format. The resulting matrix structure—constructed with a recursive partitioning process—might be heterogeneous by containing dense and sparse tiles. In contrast to the previous two index structures, the AT Matrix uses indexing primarily to access the tiles for NUMA-aware matrix multiplications.

Open Research Questions: Similar to storage synopsis in database systems, an interesting open question is the design of effective synopses for linear algebra and array operations over numeric data representations. Opportunities include summary statistics, element-wise comparisons, aggregates, and reorganization operations. Further directions includes HW-conscious index structures, automatic storage reorganization based on access patterns similar to database cracking [156], and compressed index structures.

6.5   SUMMARY

In connection to related data management techniques, in this chapter, we surveyed techniques for efficient data access in ML systems. In detail, we discussed: (1) distributed caching and buffer pool management; (2) lossless and lossy compression, and data types; (3) NUMA-aware partitioning and replication; as well as (4) memory- and disk-based index structures. Side effects originate from the impact of data sizes (e.g., compression and replication affect caching and buffer pool management, I/O, and index granularity), as well as data access patterns (e.g., compression, partitioning, and indexing influence access paths and operations performance). However, compared to their related data management techniques, many open problems remain. This includes unified buffer pool management, heterogeneous tensors and their compression and indexing, as well as means of automatic storage reorganization to specialize for data, workload, and underlying hardware.

CHAPTER 7

Resource Heterogeneity and Elasticity

As discussed in Section 5.1, it is increasingly common today to use clusters of commodity hardware for large-scale ML. Advances in cloud computing have made it easier than ever to access computing resources. For example, a public cloud such as Amazon EC2 allows users to acquire a cluster on demand and pay only for its actual usage. There is a blossoming ecosystem of tools, libraries, and platforms for ML in the cloud and cluster computing settings. While it is beyond the scope of this book to survey this field in depth, we shall provide an overview of some key challenges and how ideas from the database research community have contributed to their solutions. With this overview, we hope to illustrate the various optimization possibilities enabled by different levels of abstraction, and in particular, opportunities that become possible by having declarative specifications in the spirit of database systems.

We focus on two challenges in this chapter.

- **Resource heterogeneity** arises because most clouds consist of various types of hardware with different performance and capacities. Even though containerization and virtualization help hide some heterogeneity, in practice, cloud service providers still offer users a variety of configuration options. To achieve good performance at low cost, we need to make a number of non-trivial decisions, from how to provision resources (e.g., how many and what type of machines to acquire), to how to utilize provisioned resources effectively (e.g., how to configure *Hadoop* or *Spark* settings, and how to parallelize execution).

- **Resource elasticity** arises from the need to adapt resource usage and workload execution to performance variations, workload changes, or loss of resources due to failures or market conditions (e.g., in the case of machines with transient availability such as Amazon *spot instances* or Google *preemptible instances*). Resource elasticity is especially important to public clouds and large multi-tenant clusters, where sharing of resources occurs at scale, and to long-running ML workloads, whose execution is susceptible to constant disruptions.

To address these challenges, Section 7.1 discusses resource provisioning, configuration, and execution scheduling techniques. Then, Section 7.2 discusses recovery techniques for coping with failures or generally unavailable resources. Section 7.2 specifically deals with the scenario of working with a market of cheap yet unreliable resources. Note that these challenges and techniques are general, but we shall focus more on ML workloads and database-inspired ideas.

7.1   PROVISIONING, CONFIGURATION, AND SCHEDULING

We begin with several examples illustrating various types of provisioning, configuration, and scheduling decisions, as well as their importance to ML workloads running in the cloud and cluster computing settings.

Example 7.1   Cluster Choice   Suppose a user wants to acquire a cluster from a public cloud for one-time execution of a given ML program. The user may have a deadline for completing the program, and wish to minimize the monetary cost. A cloud service provider usually offers a large number of machine types with different hardware configurations and prices, e.g., Amazon EC2 had more than 50 "current-generation" offerings as of January 2018. The user needs to choose the type and number of machines in the cluster; this choice can have significant impact on the completion time of cost.

We borrow a concrete example from *Cumulon* [149], a system that can help users make such choices. Consider singular value decomposition (SVD) of matrices, used extensively in ML. In the randomized algorithm of [294] for approximate SVD, the first (and most expensive) step, computes a series of matrix multiplies $\mathbf{G} \times (\mathbf{A} \times \mathbf{A}^{\top})^k \times \mathbf{A}$, where $\mathbf{A}$ is an $m \times n$ input matrix and $\mathbf{G}$ is an $l \times m$ random matrix whose entries are drawn from i.i.d. Gaussian distributions of zero mean and unit variance. Here, $(\cdot)^k$ denotes matrix power, as opposed to element-wise (or Hadamard) power. Figure 7.1 shows how the cluster choice affects completion time and cost. Each curve corresponds to one machine type; given the machine type, we vary the completion time constraint (horizontal axis), and find the best cluster size (not shown explicitly) that minimizes the total cost (vertical axis).

From Figure 7.1, we can make several observations. First, some machine types are more cost-effective than others for a particular workload: e.g., m1.xlarge is better than m1.large for this job. Second, there is a trade-off between completion time and cost. Generally speaking, faster completion times require larger clusters, and at some point, they begin to translate into much higher premiums due to sublinear speedup. In this case, even though matrix multiplies are highly parallelizable, a cluster twice as big may not be able to complete the job twice as fast (which is what would be needed to achieve the same total cost). On the other hand, a cluster that is too small may not be cost-effectiveness either, because performance can degrade significantly without adequate resources (e.g., when aggregate memory is too small for input data, especially on platforms like *Spark* that heavily rely on memory).   ∎

The next example considers the setting where a cluster is already given, and we want to execute a ML program as quickly as possible; the objective here is to minimize completion time.

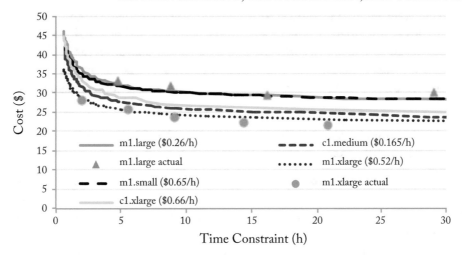

Figure 7.1: (From [149]) Costs for the key step of the randomized SVD algorithm discussed in Example 7.1 (with $l = 2,000$, $m = n = 200,000$, and $k = 5$) using different Amazon EC2 machine types under different time constraints. Curves (based on 2013 numbers) are predicted; costs of actual runs for sample data points are shown for comparison.

(In contrast, Example 7.1 minimizes monetary cost under a completion time constraint, where the factor of cost-effectiveness weighs more.)

Example 7.2 Parallelism and Configuration Settings   From Example 7.1, we have already seen that executing on large clusters can have diminishing returns. A large ML program usually involves multiple steps, some of which are less suited for execution on clusters than others. In fact, for some steps, even if a cluster is available, it may be better to execute them on a single node to avoid the overhead of distribution, especially when the single node has many cores and/or GPUs itself. *SystemML* [54, 55, 150], for example, uses a *control program* to drive the overall program execution and parallelization; its optimizer determines the appropriate degree of parallelism for each execution step, and when appropriate, will simply execute a step within the control program without distributing it to the cluster.

Important decisions also need to be made at a lower level, e.g., choosing the best config-uration settings such as the amounts of memory allocated for various aspects of the execution. To illustrate, we borrow an example from *SystemML* [150]. Consider two programs for lin-ear regression—one based on the direct-solve method (Example 2.4) and the other based on the conjugate gradient method (Example 4.1). *SystemML* automatically decides how to allocate memory to the control program and the parallel tasks (*MapReduce* in this case). For the case of 1,000 features, the direct-solve method is compute-intensive, and hence prefers a high de-gree of parallelism and only a small amount of memory for the control program. On the other

hand, the conjugate gradient method is I/O-bound and hence benefits from a large amount of memory for the control program, which can read the data once and repeatedly compute matrix-vector multiplies in memory. Therefore, the optimal memory allocation can differ significantly across programs—e.g., 2 GB for each of the parallel tasks as well as the control program for the direct-solve method vs. just 10 GB for the control program for the conjugate gradient method.
∎

Our next example deals with a more specific ML algorithm and shows how intelligent scheduling decisions help handling heterogeneity and elasticity.

Example 7.3   Scheduling Communication   Recall the SGD method introduced in Example 2.5. A popular approach for implementing distributed SGD is the *parameter server* architecture [24, 210], more broadly covered in Section 5.3. In a simple data-parallel parameter server architecture, a global parameter is stored on a parameter server; each worker has replica of this parameter, and works on its share of data independently and proposes updates to the parameter. A key decision is how to synchronize this global parameter between the server and the workers. With resource heterogeneity and elasticity, a key challenge in coping with "stragglers," or workers whose progress lags significantly behind others. If we force synchronization at the end of each step (epoch or mini-batch), the overall progress would be hindered by the slowest worker. On the other hand, if we allow workers to update their parameter replicas without waiting for each other, we risk losing convergence guarantees with stragglers.

DynSGD [159] is an example of improving the performance of distributed SGD with intelligent scheduling of synchronization. *DynSGD* represents a trade-off between the two approaches above: fast workers are allowed to lead the slowest by up to a some predefined number of steps, and they are not required to pull the global parameter every step. Furthermore, *DynSGD* adapts the "learning rate" for each local update to its "staleness": intuitively, this rate controls how much contribution a local update makes to the global parameter; the more a worker lags behind, the smaller the learning rate for (i.e., less contribution from) its local update. It was shown in [159] that *DynSGD* significantly improves the performance of distributed SGD in practice, while maintaining the same, if not better, theoretical convergence guarantees.   ∎

It is worthwhile noting that provisioning, configuration, and scheduling decisions interact with optimizations and execution strategies discussed earlier in Chapters 4 and 5. For example, cluster configuration obviously influences data partitioning and choice of physical operators. The scenario of Example 7.3 is even more complex. Here, scheduling decisions can affect the output and convergence behavior of the SGD algorithm, so the correctness and effectiveness of such decisions must be additionally established. Moreover, to achieve better performance in the presence of stragglers, *DynSGD* requires extending the basic SGD algorithm with adaptive learning rates. In other words, optimizations happen at all levels—from algorithmic design all the way to hardware provision—and interact with one other. In an ideal world, we would like to automate these optimization decisions jointly across all levels; in practice, however, we often choose levels of abstraction to work with and consider optimization opportunities that are possible at these particular levels. In the following, we briefly summarize opportunities at these levels.

Black-Box Programs: Suppose the ML program to be executed is a complete black box. Besides observing its current execution, we can try to learn from past execution traces how its performance is affected by provisioning, configuration, and scheduling decisions. We can also proactively profile the program and experiment with different decisions. For example, to choose the optimal cluster size for a black-box ML program, *TuPAQ* [317] builds a model of the execution time in terms of the task's compute, memory, and network requirements, and whether the task is compute-, memory-, or network-bound. Besides learning from past executions, control theory can also be applied to deal with dynamic environments [239].

Programs in Higher-Order, Data-Parallel Programming Models: Next, consider programs specified in data-parallel programming models with higher-order abstractions, popular in recent cluster computing platforms. In both *MapReduce* [97] and *Spark* [370], for example, a program can be thought of as a workflow of operations, each with well-understood properties designed with parallel processing in mind. Two classic examples of such operations are map and reduce. Although programmers still have considerable freedom in deciding what computation goes inside these operations, the properties of map and reduce by design make them easier to parallelize and optimize. Hence, there has been much work on automatically optimizing such programs. For example, in the context of provisioning, configuration, and scheduling for *Hadoop*, *Starfish* [142, 143] uses profiling and cost-based optimization techniques to automatically tune configuration settings; *SkewTune* [204] uses active monitoring and dynamic repartitioning to automatically mitigate the effect of stragglers; Zhang et al. [386] exploit the heterogeneity in public cloud resources to make more cost-effective provisioning decisions that may involve acquiring heterogeneous clusters. None of these systems is ML-specific. Working at this level of abstraction is appealing, because many prevailing platforms for data analytics in cloud and cluster computing settings operate at this level, so any solution can readily benefit a wide range of workloads, ML or otherwise.

Declarative ML Programs: Additional opportunities arise if we move up another abstraction level, where programs are expressed in a declarative language. Here, instead of working with generic primitives such as map and reduce, which still come with user-supplied low level code, we now have white-box programs consisting of high-level operators with well-understood semantics. For database workloads, SQL is the de facto language, and there has been plenty of work on automatic optimization for SQL-like languages in cloud and cluster computing settings. As one example, taking advantage of the declarativeness of *Pig*, a SQL-inspired language on top of *Hadoop*, *CoScan* [347] is able to identify opportunities for sharing data movement and processing costs across *Pig* programs, and intelligently merge and schedule workflows under soft deadlines. For ML workloads, because of their diversity, no single declarative language has emerged. *ScalOps* [59] is one proposal, which extends the *MapReduce* programming model with an extra `update` function for iterative computation, and allows ML tasks to be expressed as Datalog programs that are easier to optimize. However, Datalog and SQL are still low level from the perspective of many ML workloads, as standard database optimization techniques fail to exploit the semantics of high-level ML operators. Hence, as discussed in earlier chapters, another approach has been to build on the language of matrices and linear algebra, which serves a large class of ML workloads and is declarative enough to give rise to a wide range of rewrites and optimizations (Chapter 4), execution strategies (Chapter 5), and access methods (Chapter 6). For provisioning and configuration, as Examples 7.1 and 7.2 show, *Cumulon* [149, 151–153] and *SystemML* [54, 55, 123, 150] operate at this level of abstraction. Even though they are still built on top of *Hadoop* and *Spark*, they can make better decisions than systems intended for general *Hadoop* and *Spark* workloads, because their focus on declaratively specified linear algebra workloads allows them to develop better, specialized cost models, explore a richer space of alternative execution strategies, and propagate dimension and sparsity information based on operation and control flow semantics to better inform optimization.

Specific ML Algorithms or Recipes: Not surprisingly, by targeting a specific ML algorithm or ML programs that follow a particular computational recipe, we can uncover even more optimization opportunities. For instance, in the context of parameter servers discussed in Example 7.3, besides *DynSGD* [159] mentioned earlier, which focuses on update scheduling, *Dolphin* [77] focuses on dynamically tuning configuration settings of the parameter server (such as the number of worker nodes), using an elastic, distributed memory store for efficient reconfiguration. As another example, for iterative algorithms running on clusters, *PREDIcT* [270] uses sample runs of an algorithm to derive estimates of its convergence and per-iteration processing cost; key input features affecting performance (for graph processing tasks, which *PREDIcT* focuses on) are identified through domain knowledge and experimentation. Similarly, for iterative, distributed optimization algorithms, *Hemingway* [258] builds predictive models of convergence and execution times in order to select appropriate algorithms and cluster sizes. As a final example, *Omnivore* [133] optimizes deep learning tasks with intelligent choice of hardware (e.g., CPUs vs. GPUs) and synchronization strategies (e.g., synchronous vs. asynchronous training), as well as efficient hyper-parameter tuning. Generally speaking, by sacrificing some generality, these systems are able to apply more advanced optimizations tailored toward the particular computational recipes they support.

7.2   HANDLING FAILURES

In cloud and cluster computing settings, failures can occur for a variety of reasons, ranging from hardware, software, and communication errors to complete loss of resources due to market conditions (discussed further in Section 7.3). We limit our discussion in this section to node failures during the execution of a program on a cluster. When a node participating in some distributed computation fails, we lose the execution state on this node, including contents of the memory and local storage attached to this node. Clearly, failures pose great threats to long-running programs, which are typical of ML workloads. Recall from Section 7.1 that various techniques for provisioning, configuration, and scheduling are available at different levels of abstraction. Here, we will see that techniques for handling failures very much depend on the levels of abstraction as well. In the following, we discuss these techniques by the levels of abstraction they target, in the same order (from low to high) as they were presented in Section 7.1.

Black-Box Programs: Given a black-box ML program, our options are limited. Besides the fallback option of restarting the program in the event of a failure, we can periodically checkpoint the program execution (e.g., to reliable distributed storage), and upon failure, restart from the last checkpoint. Process migration techniques may be used to recover from failures of individual nodes without restarting others. In general, however, checkpointing can be very expensive because it involves remembering the states of all participating processes and their communication channels. In particular, if nodes produce large amounts of intermediate results locally (which is not atypical in ML workloads), such data must be persisted as part of a checkpoint.

Programs in Higher-Order, Data-Parallel Programming Models: Moving up one level, with programs specified in programming models with higher-order abstractions such as *MapReduce* and *Spark*, we can do better. For example, fault tolerance features are built in all the layers of the *Hadoop* stack. *HDFS* relies on replication to handle node failures. Then, assuming reliable *HDFS* storage, *Hadoop MapReduce* persists all task outputs in *HDFS*, and handles failures of individual tasks by restarting them. If a particular task fails, we simply reschedule it on a different node. The restarted task will always have access to its input data in *HDFS*, because earlier task outputs—which can serve as its input—have all been persisted; there is no need to restart tasks that have completed earlier.

Lineage is another technique available for handling failures at this level of abstraction. For example, in contrast to *Hadoop*'s approach of persisting all intermediate results to reliable storage, *Spark* handles data in memory for efficiency, and achieves fault tolerance using lineage of its RDDs [370]. If a partition of an RDD is lost due to node failure, the lineage of the RDD has enough information about how it was derived from other RDDs to be able to recompute just that partition. *Spark* also offers checkpointing support, but does not do so by default. Automatic checkpointing for *Spark* has been introduced in *Flint* [312], a system on top of *Spark* intended to support spot instances (more on this topic in Section 7.3). *Flint* automatically selects the checkpointing interval and dynamically adapts it based on the costs of checkpointing and recomputation as well as the observed meantime to failure.

Declarative ML Programs: Moving up yet another level of abstraction, we can do even better when ML programs are expressed with high-level operators, for example, those for linear algebra. First, recovery can be more flexible and fine-grained, as the following simple example illustrates.

Example 7.4   Recovering Lost Tiles from a Matrix Product   Suppose we compute $C = A \times B$ in a block-wise fashion (see Example 2.3). In a cluster setting, blocks of C would be computed in parallel. As shown in Figure 7.2, a particular block of C (shaded) is computed by a task that sums together the results of multiplying pairs of submatrices (shaded) from A and B (multiplications can be further parallelized over the pairs). Suppose that for subsequent computation, each block of C been partitioned and stored as smaller tiles, and one such tile (with dotted outline) is lost, while other tiles remain intact.

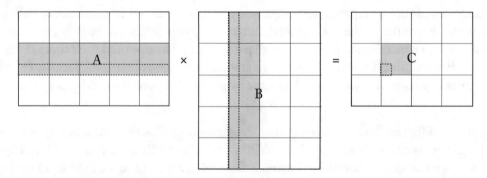

Figure 7.2: The lineage of a block (shaded) of the result matrix C of $A \times B$ vs. the lineage of a tile (with dotted outline).

For *Spark*, which tracks lineage of data but does not understand the semantics of matrix multiply, recovering the small lost tile of C would necessitate rerunning the task that generated the entire block of C, far more than what is necessary. On the other hand, knowing the semantics of matrix multiply, a system like *Cümülön* [152] can deduce that recovering this lost tile only requires multiplying the two skinny submatrices of A and B (with dotted outlines). Note that this recovery computation differs from the original tasks that computed the block of C. In other words, unlike *Spark*, *Cümülön* is not limited to rerunning parts of the original workflow. Such flexibility translates into less recovery work.

A reasonable question is whether we could achieve the same fine-grained recovery within *Spark*, by breaking $A \times B$ up into more tasks, each computing a small tile of C instead of an entire block. While doing so does make recovery more efficient, it will incur higher overhead during normal execution, and may fail to bundle related computation on the same node to achieve a good compute-to-I/O ratio. To elaborate, note that as each input tile needs to be multiplied with a number of certain other tiles; it is beneficial to schedule multiplications involving a block of tiles together on the same node for maximum data reuse. However, doing so would require the *Spark* scheduler to be aware again of the semantics of matrix multiply.   ∎

Besides fine-grained recovery, another advantage of declarative ML programs is that they are amenable to more sophisticated analysis that lead to more informed optimizations. For example, *Cümülön* [152] analyzes the program to determine data reuse and estimate recovery costs, in order to decide what intermediate results are worth checkpointing and when. In contrast, targeting generic *Spark* programs, *Flint* [312] has to resort to simpler policies: it checkpoints all most recent RDDs at the end of each interval, and it checkpoints RDDs that result from shuffle actions more frequently because such actions have wide dependencies—a good heuristic without further knowledge of the program.

Specific ML Algorithms or Recipes: Finally, consider recovery options for specific ML algorithms or computational recipes. A key observation is that many ML algorithms can tolerate missing input or errors by design. Instead of recovering to a state where it appears as if failures never occurred—which may be expensive—we can sometimes convert failures into "soft" ones that algorithms can handle themselves.

For instance, in Example 7.3 of Section 7.1, we have seen how distributed SGD implemented using parameter servers can deal with stragglers in a graceful manner. Similar ideas have also been applied to failure handling in this setting. For example, Narayanamurthy et al. [243] note that in an iteration of distributed batch SGD, if a worker responsible for one partition of the data fails, instead of waiting for this worker to recover and hence holding up overall execution progress, one can continue with an approximation of the contribution from this partition (using values from previous iterations), until the worker comes back up in subsequent iterations.

More generally, Schelter et al. [300] propose algorithm-specific "compensations" to handle failures in iterative ML algorithms. When a failure occurs, the system would allow the current iteration to finish, and then execute a user-supplied compensation function that brings the execution state to a "consistent" one from which the algorithm will still be able to converge. The compensation function is of course algorithm-specific, but the general framework has been shown to be effective with a range of algorithms such as link analysis and centrality in networks, path enumeration in graphs, and alternating least squares for matrix factorization [300].

7.3   WORKING WITH MARKETS OF TRANSIENT RESOURCES

Many cloud service providers offer computing resources at a deep discount but with only transient availability—they can be revoked at any time depending on the market condition. For example, besides the regular (*on-demand* or *reserved*) instances with fixed prices and guaranteed availability, Amazon EC2 also offers *spot* instances, whose market prices vary over time. Users set a bid price and will get the spot instances if the bid price is no lower than their market price. While in use, these machines are charged by hours, at their market price at the beginning of each hour. Once the market price rises above the original bid price, these machines will be taken away instantly, although the last partial hour of usage will not be charged. Spot market prices vary not only over time, but also across machine types and regional markets. Compared with the fixed prices of regular instances, spot market prices are often substantially (say, up to 90%) lower, but they can also quickly overtake the fixed prices and occasionally remain high for extended periods of time. As another example, Google's *preemptible* instances do not have fluctuating prices; they are charged by minute and subject to instant revocation based on the market condition.

Making effective use of such markets of cheap yet unreliable computing resources can be especially challenging for long-running ML workloads. While loss of resources can be regarded as failures, they are perhaps the worst kind possible, because a single spike in a market can revoke all machines acquired therein, with little or no time to react. Bidding strategies are also not obvious. For example, determining the cluster size involves new trade-offs: a large transient cluster may get a job done faster for cheaper, but also runs the risk of losing time and money for work lost in the event of a revocation. As another example, for Amazon spot instances, it may seem counterintuitive to bid at a price higher than the fixed price for the same machine type, but this is common and often a good strategy because it lessens the chance of revocation without significantly increasing the cost on average (recall that machines are charged at their market price, not their bid price).

As done in earlier sections of this chapter, we will explore techniques for working with markets that target the various levels of abstraction laid out first in Section 7.1. Before proceeding with that exploration, however, we shall first discuss several ideas that cut across multiple abstraction levels (example systems cited below will be discussed in more detail later).

- **Leverage more reliable resources.** They can be distributed storage services such as Amazon S3 or Elastic File System (for checkpointing [312, 324] or storing intermediate results [75, 153]), as well as regular machines with guaranteed availability (for replicated execution [324] or storing important state [139]).

- **Diversify the resource portfolio.** Earlier, in Section 7.1, we mentioned how heterogeneous clusters can be more cost-effective for some workloads [386]. Here, we can push the idea further to exploit the observation that markets for different resource types and across regions often follow different patterns. When resources from one market are not available or cost-effective, we can turn to other markets [139, 312, 324, 387]. For Amazon EC2, even within a single market, we can acquire sets of machines at different bid prices, which offer different trade-offs between expected cost and reliability that can be exploited [139, 153].

- **Model the markets.** To inform optimization, we need to model the markets, e.g., from historical Amazon EC2 price traces. Such models offer useful estimates such as mean time to failure [75, 139, 312, 387], and revocation probability before a target completion time [324, 387] or the end of a billing period [139]. Beyond single-point estimates, some systems take a more careful approach to modeling in order to quantify the risks associated with optimization decisions, which can be high when working with markets. They may provide a high-probability guarantee that the actual cost [152] or time [387] does not exceed some target, or optimize a combination of cost expectation and variance [153].

- **Adapt to the markets.** Runtime adaptation is an effective method for coping with market uncertainty. At the very least, any system that uses transient resources must be able to react in response to their revocation. When that happens, we can re-optimize remaining execution based on new market conditions [152]. Some systems also monitor market conditions and adapt proactively. For example, we can dynamically acquire additional resources or release current ones based on market conditions [139, 153], without waiting for revocation to happen.

- **Consider provider specifics.** Different cloud service providers offer transient resources in different ways, and some of the provider-specific details—such as billing and revocation policies—need to be considered in devising practically effective solutions. Because of Amazon EC2's popularity, many existing solutions are specific to Amazon spot instances. Perhaps the most commonly exploited are Amazon's policies of billing by hour and not charging the last partial hour in the event of a revocation. For example, releasing a machine before the billing hour ends would not be a good idea, since the remaining time must be paid for anyway [153, 387]. Furthermore, since revocation results in a free partial hour, one could strategically bid low and aim to complete within an hour [369]. In general, however, if it is not feasible or cost-effective to complete the work within an hour, then the time and cost overhead caused by revocations must be carefully considered [139, 153]. There is some recent work [153] toward developing solutions for a more general framework to accommodate some of the differences in how cloud service providers offer transient resources.

Having seen these general ideas above, we now present techniques targeting the various levels of abstraction introduced in Section 7.1.

Black-Box Programs: In Section 7.2, we have discussed techniques for handling failures for a black-box ML program. When working with markets, we have a few additional options besides checkpointing. First, some cloud service providers give short notices before revocations (e.g., two minutes in advance for Amazon EC2). If the program does not have a large amount of state, such a notice would allow reactive migration in response to a revocation event. Second, in parallel to executing the program with transient resources, we can also execute it on reliable resources. While replicating execution incurs additional cost, the hope is that the execution on fast and cheap transient resources will finish quickly, allowing us to stop the execution on reliable resources; on the other hand, the execution on reliable resources provides a fallback option in the event of a revocation. For example, targeting batch jobs on Amazon EC2, *SpotOn* [324] considers a range of options—proactive checkpointing, reactive migration, and replicating execution—as well as multiple markets, and chooses the most appropriate strategy depending on the situation. However, for parallel black-box programs, checkpointing and migration are more difficult, so *SpotOn* currently only supports replicating their execution.

To exploit markets of transient resources fully, we ideally want to support elastic—and oftentimes higher-than-usual—degrees of parallelism at run time. One recent trend is *serverless computing*, as exemplified by Amazon Lambda, which offers "functions as a service" where programmers can register functions in the cloud and compose them into programs; the cloud would provide storage for function input/output, mechanisms to trigger function execution, and the ability to automatically and dynamically scale to a large number of executions. While serverless computing has many compelling use cases, programmers need to rethink how to restructure their programs in this fashion, which may be difficult for many workloads or may incur high overhead. A recent critique of serverless computing [140] also identified a number of shortcomings of current serverless architectures, such as data shipping and reliance on slow storage for communication. Regardless of how serverless computing evolves in the future, a case can be made for programming at higher levels of abstraction, to allow automatic optimization of programs using serverless computing as an execution option.

Programs in Higher-Order, Data-Parallel Programming Models: There has been a large body of work using transient resources to support such programs including, but not limited to, ML workloads. Here we sample a few. In the context of *Hadoop*, one of the earliest work along these lines is by Chohan et al. [75], which uses additional Amazon spot instances to accelerate program execution; all intermediate results are stored in S3, or *HDFS* running on regular instances. The *Hadoop* scheduler, when assigning tasks to available machines, naturally leverages the extra spot instances to increase the degree of parallelism. Amazon's own *Elastic MapReduce* service takes advantage of spot instances in a similar fashion. A recent feature called *instance fleets* lets users specify rules for acquiring and maintaining (in response to revocations) a diverse portfolio of spot and non-spot instances of different machine types for *MapReduce*.

Handling *Spark* workloads is more challenging, since intermediate results are cached in memory and may be lost in a revocation event. *Flint* [312] uses *Spark*'s lineage information to checkpoint relevant RDDs proactively (as discussed in Section 7.2) using Amazon's *Elastic Block Store* as stable storage. *Flint* adapts checkpointing frequencies, and takes advantage of multiple markets to maintain the desired cluster size in response to revocations, bidding always at the fixed, on-demand price. *Flint* does not, however, proactively change the cluster.

Dyna [387] does not assume any particular data-parallel programming model, but works with a workflow of tasks, which can also represent the execution plan of a *MapReduce* or *Spark* program. With the knowledge of the workflow, *Dyna* has the flexibility of executing some tasks in parallel and deciding where to execute each task. *Dyna* also considers multiple Amazon EC2 markets, and tries execution on faster spot instances before falling back to regular ones—but only if doing so reduces the expected cost while ensuring that the estimated completion time (accounting for revocations) meets the target with high probability.

Support for elasticity afforded by data-parallel programming platforms such as *Hadoop* and *Spark* can be leveraged more aggressively when using transient resources. Although not targeting any specific platform, Zafer et al. [369] propose a strategy that can be applied in this setting. Exploiting Amazon's hourly charging policy, this strategy always bids for a cluster of spot instances that would complete the given program within an hour—if the cluster is revoked, there would be no charge because an hour has not passed. The strategy starts with a low bid price, and restarts with an increased bid price whenever the cluster is revoked. This strategy is shown to be optimal [369], but only if the program has perfect (linear) speedup. Unfortunately, this assumption is often not met in practice, and the strategy also depends crucially on Amazon's current charging policy.

Declarative ML Programs: As we have seen in earlier sections of this chapter, ML programs expressed in declarative languages enable more sophisticated optimizations. For example, starting with a "baseline" execution plan optimized for regular (on-demand, non-spot) instances, *Cümülön* [152] seeks to lower the expected execution cost by adding spot instances, while ensuring that the probability of significantly exceeding the baseline cost is low. Other than storage attached to the spot and regular instances, *Cümülön* does not assume any external stable storage; data not written to regular instances can be lost in a revocation event. Sending every write to regular instances can easily overwhelm them, however, so *Cümülön* relies on a combination of caching and selective checkpointing to save intermediate results: caching implicitly persists any data read by regular instances during execution, while selective checkpointing adds explicit checkpoint operators to strategic points in the execution plan. In the event of a revocation, *Cümülön* recovers lost results using the fine-grained lineage information derived from the semantics of linear algebra operators, as discussed in Example 7.4. *Cümülön* employs a market price model that captures diurnal and weekly periodicity, and carefully considers the bidding price and number of spot instances as well as the timing of their use. All these features and the optimization decisions involved are only possible because *Cümülön* works with declarative linear algebra workloads, whose behaviors are relatively easy to predict. Lower levels of abstraction lead to less predictability, which, when coupled with unpredictability of the market, will make it exceedingly difficult to guarantee the quality of optimization decisions.

Cümülön only makes a one-time decision on how to bid for spot instances, and assumes a single batch of them at any time during execution. In response to a revocation event, it can re-optimize and acquire a new batch of spot instances, but this adaptation is reactive. In comparison, *Cümülön-D* [153] adapts more proactively—it would consider acquiring more spot machines when the spot price drops, or releasing them in anticipation of price hikes. The dynamic optimization problem is modeled and solved as a Markov decision process; to avoid runtime optimization overhead, *Cümülön-D* precomputes a "cookbook" that allows the appropriate adaptation to be looked up at run time for any given market price and execution progress. This highly dynamic adaptation also motivates a simpler system to tame model complexity and adaptation overhead: *Cümülön-D* requires an external stable storage service such as Amazon Elastic

File System, which eliminates the need for complex recovery. The differences between *Cümülön* and *Cümülön*-D illustrate the design trade-offs in supporting declarative programs, for which the space of possibilities is rich. *Cümülön* has a more sophisticated system with more "smarts" built in, but predicting its behavior (especially in conjunction with revocations) becomes more complicated. On the other hand, by making some simplifying assumptions and giving up some optimization opportunities at lower levels, *Cümülön*-D offers more sophisticated optimizations at a higher level to support proactive adaptation.

Specific ML Algorithms or Recipes: While it is possible to tailor the use of transient resources to specific ML algorithms, a more general approach is to build solutions that can work for a family of ML algorithms sharing the same computational recipe. Consider, for example, *Proteus* [139], which targets parameter server workloads where workers are stateless. Such workloads stand to benefit from transient resources naturally. The bulk of work can be carried out by workers running on transient machines. The more critical work of servers can run on regular machines; if they become a bottleneck due to a large number of transient machines, *Proteus* will instead use regular machines for online backup, processing updates that are coalesced and streamed in the background from active servers running on transient machines. *Proteus* adaptively allocates machines from multiple Amazon spot markets, and accordingly transitions the computational roles played by spot and regular machines automatically. *Proteus* acts proactively in response to market conditions, and can take advantage of Amazon's charging policy to get some work done for free (by bidding aggressively and hoping for revocation within an hour). In general, however, aiming simply to maximize the amount of free work is not a good strategy, because frequent revocations may incur significant overhead for some workloads. Therefore, *Proteus* seeks to minimize average cost per unit work instead, taking into account both the opportunity and risk of aggressive bidding.

7.4   SUMMARY

In this chapter, we discussed how to handle resource heterogeneity and elasticity when running large-scale ML workloads in the cloud and cluster computing settings. Here, automatic optimization is highly desirable because it is difficult for users to choose among myriads of complex, interlocking options in a sometimes unpredictable environment. The increasing varieties of hardware (e.g., CPU vs. GPU), platforms (e.g., storage, compute, and application), and pricing policies (e.g., spot vs. regular) undoubtedly add to the challenges. These problems are not unique to ML (or database) workloads, and there are many ideas and techniques for coping with them—some targeting specific levels of abstraction and others being more general. As we have seen throughout this chapter, higher levels of abstraction and better understanding of the workloads enable more sophisticated optimizations, but on the other hand they tend to become less general. Recent work targeting workloads with declarative specifications or specific computational recipes seems promising, although much future work remains in finding the "sweet spot"—or perhaps multiple of them—between generality and effectiveness of automatic optimization for ML workloads.

CHAPTER 8

Systems for ML Lifecycle Tasks

In the previous chapters, we focused on the specification, execution, and optimization of ML algorithms in various settings. However, the process of running ML algorithms to train ML models is only one step, albeit a major one, in the end-to-end lifecycle of ML applications, as depicted in Figure 1.1 in Chapter 1. This lifecycle also involves the processes of sourcing and preparing data for ML, model selection and model management, and deployment of ML models into production. Tackling these challenges requires ideas and techniques that combine not just ML and data management, but also other fields of computing, including human-computer interaction and operating and distributed systems. We now dive into these auxiliary steps in the ML lifecycle in depth.

8.1 DATA SOURCING AND CLEANING FOR ML

ML does not exist in a vacuum—it is impossible in general to train ML models without training data from the very *data generating process* that we aim to make predictions about using ML. Thus, the very first step in any applied ML endeavor is gathering the training data and massaging it into a form needed for even starting the process of ML training. Moreover, ML is a classic example of "garbage in garbage out"—if the training data distribution is not representative of the data distribution where the ML models are deployed or if the training data is ridden with data errors, ML models could fail in unexpected ways [269]. We call this whole process of getting the training data in place as "sourcing" data for ML, which includes diverse tasks such as procuring the data from their sources, representing the data in an ML-friendly manner, getting high-quality labels for supervised ML, validating and cleaning the values of the features and labels, and overseeing the ML predictions served and all ML-related data in general throughout the application's life. Such validation often includes automated components such as outlier detection, for which there are many algorithms [145], but often applied in a custom dataset-specific and human-in-the-loop manner. According to recent surveys of data scientists in practice, all data-related processes typically consume 80–90% (if not more) of the time and effort spent by most data scientists [1, 2]. We categorize existing data management-oriented research in this space into three groups: procuring data for ML, cleaning data for ML, and data labeling frameworks.

Procuring Data for ML: Most organizations have large databases with different types of data and many tables (even up to billions [32]). There are also many publicly available sources of datasets, both free data (e.g., Freebase or Wikipedia) and commercial data sold on data marketplaces [4, 14, 41]. Given an applied ML task, it is part of a data scientist's responsibility to identify and procure all potentially relevant datasets, inspect them, and transform them into a form that can let ML modeling commence. Naturally, there is a growing work on software infrastructure for better governance of ML-related data. For instance, *TFX* [42] is an "ML platform" built around *TensorFlow* for integrated management of data and ML tasks. It supports procuring data from various sources, including DBMSs, flat files, and data streams, and feeding such data pipelines to various ML training, testing, and serving modules by leveraging Apache Beam and other such flexible data infrastructure. This requires *loose coupling* between the data and ML system, which in turn requires flexible schema representations for data. *TFX* uses semi-structured JSON-based ProtoBuf formats for data combined with a set of constraints to enforce data integrity. *TFX* also supports semi-automatic business rules that can trigger alerts to ML DevOps engineers based on issues with the data sources or quality.

Sometimes, even procuring the right data could be a headache, say, because it is owned by a different team within the same organization. In this context, *Hamlet* [202] and *Hamlet*++ [307] showed that in many cases of ML over multi-table relational data, procuring extra tables for joining with the main table may not really be needed. By applying learning theory, they showed that key-foreign key dependencies present in a multi-table database imply that the features brought in by such joins may not help improve prediction accuracy. But avoiding such joins introduce a twist to the bias-variance tradeoff of ML in that it may not alter the bias but it could cause the variance to rise in some cases. *Hamlet* presented some learning theory-inspired and easy-to-apply decision rules that only look at the metadata of the database to predict if the variance will rise significantly [202]. While *Hamlet* focused on linear classifiers such as logistic regression and Naive Bayes, *Hamlet*++ showed that similar results hold for more complex classifiers such as decision trees, SVMs, and neural networks as well.

In some cases, training data may not be available in the organization itself, which leads practitioners to purchase data sold on data marketplaces. These are platforms where buyers and sellers interact to exchange commercially valuable datasets. But instead of buying an expensive dataset wholesale, one could imagine purchasing only subsets of the data computed by a relational query and pay a lower price. This led to the framework of query-based pricing [41]. Building upon this idea, *Nimbus* studied the possibily of releasing only ML model instances trained on subsets of the data for cheaper prices compared to procuring the whole dataset [68, 69]. This leads to new tradeoffs between cost and accuracy, as well as between optimizing for revenue of the seller and coverage of potential customers with different purchasing power. Applying techniques from micro-economics and game theory, *Nimbus* showed that it is possible to design a practical data marketplace for selling ML models with formal guarantees on the prediction accuracy and arbitrage-freeness of the sale.

Cleaning Data for ML: Data cleaning is a long-standing topic in the database literature, even for regular SQL analytics [76, 278]. Many of those issues still matter for ML but have interesting accuracy-oriented implications. For instance, handling missing values in features is still unavoidable. But disambiguating and deduplicating entities in categorical features may or may not be essential depending on the number of training examples due to the bias-variance trade-off. For instance, both "CA" and "California" can appear as the representation for the state of California in a categorical feature named State. ML models can still work without accuracy issues, if both representations have enough training examples. Otherwise, deduplicating and consolidating these value representations can help improve accuracy. Identifying and handling outliers and erroneous data values is also an issue but what is an outlier depends on the task. For instance, the value "-1" in a numeric feature named Age could corrupt the ML model and lead to serious accuracy issues, but the same value in a categorical feature named State can be treated as just another (say, unknown) category without serious accuracy issues.

A recent line of work focuses on human-in-the-loop cleaning and aims to reduce human effort for fixing errors in the data either by exploiting statistical properties of ML. *Active-Clean* [194] integrates iterative data cleaning operations with stochastic gradient descent-based training of convex ML models. They observe that it is risky in general to perform iterative cleaning with training in the loop because it might lead to statistically spurious conclusions caused by the Simpson's Paradox. They then propose new sampling mechanisms that exploit the convexity of the loss function to reduce the number of examples that need to be cleaned by a human in the loop during training itself, while still offering convergence guarantees and ensuring the model trained is accurate. *BoostClean* [195] is an automated data cleaning tool to detect and repair violations of domain value constraints for features in the training data. Based on a library of functions for detecting and repairing data errors, *BoostClean* casts this problem as a form of boosting to obtain the best ensemble of functions from the library that improves the accuracy of the downstream ML model. Related is *HoloClean*, which casts data repair as a holistic probabilistic inference task that jointly processes various sources of constraints, including domain-specific integrity constraints, outlier detection methods, and knowledge bases, while also exploiting the statistical properties of the data. It exploits *DeepDive* under the covers and introduces new optimizations and approximations to enable its compilation and execution stack to scale to large datasets.

TFX [42], mentioned earlier, also helps with validating the quality of both training and serving data for ML-based Web products at Google. It allows for creating application-specific rules for monitoring the accuracy behavior of deployed ML models and connecting them with training-related issues such as wrong feature values, outliers, and concept drift. Finally, *DataLinter* [155] is a tool that automated the application of a list of ML-specific data quality checks such as encodings of categorical features, distributions, missing value handling, etc. They call such issues "lints" and package them into a tool that can help data scientists, especially novices, avoid many routine but widespread data quality pitfalls in applying ML for data analytics.

Data Labeling Frameworks: All supervised ML models require labeled examples for training. While in many applications, the labels are automatically created as part of the data-driven application's lifecycle (e.g., past customers that have churned or not in customer churn prediction), such labeled data may not be forthcoming in all applications. In some applications, especially in vision, one can generate high-quality synthetically labeled data using simulators that exploit the knowledge of the underlying physics. For instance, [164] present a technique called "domain randomization" that involves creating and composing 3D models of objects, adding irrelevant geometric shapes to the scene to make it harder to identify the objects, and overlaying random textures. They show that training data generated with this approach still allows deep CNNs to yield high accuracy for object recognition tasks in self-driving car scenarios. However, many new consumer-facing applications of AI, as well as many domain scientific applications may not have large labeled datasets to begin with or not have fine-grained knowledge of the underlying mechanisms that produce the data to be able to simulate it well. The common solution in such cases is to have "subject-matter experts" from that domain manually annotate a large unlabeled corpus. But such manual labeling could be expensive, and there may not be enough experts willing to label data. Crowdsourcing presents an alternative to collect labels from common crowd workers that may not be experts. But not all applications are amenable to crowdsourcing, perhaps due to privacy constraints or the sheer complexity of the prediction tasks. The paradigm of "weak supervision" can help such cases [20]. Essentially, we drop the assumption that labels have to be perfect and instead, we allow labels to be approximate and noisy.

Snorkel [284] is a framework that helps denoise labeled data produced by various sources of weak supervision. It produces probabilistic training data wherein a label is not a point value but a probability distribution over the target vocabulary. The sources of weak supervision could be diverse, including labeling functions programmed by domain experts, say, in the form of Python scripts that capture various domain-specific heuristics, patterns, and intuitions, as well as crowdsourced labels, data augmentation techniques such as label-preserving translations and rotations of images, external knowledge bases (e.g., Freebase), and so on. Denoising is performed by learning a probabilistic graphical model that is generative in an unsupervised manner. By tracking the provenance of labeling sources in this manner and denoising their inputs, *Snorkel* often boosts the accuracy of downstream discriminative models. *Snuba* and *Babble Labble* build upon *Snorkel* to further reduce per-example manual labeling effort. *Snuba* automates weak supervision when unlabeled data is available along with some labeled examples [334]. It learns multiple simple classifiers on the labeled data and produces such heuristic automated labeling functions iteratively until a large part of the unlabeled data is covered. *Babble Labble* allows uers to provide natural language explanations for their labeling heuristics, which it then converts to labels using a semantic parser [136]. Such a high level of abstraction is sometimes feasible in text analytics tasks and reduces the barrier for domain experts without programming skills to provide weak supervision.

Finally, *Snorkel Metal* generalizes the idea of Snorkel to multi-task learning [384] by allowing users to specify hierarchically-related labeling functions for hierarchically related subtasks defined with a "task schema" [285]. By allowing downstream models for these tasks to share both supervision and internal learned features, *Metal* can potentially boost accuracy for all tasks. Taking this idea even further, the "massively multi-task" (*MMT*) vision overhauls weak supervision for neural networks in large organizations to improve ML engineers' productivity [15, 286]. In *MMT*, there is a single multi-task model, analogous to a single central code repository. Each prediction task's weak supervision signals are "checked in" to update the *MMT* model. If smaller models are needed for specific tasks, they can then be supervised by the *MMT* model. Overall, *MMT* pools the human effort that goes into weak supervision across tasks and enables ML users to share the benefits of both labeling and jointly learned features across tasks.

8.2   FEATURE ENGINEERING AND DEEP LEARNING

Most ML models simply cannot be used directly on most raw data attributes, or they might yield poor generalization errors if used directly. For instance, in our running example of customer churn prediction, two common customer attributes are `Name` and `Address`. If used directly as features for ML, these attributes will be treated as categorical features with very large domains, since the number of unique names or addresses is likely very large. Even worse, these attributes may not be "generalizable," i.e., when the trained ML model is deployed for prediction in the application, new values of names or addresses might arise that ML model will not know how to handle (unless it is mapped to a special "unknown" category). Thus, data scientists almost always have to apply some knowledge about the data and application domain to covert the raw data into a clean *representation* for ML, i.e., obtain the well-defined *feature vector* with numeric or categorical features with fully known domains. This overarching process of converting the raw data into the precise feature vector to use for ML is called *feature engineering*, *feature extraction*, or *representation extraction*.

Forms of Feature Engineering: Feature engineering involves a wide swathe of data transformations depending on the data types and how helpful different attributes of the data are for prediction. We categorize a few major forms of such transformations. Of course, this is not an exhaustive list, since they are far too diverse in practice to enumerate succinctly.

1. **Recoding and Value Conversions:** Even on tabular (relational) data with well-defined categorical and numeric features, simple forms of feature engineering might be needed for different ML models, including one-hot encoding of categorical features, binning of numeric features, and scaling of numeric features. ML models that operate on numeric feature spaces (e.g., logistic regression or neural networks) cannot directly handle categorical features that draw values from a discrete set. One-hot encoding converts a categorical feature X with domain D_X to a binary (0/1) feature vector of length $|D_X|$ (or strictly, $|D_X| - 1$) with exactly one of these features being non-zero corresponding to the value of X present in a given example. Similarly, for some ML models such as Bayesian Networks or MLNs, numeric features are often discretized and converted to categorical features by binning based on their values.

Many ML models that operate on numeric feature spaces require feature scaling, also called "normalization" or whitening. This involves updating the feature by subtracting its mean (over the training set) and dividing by the standard deviation. In the case of sparse features with many zeros, normalization may also be done with the difference of the maximum and minimum values to help preserve sparsity. Such transformations rebalance the influence of different features that vary widely in the ranges of their values on the ML model. Finally, data cleaning concerns such as entity matching and value standardization also become a part of feature engineering for ML workloads. For example, the values "CA" and "California" correspond to the same entity in a categorical feature representing state. But unlike value standardization for SQL workloads, ML presents semantic differences in how to interpret the values. For instance, one could present processor speed "2.3 GHz" as a string-valued attribute for SQL queries but one might have to write a string processing script to convert this value to a numeric feature value "2.3" with the implicit semantics that the units are GHz for this feature.

2. **Feature Selection:** Still focused on structured (relational) data with well-defined categorical and numeric features, feature selection techniques such as subset selection and feature ranking are sometimes used to explicitly reduce the number of features used for ML modeling [132]. Having fewer features could improve interpretability of some models, but more importantly, it could also improve the prediction accuracy of some models due to the bias-variance tradeoff [308]. Optimal subset selection is NP-Hard and a variety of search heuristics, including forward selection, backward selection, and stepwise elimination exist. In many applications, such feature selection often happens in a human-in-the-loop fashion due to special domain-specific constraints on what features the data scientist wants to include or exclude.

3. **Dimensionality Reduction:** Procedures such as principal component analysis (PCA), linear discriminant analysis (LDA), singular value decomposition (SVD), and general non-negative matrix factorization (NMF) are also common for reducing the number of features, especially for compressing large sparse feature vectors into smaller dense feature vectors [123]. Such techniques yield similar benefits as feature selection in terms of accuracy, but they construct complex combinations of the base features, while feature selection techniques retain the semantics of the base features.

4. **Temporal Feature Extraction:** Time series data can be viewed as structured data that do not satisfy the IID assumption because of correlations of values over time. Thus, when applying ML models to such data, one might have to extract temporally-aware features for forecasting or other prediction applications. There is a large body of work in the data mining literature on extracting features from such data types, including detecting "motifs" (patterns that convey some information and likely occur often), similarity metrics such as

dynamic time warping for comparing pairs of time series, window-based feature replication, etc.

5. **Textual Feature Extraction:** In many structured datasets, some attributes could be textual, e.g., reviews in a recommendation system. Similar to time series feature extraction, a wide variety of textual feature extraction techniques are commonly used. One popular technique is *bag-of-words*, which converts the text to a large sparse feature vector of counts of words from a given vocabulary, and *n-grams*, which looks at fixed-length sequences of tokens from the vocabulary that occur in the text. In many applications, bespoke domain-specific extraction scripts are common for dealing with textual data, including the use of entity dictionaries (e.g., names of all restaurants in a city or names of all celebrities), regular expressions for detecting specific patterns (e.g., are there words that are all in upper case or are there multiple exclamation marks), and more specific features that a data scientist thinks could be informative for ML modeling.

6. **Textual Embeddings:** The state of the art for feature extraction from textual data types in many applications are the so-called "distributed representations" such as Word2Vec, GloVe, and Doc2Vec [205, 237, 266]. These are essentially shallow neural networks that map each token in the vocabulary to a small dense feature vector, called an *embedding*, instead of a large sparse feature vector as is obtained from bag-of-words or n-gram feature extraction. Such embeddings are typically constructed by solving an optimization problem that creates a representation based on the occurrence context of a token in terms of predicting its neighboring tokens. The training procedures for some embeddings resemble matrix factorization algorithms, albeit trained in an application-agnostic manner on a general corpus [237]. Such embedding features have been found to have remarkable analogizing properties. For instance, with Word2Vec, if one subtracts the vector of "man" from "king" and adds "woman," the token that is closest to the resultant vector is "queen." Such properties help improve prediction accuracy in many NLP tasks.

7. **Recurrent Neural Networks (RNNs):** Generalizing further from textual embeddings, RNNs are complex sequential ML models that integrate feature extraction and predictive modeling. In a sense, they construct a hierarchy of linear and non-linear transformations that also take into account the sequential dependencies in the data [124]. In fact, a form of RNNs known as long short-term memory (LSTM) networks can learn very long dependencies automatically by employing an internal state vector that is selectively modified based on the sequential patterns [215]. LSTMs now yield state-of-the-art accuracy in several sequential ML tasks, including on time series, speech, and audio data [28], and for NLP tasks such as sentiment mining and machine translation [326]. It should, however, be noted that in place of complex manual feature extraction for such sequential data types, RNNs often require more tedious and computationally expensive neural architecture exploration and hyper-parameter tuning efforts.

8. **Convolutional Neural Networks (CNNs):** In the same spirit as RNNs, CNNs integrate feature extraction and predictive modeling for images and similar data types such as video. CNNs also construct a hierarchy of linear and non-linear transformations, but they exploit spatial locality of information in the input using operations called *convolutions*. These feature extractors are parametrized, with the parameters learned automatically during training with backpropagation [124]. CNNs now yield the state-of-the-art accuracy in several image and video prediction tasks, including the famous ImageNet classification contest [100]. Certain forms of CNNs also excel on sequential data such as speech [83], short text, and time series data. However, as with RNNs, CNNs also often require tedious and computationally expensive neural architecture exploration and hyper-parameter tuning efforts.

Several recent works have focused on abstracting and optimizing the dataflow of different forms of feature engineering from the data management standpoint, especially on structured data. At a high level, these systems propose a representation language or API for a class of feature engineering tasks that is more "declarative" than manually executing these tasks one by one in a lower-level language. Almost all of them then introduce execution optimization techniques inspired by relational query optimization to reduce runtimes resource costs. We categorize these systems based on the kinds of dataflows and feature engineering tasks they target.

Feature Selection Systems: A key example system in this category is *Columbus* [186, 373, 374], which considers feature selection on structured data as not a one-shot algorithm but rather a human-in-the-loop "dialogue with the algorithms." Focusing on the R environment, *Columbus* introduces a domain-specific language (DSL) for exploratory feature selection, in particular, various subset selection heuristics for linear and logistic regression models. By composing scripts in this DSL, the data scientist can focus on the logic of *what* feature subsets they want to explore rather than write lower-level R code that tells the system *how* to execute them. Under the covers, *Columbus* compiles the script to an abstract representation of the projections to perform on the dataset and accuracy budgets. It then applies a suite of materialization optimizations, including lazy vs. eager materialization of projections, materialization of the QR decomposition, coreset sampling, and warm starting of models. The former two techniques improve runtimes without affecting accuracy, while the latter two balance runtime-accuracy tradeoffs. *Columbus* uses a simple cost-based and accuracy-aware optimizer to pick which combinations of techniques to use on a given input instance.

More General Feature Engineering Workflows: This class of systems focus on more general feature engineering tasks, typically abstracted as workflows of data transformations or even general programs.

Brainwash [34] envisions a system architecture for rapid exploration of different forms of feature extraction (regardless of data type) by treating them all as custom user-defined functions.

While this approach means it may not be able to exploit any specific algebraic or ML-specific properties to optimize such workflows, it could enable auxiliary support such as reuse of workflows by matching templates, materialization of intermediate results, and recommendations of features based on past workflows. *DeepDive* [377] supports a similar architecture for extracting features from unstructured data for the task of knowledge base construction (KBC). While it exposes a logic-based language called DDLog to the user, *DeepDive* supports user-defined functions for feature engineering written in Python embedded into DDLog scripts. This allows *DeepDive* to incorporate complex, ad-hoc, domain-specific information for feature extraction into its core SRL-based framework.

KeystoneML [316] focuses on pipelines of feature extraction operations for structured data and images. It introduced optimizations for selecting between different algorithmic operators, especially solvers for numerical optimization problems, when executing such pipelines end-to-end. It uses a cost model for runtime performance to pick between different solvers based on the properties of the data input. *Zombie* [35] is different from the above systems in that it does not focus on multi-stage workflows but rather a single step of evaluating the utility of a given piece of feature engineering code. Instead of blindly processing all of the raw data to extract features and then check if ML accuracy has improved, Zombie introduces indexing-based techniques to steer the data processing to focus on "more useful" data subsets earlier on. This could enable faster exploration and earlier stopping when exploring and evaluating newly engineered features.

Handling Deep Learning Features: Finally, general deep learning frameworks such as *TensorFlow* and *PyTorch* enable data scientists to specify learning-based feature extraction as part of the neural architecture itself. In this sense, they can be viewed as systems for feature engineering as well. As of this writing, there is not much work specifically on data management for deep learning-based feature engineering, except perhaps for *ModelHub* [235] and *Vista* [241].

ModelHub is a tool that enables users to snapshot, store, version, and reuse deep neural network models. In particular, it focuses on deep CNNs for computer vision applications. To reduce storage costs, *ModelHub* employs compression across model versions and snapshots during a training run. This leads to a tradeoff between storage space and model re-creation times for retrieval, which *ModelHub* optimizes based on user preferences. We can view *ModelHub* as a feature engineering system in that it supports reusing pre-trained CNNs for *transfer learning*, an emerging popular approach to using CNNs in data-constrained applications. In particular, to remove the last layer(s) of a pre-trained CNN and "fine tune" it on a new dataset is to treat the lower parts of that CNN as just a feature extractor.

Vista [241] observes that users typically explore multiple layers of pre-trained CNNs as the feature representation of images. This is a "model selection" process that uses CNNs for feature engineering [200]. *Vista* observes that this process could have computational redundancy due to repeated partial CNN inference—an instance of the classical database issue of view materialization tradeoffs. *Vista* optimizes such tradeoffs based on user preferences and enables more declarative execution of this workload at scale. It builds on top of a deep learning framework such as *TensorFlow* for CNN inference combined with a distributed memory-based dataflow system such as *Spark* for efficient, scalable, and fault-tolerant execution of this workload.

8.3   MODEL SELECTION AND MODEL MANAGEMENT

Model Selection: Model selection is the overarching process of obtaining a "satisfactory" *prediction function* using a given (labeled) dataset, wherein satisfactory is defined by the application user using metrics such as accuracy and/or cost. This process lies at the heart of obtaining "good" accuracy with ML because it lets a user control the bias-variance tradeoff in a structured manner [308]. It is typically an iterative human-in-the-loop process but most existing ML systems provide little support for optimizing this process end-to-end. The model selection process is typically both data-intensive and compute-intensive. Thus, it is crucial to understand this process in more detail from the systems standpoint. At a high level, model selection subsumes feature engineering and also includes at least two other key ML-related processes: *algorithm selection* and *hyper-parameter tuning*. It is a combination of decisions for these three processes, dubbed a "model selection triple" in the literature, that determines what prediction function is ultimately picked [200]. Figure 8.1(A) illustrates this process.

Algorithm Selection: Recall that feature engineering is the process of creating the feature vector representation to be used for ML. Algorithm selection, on the other hand, is the process of deciding which *hypothesis space* of prediction functions to use for the application. For example, for a binary classification application such as spam detection, one could use decision trees, Naive Bayes, logistic regression, SVMs, neural networks, or other types of ML classification models. Even for a given ML model, e.g., logistic regression, one could use stochastic gradient descent (SGD) or a batch gradient method as the numerical optimization procedure for training. Similarly, for a neural network, one has to specify its *architecture*, which includes the number and types of layers, number of neurons, and types of activation functions. All these decisions are part of algorithm selection because they affect the hypothesis space of prediction functions available for use. In practice, algorithm selection is not guided only by prediction accuracy but rather a complex mix of technical and non-technical factors beyond just accuracy, including runtime, resource cost, availability and ease-of-use of training tools, and user-specific judgments on the "interpretability" of a prediction function.

Hyper-parameter Tuning: This is the process of deciding what hyper-parameter values, which are tunable "knobs," to use for a chosen ML model and training algorithm. Almost all ML models and training algorithms have such knobs because they let users control the bias-variance tradeoff and/or configure the training to be more effective. For example, logistic regression with SGD has at least 4 hyper-parameters: balance between L1 and L2 regularization (also called elastic net regularization), regularization strength, step size (also called learning rate), and step size decay rule. On top of these, one can also view the *convergence criterion* as another hyper-parameter, e.g., number of training iterations or a threshold for

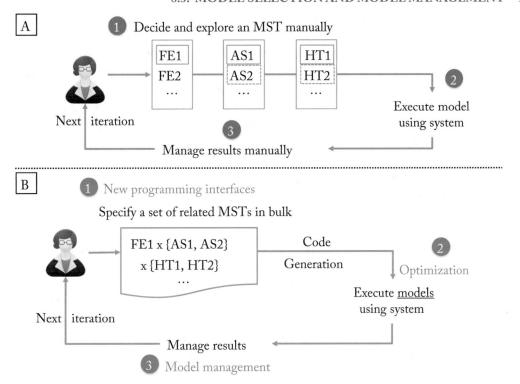

Figure 8.1: (A) Illustrating how model selection is handled by most ML systems today. The data scientist decides the feature representation with feature engineering, followed by algorithm selection conditioned on the feature representation and hyper-parameter tuning conditioned on the preceding two decisions. This "model selection triple" (MST) is the key object of exploration in model selection. (B) Often, the data scientist can group different logically related MSTs for bulk execution, e.g., combining many hyper-parameters in one go. Research in model selection and model management systems can be categorized at a high-level into new programming interfaces to enable such bulk specification of MSTs, optimization techniques for executing a set of MSTs, and model management systems and techniques to better manage the results.

the fractional drop in the loss value or validation error across iterations. As with algorithm selection, hyper-parameters configurations are typically picked using heuristics that combine technical and non-technical factors. A popular heuristic is "grid search," which requires the user to specify a small set of values for each hyper-parameter and construct the cross-product of all such sets. "Random search" is another popular heuristic that picks a random subset of the preceding set of combinations. More sophisticated hyper-parameter search procedures, including Bandit-based approaches [209] and Bayesian optimization [315], have been studied for various ML models, and this remains an active area of research in the ML community.

Model selection is a process that is rife with data management challenges, as identified and characterized in [200]. These challenges can be split into three high-level issues: programming interfaces, execution optimizations, and model management. The programming interface for model selection determines the abstraction level at which users engage in the model selection process. Execution optimizations are database-inspired systems techniques that help reduce runtimes or other resource costs. Model management involves capturing, storing, and managing the provenance of models generated during this process. Many systems that support model selection-related tasks tackle one or more of these challenges, which is how we split the rest of this subsection's discussion. Figure 8.1(B) illustrates how such systems and ideas relate to the model selection process and help improve it.

Programming Interfaces: At one extreme, users can specify each training configuration one by one in their favorite ML tool, e.g., *Scikit-Learn*. At the other extreme, users can be removed from the loop by an automated search process that is hardcoded by the ML system developer. The latter approach is often called *AutoML*. Examples of AutoML systems include *AutoWeka* [330], *Auto-SKLearn* [116], *MLBase* [193] and its component *TuPAQ* [317], and *QuIC-M* [49]. *AutoWeka* imposes a customizable search procedure on top of Weka's ML implementations so that users need to exert almost no effort for model selection, while *Auto-SKLearn* does something similar for the ML algorithms in *Scikit-learn*. *MLBase* goes further by abstracting out high-level ML tasks, such as classification, themselves as operators. Under the covers, *MLBase* and *TuPAQ* hardcode multi-armed bandit-style explore-exploit techniques for performing algorithm selection and hyper-parameter tuning automatically. *QuIC-M* builds upon this idea to also support different data types, more automation for data preparation and feature extraction steps, and sampling-based estimates of the convergence behavior of iterative models for faster model selection. *Google AutoML* automates the creation of computer vision-focused CNNs based on a user-given dataset and cost budgets [5].

Other systems and tools explore semi-automated programming interfaces, some inspired by the database notion of declarative query specification. For example, *Longview* [26] provides simple APIs for model selection in an RDBMS context, while *Sherlock* [336] provides more automated model search APIs. *ModelHub* [235], which we discussed earlier, provides a higher-level API for retrieving and reusing pre-trained CNNs as part of fine tuning and transfer learning for computer vision applications. Libraries such as *glmnet* in R, *Keras*, and *TFLearn* [18] also provide APIs for various parts of model selection, especially hyper-parameter tuning. In the commercial arena, *AzureML* provides programmatic (and GUI-based) mechanisms to specify "parameter sweeps" for automating hyper-parameter tuning. Similarly, *FBLearnerFlow* [6] is a tool from Facebook for specifying and orchestrating large-scale model selection executions and experimentation. Finally, *SageMaker* [3] is a cloud-based tool from Amazon for visually and programmatically specifying and managing model selection workflows.

Execution Optimizations: A few systems have studied RDBMS-inspired execution optimizations for some parts of the model selection process, some of which are adapted to the ML setting in an accuracy-aware manner. These can be categorized into two: exact optimizations that do not affect ML accuracy and approximate optimizations that do affect accuracy but have empirical mechanisms to guard against substantial drops in accuracy.

As an example of the first category, *TuPAQ* [317] batches data scans for training different algorithms and hyper-parameter combinations. *Columbus* [374] also exploited batched data scans but in the context of exploratory feature subset selection. This optimization reduces the I/O cost on large-scale datasets, while yielding the same eventual ML models. Another example is *Helix* [358], which abstracts feature extraction and ML training workflows for classical ML models in a higher-level API. This allows *Helix* to apply database-inspired view materialization optimizations for reusing intermediate data across model selection iterations, thus potentially reducing runtimes for human-in-the-loop training.

As an example of the second category, [275] applies online aggregation-style techniques to hyper-parameter tuning for iterative gradient descent-based ML. In particular, they use empirical mechanisms to stop the exploration of certain combinations automatically if they do not improve accuracy. Along similar lines, *Hemingway* [258], which we discussed earlier in Chapter 7, automates the task of estimating the number of iterations needed for gradient descent-based ML to converge to a desired accuracy in conjunction with deciding how many nodes to use in a cluster for a desired runtime. Finally, [212] takes an even higher-level view of the model selection process by considering multi-tenancy, especially for neural network models. They introduce a Bayesian optimization technique that can learn from the execution results of other users to decide which model to use for a given user's model selection. They do so by maintaining a database of previously trained models and datasets and using an explore-exploit technique to better predict which models might be most useful for a new dataset relative to manual decision baselines.

Model Management: The process of model selection almost always leads to the creation of a large number of trained model instances, often even in the millions [6]. Thus, at this scale, models themselves become a new form of data. Model management is the task of managing the storage, retrieval, versioning, and provenance of models and their associated model selection metadata. Such capability might be needed for various reasons: reproducibility, auditing, reuse, and discovery of pre-existing models. We classify tools and frameworks for model management into three categories based on their primary intended functionality: model serialization formats, tools for model capture and storage, and model metadata management.

The first category includes at least three popular formatting frameworks for model serialization and sharing: Portable Model Mark-up Language (PMML) [13], Portable Format for Analytics (PFA) [12], and Open Neural Network Exchange (ONNX) [11]. PMML is an XML-based meta-language for serializing ML model parameters and some associated metadata. PFA is a successor to PMML that is JSON-based and supports more functionality for capturing new forms of ML models and feature extraction pipelines used to create those models. Finally, ONNX is a formatting and sharing mechanism targeting deep neural networks, especially those trained with Torch, PyTorch, Caffe, CNTX, and MXNet. Google has similar formats for models trained with TensorFlow. The second category includes *Longview* [26], *ModelHub* [235], *ModelDB* [337], and *MISTIQUE* [335]. *Longview* uses an RDBMS to store models and their metadata. *ModelHub*, *ModelDB*, and *MISTIQUE* primarily use custom file formats for storing models, especially neural networks. *ModelHub* also uses an RDBMS in addition for the associated metadata. Both *ModelHub* and *MISTIQUE* introduce ML model-specific compression techniques to save space when archiving and versioning a large number of models and/or some feature extraction pipelines. In the final category are *TFHub* [16], Amazon's ML metadata management tool [299], *MLFlow* on *Spark* from Databricks [8], *GroundFlor* [119] for capturing and managing context data from ML experimentations, and model "discovery" tools [236] that help users locate relevant models based on their metadata and other desired properties.

Privacy in ML Systems: In the context of model selection, there are many reasons for altering the ML algorithm and/or hyper-parameters beyond accuracy or runtime. A key reason is *privacy*—some applications, especially in health sciences, require guarantees that the ML model learns only population-level aggregate knowledge that cannot reveal exact information about specific individuals in the dataset. *Differential privacy* has emerged as a popular rigorous notion of privacy for data analytics, including ML [108]. It is a cryptography-inspired approach that involves injecting some carefully structured forms of noise into what the model learns. For instance, [379] present a mechanism to modify the objective function of a class of optimization problems, including linear and logistic regression, to make them differentially private. There is a large body of work in the theory and ML literatures on making ML algorithms differentially private, and that topic is beyond the scope of this book. But we note that differentially private ML algorithms are only beginning to become mainstream. Most ML systems still do not offer differentially private ML algorithms, with the key concerns being the development overhead of rewriting the ML implementation, potential degradation of accuracy due to an inherent tradeoff with privacy, and runtime overhead. To this end, [356] presented a new "bolt-on" approach to make a class of popular ML algorithms differentially private without needing to modify their implementations. They use a classical technique called output perturbation that adds noise to the model parameters after training rather than during training. Thus, they avoid any changes to the ML system's internals, unlike prior approaches. They also proved that this approach can also offer better accuracy, yielding another benefit. This approach was prototyped in Python and integrated with the in-RDBMS ML system *Bismarck*, which we discussed in Chapter 2. While prior approaches required tedious code changes to the low-level UDFs of *Bismarck*, this approach did not require modifying the UDFs.

8.4   INTERACTION, VISUALIZATION, DEBUGGING, AND INSPECTION

As with many other forms of computing, going beyond programmatic interfaces could make ML-based data analytics more accessible to users at various levels of expertise. In this light, there is some work on interactive tools and techniques for handling both ML tasks and artifacts. We split such work into two high-level categories: interactive exploration tools, which primarily aim to make it easier for the user in the loop to interactively perform ML tasks, and ML debugging tools, which primarily aim to help users interactively debug the behavior of ML models.

Interactive Exploration Tools for ML: Enterprise ML tools such as SAS have long had interactive visual interfaces, including drag-and-drop workbenches. More recently, cloud ML services such as *AzureML Studio* [7] and *Amazon SageMaker* [3] provide support for easy construction, scaling, and management of end-to-end ML workflows in a visual manner. Going beyond such visual interaction tools, a few recent systems target other modalities of interactive specification. *QUIC-M* [49] enables users to interactively construct ML models on a pen-and-touch board. Users can touch and drag to subselect data and specify the features. It uses data sampling and Bayesian hyper-parameter optimization techniques under the covers to quickly perform model selection and obtain approximate ML models and lets users interactively explore the results. *Helix* [358] offers a new dataflow language integrated into Scala for specifying and interactively refining ML pipelines. It optimizes the dataflow DAGs and injects materialization decisions to reuse partial computations and datasets across iterations to improve runtime performance. Finally, *Ava* [162] provides a chat-bot front-end to make it easier to build models interactively. It enables users to specify a few feature extraction and model training tasks in natural language and uses natural language translation to pick from a repository of "storyboards" for typical model building templates.

ML Debugging and Inspection Tools: As with regular software, ML-based software can also fail in unexpected ways. Thus, inspecting and debugging ML artifacts is an important topic that is receiving more research attention. We categorize work in this space into three groups: debugging ML results and/or data, interpreting/explaining/debugging trained ML models, and enforcing auxiliary constraints such as "fairness."

We discussed earlier in this chapter about the issues of data validation and cleaning for ML. But in many cases, even after model building is (partially) over, data scientists want to assess the behavior of their models on various subsets of the data to identify if any particular parts are causing accuracy issues or to take further action on improving the data or model building process. In this regard, [167] introduced the concept of an "ML cube" inspired by data cubes for exploring and comparing ML prediction results on different slices of the data. These slices can be interactively specified using predicates on the values of some features. They built a graphical tool, *MLCube Explorer*, to enable users to explore various slices, drill down in to data subsets, and compare various accuracy measures of trained models. *Flipper* [333] is a framework for debugging programmatically generated labeled data. It offers users an easy-to-interpret higher level description of issues in the training data rather than have users manually sample and inspect examples randomly to fix the labeled data generation code. These descriptions essentially abstract features of the data automatically and present them in various modalities, e.g., textual descriptions. Finally, *SliceFinder* [79] is a framework for automating the process of finding data subsets where the ML model has poorer accuracy than the overall dataset. As with *MLCube*, slices are defined by predicates on some feature values that are interpretable and meaningful for the application users to take further action, e.g., sourcing more labeled data for some groups. It uses a set of heuristics to rank and surface "problematic" slices to the user.

A more recent line of work aims to help "debug" complex ML models to help shed light on their prediction behavior. *PALM* [196] is a tool to summarize the effects of different parts of the training data on a "black-box" model such as deep neural network. It does so by approximating the complex model with a two-part model that may be easier to interpret: it constructs a partitioning of the feature space with a decision tree and learns a smaller complex model for each partition. This could perhaps help users prioritize which parts of the data to inspect when explaining a given prediction of the model instead of looking at the raw training examples themselves, say, with nearest neighbor searches. *Luigi* [306] is an abstraction to inspect and understand the internals of a recurrent neural network. It expects the users to specify higher-level logic (say, automata or a general Python program) for expected model behavior, which they call "hypothesis functions," and returns sets of hidden layer neurons ranked by how much those neurons are faithful to the given logic. This could perhaps help users understand where and why parts of the RNN violate expected behavior. Finally, *MISTIQUE* [335] automatically captures and stores intermediates of models produced during the model selection process and/or internal of a complex model such as a deep CNN to aid post-hoc inspection and debugging. It employs lossy forms of compression to reduce the storage footprint of such artifacts and is integrated with standard ML tools in Python.

Finally, *Krypton* [242] is a tool for reducing the runtime of a popular approach to explain CNN predictions called occlusion-based explanations. This approach produces a "heatmap" over the input image to help the user see which parts of the image mattered the most for the predictions. Essentially, one occludes a part of the image with a dark patch, performs re-inference with the CNN, notes the drop in the predicted labels' probability, and then moves the patch all over the image with some stride to obtain the heatmap. In *Krypton*, this process is cast as a new instance of the incremental view maintenance problem, with each CNN layer viewed as a "query" over a tensor. It introduces an algebraic framework that materializes all CNN features from all layers and incrementally updates only parts of the layers' outputs depending on which pixels were occluded. The updates are automatically propagated across the CNN. A new multi-query optimization technique that batches the re-inference requests across patches is used on both CPUs and GPUs. Finally, it also introduces some approximate inference optimizations that reduce CNN computations further by exploiting the properties of human perception to produce approximate heatmaps.

Apart from the above approaches, there is a long line of work on debugging, inspection, explanations, and interpretability of ML models in the core ML/AI communities [291, 371], as well as a spurt of recent work in the visualization and human-computer interaction communities [19]. Covering all of these approaches is beyond the scope of this book, but we refer interested readers to recent surveys and tutorials on this topic [146]. A more recent line of work related to model inspection is in instilling a sense of "fairness" and avoiding "discrimination" of people by ML models [107]. As complex ML models become ever more widespread, quantifying notions of fairness that are easy to understand and adopt across diverse applications, as well as easy to enforce and verify will become a more pressing challenge.

8.5   MODEL DEPLOYMENT AND SERVING

Deployment is the last major stage of the ML lifecycle, as illustrated in Figure 1.1. Historically, model deployment was not particularly complex, since it was relatively straightforward to provide APIs to integrate ML prediction routines with standard software systems that managed data. ML models would also be (re)trained only every quarter or so. But in the last decade, the adoption of ML has exploded in both the number and kinds of tasks, some of which require more rapid turnaround times. This has led to new systems-oriented issues in the model deployment stage. In particular, there is a growing need for closer integration of complex ML prediction infrastructure with regular querying support for monitoring, preparing for the next iteration of the ML lifecycle, and enforcing post-prediction business logic. There is also a growing need to reduce latency and improve throughout for serving ML predictions in applications where prediction requests might arrive at a high rate, e.g., Web-based services accessed by people around the world, the Internet of Things (IoT), and real-time video monitoring. We now dive into these two main kinds of model deployment systems and techniques.

Complex ML Predictions on Data Infrastructure: ML prediction routines integrated with data infrastructure have long been a part of in-RDBMS data mining toolkits. But more recently, as ML models have become complex, e.g., due to deep learning, treating such routines as just black box user-defined functions could lead to unexpected efficiency issues or loss of optimization opportunity for query processing. For instance, *Staccato*, which we discussed in Chapter 2, focuses on reducing the inference runtime of a form of probabilistic graphical models for optical character recognition (OCR) data in the context of querying such content in conjunction with structured data in an RDBMS. It introduces a new approximation scheme for storing the output of OCR using such models that can gracefully trade off accuracy for faster execution [203]. Along similar lines, the abstraction of "probabilistic predicates" helps integrate predicates that involve ML prediction functions over complex data types such as images and video with regular relational query processing [220]. By pre-training a series of cheaper ML models based on available predictions, they can short-circuit the predictions by reordering the application of expensive ML prediction functions with the cheaper ones. The reordering is based on a heuristic that users can tune based on their desired accuracy. In ML parlance, such a sequence of models for prediction is called a "cascade." [340].

Vista [241], which we discussed earlier, also opens up ML prediction functions for optimization, but focused on deep CNNs for multimodal analytics that integrate structured and image data. It focuses on transfer learning with CNNs, wherein some specified feature layer of a pre-trained CNN is used to extract features from the image and used in conjunction with the structured features to train a downstream ML model. Since no single layer would dominate in general for accuracy, this process requires a model selection step that compares multiple features layers. *Vista* elevates this process to a declarative level and optimizes the materialization tradeoffs of creating and transferring such features on top of a parallel dataflow system such as *Spark*.

ML Prediction Serving: In some applications of ML, the data on which predictions are to be made could be a fast stream with stringent latency requirements. This is common for many user-facing Web-based applications such as online advertising and recommendation systems, as well as for real-time monitoring with IoT devices and video cameras. This gives rise to new latency-throughput-accuracy tradeoffs, a problem called *model serving* [87]. We categorize work in this space into two categories: model serving for specific ML tasks and more general-purpose model serving platforms.

The first category includes *Velox* [87], *NoScope* [170], and *IDK Cascade* [346]. *Velox* focuses mainly on matrix factorization-based recommendation systems and introduces approximate search techniques to speed up ranked retrieval over inner products between user features and product features. It also explored new techniques to pre-compute and cache predictions to reduce latency. *NoScope* and *IDK Cascade* focus on classification with deep CNNs on a video stream to predict object occurrences. They observe that not all video frames need to be processed by the deep CNN, since there is often little difference across frames. Thus, similar to probabilistic predicates, they introduce cascades of cheaper classifiers, in particular, automatically trained linear models and smaller CNNs that balance the accuracy-throughput tradeoffs in a dataset-specific manner.

The second category includes systems such as *TensorFlow Serving* [17], *Clipper* [88], *Pretzel* [206], and *MacroBase* [40]. Their goal is to develop platforms to make it easier to deploy a variety of ML models efficiently into a variety of applications, possibly with latency constraints. *TensorFlow Serving* is a software framework for deploying neural networks trained in *TensorFlow* on to a variety of device environments ranging from servers to smartphones. By creating a uniform deployment environment, it obviates the need to write separate code stacks for different device types. *Clipper* is a model serving system that provides container-based abstractions to more easily deploy ML model training stacks developed in a variety of frameworks such as *Scikit-learn* and *TensorFlow*. It explores generic batching and caching tradeoffs to optimize for improving the throughout of serving predictions, while satisfying prediction latency constraints given by the user. In contrast to *Clipper*'s largely "black-box" approach that is model-agnostic, *Pretzel* proposes a "white-box" approach that represents inference workflows in a higher-level API for models built in the ML.NET framework [9]. Such an approach allows *Pretzel* to apply multi-query optimization techniques such as sharing work among different inference pipelines that involve expensive feature extraction steps. *Pretzel* materializes and reuses intermediate data, reducing memory footprints and enabling more complex resource sharing and scheduling. In this sense, it sacrifices some generality in favor of lower latency and higher system efficiency. Finally, *Macrobase* is a model serving system tailored for anomaly detection applications with various ML models. It introduces new systems techniques to improve the throughput of sketch-based outlier detection and also provides higher-level summaries to explain the outliers to users.

8.6   BENCHMARKING ML SYSTEMS

The growth in the number and complexity of ML systems could make it harder for ML users to decide which ML system(s) best match their application needs. Moreover, the publications on an ML system typically focus only on its their strengths and seldom highlight regimes where they may not work so well. The dominant approach to tackle such issues with data-driven systems is to standardize empirical comparisons via benchmarks, e.g., TPC benchmarks for RDBMSs. Benchmarks help clarify the metrics and methodologies for comparing systems on an even footing, while also helping expose hidden weaknesses in systems that can become opportunities for improvement. Surprisingly, there has been relatively little work on benchmarking modern ML systems. While linear algebra packages such as *BLAS*, *Eigen*, and *LAPACK* have been extensively benchmarked, such results focused on low-level matrix operations and single-node runtime efficiency. ML users typically care about multiple higher-level metrics such as overall ML execution runtime or costs, ML model accuracy, succinctness of specification, and scalability of execution.

We categorize existing ML systems benchmarks into two based on their scope: those that focused on a specific set of tasks and those that focus on a more general class of ML workloads. As an example of the first are the benchmarks focused on MCMC-based ML models [62] and image analytics tasks [233]. In [62], the programmability and efficiency of five ML models trained using MCMC sampling was compared on four ML systems. The models included Gaussian Mixture Model, Bayesian Lasso, Hidden Markov Model, LDA, and missing data imputation. The systems compared were *Spark*, *SimSQL*, *GraphLab*, and *Giraph*, spanning a spectrum of in-RDBMS, dataflow, and custom data processing stacks. Each system has its own pros and cons on intuitiveness of expressing the ML programs, as well as different levels of limitations on scalability. In [233], the implementation and efficiency of some large-scale image analytics pipelines are compared on five systems: *SciDB*, *Myria*, *Spark*, *Dask*, and *TensorFlow*. The tasks were based on MRI data from a neuroscience application and telescope data from an astronomy application. A key finding was that extracting good performance from such systems at scale required more programming and systems expertise than would be ideal for domain scientists in such applications, suggesting that more work is needed on automating some systems aspects.

In the second category are SLAB [329], GenBase [327], DAWNBench [82], and MLPerf [10]. The Scalable Linear Algebra Benchmark (SLAB) targets systems for scalable linear algebra-based ML (e.g., *SystemML*, *SparkR*, and *MADlib*). It compares systems both on ease of use (measured as lines of code to specify an ML task) and runtime performance at scale. It presents a hierarchy of test cases of increasing complexity ranging from low-level matrix operations to pipelines of operations to fully fledged LA-based ML algorithms. It provides a data generator to synthesize data of different scales and also includes a benchmark real-world structured dataset. In the distributed setting, these tasks capture different points on communication load and computation load. Experiments using SLAB exposed new bottlenecks in existing scalable linear algebra systems, underscoring the utility of such benchmarks. Related is the *GenBase* benchmark, which also focused on linear algebra operations on large array data drawn from the genomics domain. It compared *SciDB* with *Hadoop* and *MADlib* on *PostgreSQL*, as well as R integrated with various data backends on various queries, including linear regression, covariance matrix, and SVD. It found that *SciDB* scales well for these tasks across various dataset sizes and cluster sizes, while the other systems often faced scalability bottlenecks.

DAWNBench targets deep learning systems (e.g., *PyTorch* [264] and *TensorFlow* [22]), albeit in a more integrated cross-stack manner that measures "time-to-accuracy" for a handful of pre-specified benchmark real-world unstructured datasets. It handles a two-dimensional tradeoff space involving both the final accuracy reached and the total resource cost measured in dollars on the same hardware platform. Associated with this benchmark is an online competition with a leaderboard for ML users to post better training solutions that improve on the accuracy-cost Pareto frontier. Finally, MLPerf is a recent and wider benchmark effort for standardizing comparisons between ML systems, including software frameworks, hardware accelerators, and cloud ML platforms. It offers benchmark datasets and time-to-quality targets for a wider variety of ML tasks, including image classification, machine translation, sentiment analysis, and reinforcement learning.

8.7 SUMMARY

This chapter presented a wide-ranging discussion of several data management issues in the entire ML application lifecycle beyond just the efficiency or scalability of ML training. Since high-quality data is the bedrock of effective ML, sourcing, transforming, cleaning, and labeling data remains a perennial data management challenge for ML applications. Building ML models requires steering the higher level processes of feature engineering and model selection, as well as managing and debugging the artifacts and metadata from such processes, which are replete with data management challenges. Finally, deploying and integrating ML models with applications, monitoring their use, and benchmarking ML systems will remain active areas of inquiry as ML systems see increasing adoption. Since almost every stage of the larger ML lifecycle features open research questions, it will likely remain an active research area for the foreseeable future.

CHAPTER 9

Conclusions

ML systems draw upon ideas from a variety of computing fields beyond just ML algorithmic research, including data management, operating and distributed systems, high-performance computing, programming languages, and more. Motivated by (1) data-driven applications, (2) data-intensive workload characteristics, and (3) data systems support for ML, we took a data-centric view and reviewed approaches for integrating ML in data systems as well as data management techniques in ML systems. In the following, we draw several conclusions regarding the existing state of the art, as well as major open problems and directions for future work.

ML with SQL and UDFs: Although many ML algorithms can be expressed in SQL and can be reasonably well supported via UDFs, several projects have recognized that numerical computing in SQL often leads to unnatural specifications from an ML user standpoint and performance degradation. Moreover, UDFs themselves are a too low-level programming abstraction for most ML users. While there are use cases that require ML directly over RDBMS-resident data with SQL and UDFs, it is also crucial to understand and address the majority of use cases that do not, including ML over parallel dataflow systems and custom scalable ML systems. As our discussions in the various chapters showed, many concepts and techniques from the database world, including query processing and optimization and storage management, are broadly applicable with appropriate adaptation to ML systems regardless of the execution environment, as well as to the larger ML lifecycle.

Specification Languages: High-level specification languages have the potential to simplify ML applications and their deployment, while providing the flexibility of exploring new and customizing existing ML algorithms. However, the current abstractions range from fixed algorithm and operator libraries for local and distributed computation, over specialized systems for graph analytics and deep learning, to linear algebra systems. More often than not, users have to manually decide upon local vs. distributed operations, sparse and dense representations, operator placement and many more. It would be unrealistic to hope for a single, generic specification language because these abstractions target very different users. We should work toward consolidating the abstractions for different aspects in the entire ML lifecycle, common exchange formats such as PMML, PFA, and ONNX, and building more on each other's work. That said, we should also be aware of potential commercial incentives that could hinder such consolidation due to the desire to monetize ML systems in custom cloud environments (e.g., *TensorFlow* in Google Cloud, *MXNet* in AWS, or *CNTK* in Microsoft Azure).

Program Optimization: Given the goal of higher level specification languages, automatic program optimization is crucial for achieving the same—or even better—performance as manually constructed execution plans. Program optimization for linear algebra operations is very similar to query optimization with well-defined high-level operators, rewrites, size estimation, alternative evaluation orders, and different physical operators. However, challenging differences include the prevalent use of operator DAGs instead of trees, the larger scale of even thousands of operators, as well as conditional control flow and complex function call graphs, which require advances on different levels of typical compilation chains.

Physical Design: Most ML systems require the explicit specification of dense or sparse data formats and operations, local or distributed data representations and operations, data types, and data access optimizations such as indexes, NUMA partitioning, lossless compression, and lossy sparsification or quantization. Especially regarding lossy techniques, we might need to introduce a proper notion of *contracts* that specify the degrees of freedom of the data representation. Fundamentally, we should aim at specifying ML algorithms and models with physical data independence, which—similar to the relational model—has the potential to isolate the applications from low-level optimizations, and thus, can simplify application deployment and allow for automatic optimizations with regard to data characteristics.

Diversity of ML Algorithms: With the current hype around deep learning, there is a popular perception that neural networks and SGD will make all other ML algorithms obsolete. However, this perception is still far from the reality in most real-world applications [2]. The range of existing ML learning algorithms is very diverse, ranging from statistical and numerical computing to unsupervised and supervised ML algorithms, including higher-order optimization. To foster new advances, we should aim to support this diversity in ML algorithms and ML systems. Furthermore, in contrast to research in the ML/AI community, the choice of ML algorithms to use in real applications is almost always a tradeoff between accuracy benefits and monetary costs. Slightly reduced accuracy may be acceptable in many cases if it means vastly more efficient training and scoring. Finally, ML models are just one part of a larger data pipeline in an ML application. ML models are typically combined with application-specific rules (in terms of queries, dictionary lookups, and regular expressions), dedicated extractors, and other ML models, orchestrated in a larger workflow. We should embrace this diversity.

Heterogeneous Data Sources: While deep learning can eliminate the need for feature engineering on many forms of unstructured data (e.g., images or text), a majority of ML applications still rely on explicitly constructed features from multiple data sources, both structured and unstructured, in heterogeneous data formats that require various pre-processing techniques. Such heterogeneity and data sourcing tradeoffs render it almost impossible to directly feed raw inputs to an ML algorithm in most cases. Thus, many ML systems build on top of Spark or other dataflow systems to support more seamless data sourcing and preparation and/or provide dedicated data types such as Dataset in *TensorFlow* and Frame in *SystemML* to support simple feature pre-processing. Providing better support in ML systems for such heterogeneous data sources, data preparation and cleaning, feature engineering, training, and scoring would be valuable for many applications.

Lifecycle Management: It is clear that data management issues are abound throughout the ML lifecycle beyond training, scoring, and feature engineering. Tackling such issues requires an integrative approach combining data management with other areas of computing or even other fields. Using ML en masse in organizations requires more principled approaches to ML provenance and metadata management in the context of ML workflows. Improving the ecosystem for data preparation and exploration, model building, and model inspection requires a closer integration with visualization and human-computer interaction techniques. Building and debugging holistic ML platforms for modern Web services requires an understanding of the emerging design patterns of ML-powered software ("Software 2.0" [15]), which requires a closer integration with software engineering and programming languages. Finally, as ML-driven decision making permeates society, there is also a need for understanding how data is (ab)used in ML applications, which requires a closer integration with the fields of microeconomics, algorithmic fairness, ethics, and more.

In summary, we believe that the rapidly changing field, the increasing complexity of ML systems, and the diversity of the ML systems community call for declarative—or more generally, higher-level—abstractions and well-defined system architectures. In the database community, we witnessed how SQL enabled the adoption of new hardware, storage advances, and scaling from out-of-core to distributed processing with minimal disruption to application users. Achieving similar benefits for ML applications will be a multi-decade effort but it will help in (1) protecting the investments into the ever growing number of ML applications, (2) fostering more automation of data processing, optimization, and tuning issues in ML systems to reduce manual grunt work, and (3) focusing research on challenging and interesting technical problems across the whole stack and spectrum of ML systems.

Bibliography

[1] 2017 CrowdFlower data scientist report. `https://www.kdnuggets.com/2017/05/crowdflower-data-science-report-available.html` 2, 101

[2] 2017 Kaggle survey on the state of data science and machine learning. `https://www.kaggle.com/surveys/2017` 2, 30, 101, 124

[3] Amazon SageMaker. `https://aws.amazon.com/sagemaker/` 112, 115

[4] BDEX (big data exchange) DataMarket. `http://www.bigdataexchange.com/` 102

[5] Google cloud AutoML. `https://cloud.google.com/automl/` 112

[6] Introducing FBLearner flow: Facebook's AI backbone. `https://code.fb.com/applied-machine-learning/introducing-fblearner-flow-facebook-s-ai-backbone/` 112, 113

[7] Microsoft AzureML studio. `https://studio.azureml.net/` 115

[8] MLFlow: An open source platform for the machine learning lifecycle. `https://mlflow.org` 114

[9] ML.NET: An open source and cross-platform machine learning framework. `https://dotnet.microsoft.com/apps/machinelearning-ai/ml-dotnet` 119

[10] MLPerf benchmarks. `https://mlperf.org` 120

[11] Open neural network exchange (ONNX) format. `https://onnx.ai/` 113

[12] Portable format for analytics (PFA). `http://dmg.org/pfa/` 113

[13] Predictive modeling markup language (PMML). `http://dmg.org/pmml/v4--3/GeneralStructure.html` 113

[14] Qlik DataMarket. `https://www.qlik.com/us/products/qlik-data-market` 102

[15] Software 2.0 blog post by Andrej Karpathy. `https://medium.com/@karpathy/software-2--0-a64152b37c35` 105, 125

[16] TensorFlow hub. `https://www.tensorflow.org/hub/` 114

[17] TensorFlow serving. `https://www.tensorflow.org/serving/` 118

[18] TFLearn high-level API for TensorFlow. `http://tflearn.org/` 112

[19] The building blocks of interpretability. `https://distill.pub/2018/building-blocks/` 117

[20] Weak supervision: The new programming paradigm for machine learning. `https://dawn.cs.stanford.edu/2017/07/16/weak-supervision` 104

[21] D. J. Abadi, S. Madden, and M. Ferreira. Integrating compression and execution in column-oriented database systems. In *SIGMOD*, 2006. DOI: 10.1145/1142473.1142548 76

[22] M. Abadi et al. TensorFlow: A system for large-scale machine learning. In *OSDI*, 2016. 35, 37, 43, 46, 47, 56, 57, 64, 65, 75, 120

[23] M. Abadi et al. TensorFlow: A system for large-scale machine learning. *CoRR*, 2016. 63, 78

[24] A. Ahmed, M. Aly, J. Gonzalez, S. M. Narayanamurthy, and A. J. Smola. Scalable inference in latent variable models. In *WSDM*, 2012. DOI: 10.1145/2124295.2124312 62, 88

[25] A. V. Aho, M. S. Lam, R. Sethi, and J. D. Ullman. *Compilers: Principles, Techniques, and Tools*. Addison-Wesley, 2007. 37

[26] M. Akdere, U. Cetintemel, M. Riondato, E. Upfal, and S. Zdonik. The case for predictive database systems: Opportunities and challenges. In *CIDR*, 2013. 112, 114

[27] D. V. Aken, A. Pavlo, G. J. Gordon, and B. Zhang. Automatic database management system tuning through large-scale machine learning. In *SIGMOD*, 2017. DOI: 10.1145/3035918.3064029 6

[28] A. Graves, A.-R. Mohamed, and G. Hinton. Speech recognition with deep recurrent neural networks. In *ICASSP*, 2013. DOI: 10.1109/ICASSP.2013.6638947 107

[29] A. Alexandrov, R. Bergmann, S. Ewen, J. Freytag, F. Hueske, A. Heise, O. Kao, M. Leich, U. Leser, V. Markl, F. Naumann, M. Peters, A. Rheinländer, M. J. Sax, S. Schelter, M. Höger, K. Tzoumas, and D. Warneke. The stratosphere platform for big data analytics. *VLDB Journal*, 23(6), 2014. DOI: 10.1007/s00778-014-0357-y 54

[30] A. Alexandrov, A. Kunft, A. Katsifodimos, F. Schüler, L. Thamsen, O. Kao, T. Herb, and V. Markl. Implicit parallelism through deep language embedding. In *SIGMOD*, 2015. DOI: 10.1145/2723372.2750543 35, 36, 42, 43, 55

[31] R. Allen and K. Kennedy. *Optimizing Compilers for Modern Architectures: A Dependence-based Approach.* Morgan Kaufmann, 2001. DOI: 10.1109/MC.2002.993777 38

[32] A. Halevy, F. Korn, N. F. Noy, C. Olston, N. Polyzotis, S. Roy, and S. E. Whang. Goods: Organizing Google's datasets. In *SIGMOD*, 2016. DOI: 10.1145/2882903.2903730 101

[33] R. R. Amossen, A. Campagna, and R. Pagh. Better size estimation for sparse matrix products. *Algorithmica*, 69(3), 2014. DOI: 10.1007/s00453-012-9692-9 39

[34] M. Anderson, D. Antenucci, V. Bittorf, M. Burgess, M. Cafarella, A. Kumar, F. Niu, Y. Park, C. Re, and C. Zhang. Brainwash: A data system for feature engineering. In *CIDR*, 2013. 108

[35] M. R. Anderson and M. Cafarella. Input selection for fast feature engineering. In *ICDE*, 2016. DOI: 10.1109/icde.2016.7498272 109

[36] M. Armbrust, D. Bateman, R. Xin, and M. Zaharia. Introduction to spark 2.0 for database researchers. In *SIGMOD*, 2016. DOI: 10.1145/2882903.2912565 5

[37] J. V. Arthur, P. Merolla, F. Akopyan, R. Alvarez-Icaza, A. Cassidy, S. Chandra, S. K. Esser, N. Imam, W. P. Risk, D. B. D. Rubin, R. Manohar, and D. S. Modha. Building block of a programmable neuromorphic substrate: A digital neurosynaptic core. In *IJCNN*, 2012. DOI: 10.1109/ijcnn.2012.6252637 69

[38] A. Ashari, N. Sedaghati, J. Eisenlohr, and P. Sadayappan. An efficient two-dimensional blocking strategy for sparse matrix-vector multiplication on GPUs. In *ICS*, 2014. DOI: 10.1145/2597652.2597678 70

[39] A. Ashari, S. Tatikonda, M. Boehm, B. Reinwald, K. Campbell, J. Keenleyside, and P. Sadayappan. On optimizing machine learning workloads via kernel fusion. In *PPoPP*, 2015. DOI: 10.1145/2688500.2688521 34, 45, 70

[40] P. Bailis, E. Gan, S. Madden, D. Narayanan, K. Rong, and S. Suri. MacroBase: Prioritizing attention in fast data. In *SIGMOD*, 2017. DOI: 10.1145/3035918.3035928 118

[41] M. Balazinska, B. Howe, and D. Suciu. Data markets in the cloud: An opportunity for the database community. *PVLDB*, 4(12), 2011. 102

[42] D. Baylor, E. Breck, H.-T. Cheng, N. Fiedel, C. Y. Foo, Z. Haque, S. Haykal, M. Ispir, V. Jain, L. Koc, C. Y. Koo, L. Lew, C. Mewald, A. N. Modi, N. Polyzotis, S. Ramesh, S. Roy, S. E. Whang, M. Wicke, J. Wilkiewicz, X. Zhang, and M. Zinkevich. TFX: A TensorFlow-based production-scale machine learning platform. In *KDD*, 2017. DOI: 10.1145/3097983.3098021 102, 103

[43] N. Bell and M. Garland. Implementing sparse matrix-vector multiplication on throughput-oriented processors. In *SC*, 2009. DOI: 10.1145/1654059.1654078 56

[44] G. Belter, E. R. Jessup, I. Karlin, and J. G. Siek. Automating the generation of composed linear algebra Kernels. In *SC*, 2009. DOI: 10.1145/1654059.1654119 50

[45] J. Bergstra, O. Breuleux, F. Bastien, P. Lamblin, R. Pascanu, G. Desjardins, J. Turian, D. Warde-Farley, and Y. Bengio. Theano: a CPU and GPU math expression compiler. In *SciPy*, 2010. 35, 40, 43

[46] A. Beutel, P. P. Talukdar, A. Kumar, C. Faloutsos, E. E. Papalexakis, and E. P. Xing. FlexiFaCT: Scalable flexible factorization of coupled tensors on Hadoop. In *SDM*, 2014. DOI: 10.1137/1.9781611973440.13 55

[47] J. Bezanson, A. Edelman, S. Karpinski, and V. B. Shah. Julia: A fresh approach to numerical computing. *SIAM Review*, 59(1), 2017. DOI: 10.1137/141000671 35, 36, 38, 50

[48] S. Bhattacherjee, A. Deshpande, and A. Sussman. PStore: An efficient storage framework for managing scientific data. In *SSDBM*, 2014. DOI: 10.1145/2618243.2618268 77, 78

[49] C. Binnig, B. Buratti, Y. Chung, C. Cousins, T. Kraska, Z. Shang, E. Upfal, R. Zeleznik, and E. Zgraggen. Towards interactive curation and automatic tuning of ML pipelines. In *SIGMOD DEEM Workshop*, 2018. DOI: 10.1145/3209889.3209891 112, 115

[50] C. Binnig, N. May, and T. Mindnich. SQLScript: Efficiently analyzing big enterprise data in SAP HANA. In *BTW*, 2013. 52

[51] V. Bittorf, M. Kornacker, C. Ré, and C. Zhang. Tradeoffs in main-memory statistical analytics from impala to DimmWitted. In *IMDM*, 2014. 80

[52] D. W. Blalock, S. Madden, and J. V. Guttag. Sprintz: Time series compression for the Internet of Things. *IMWUT*, 2(3), 2018. DOI: 10.1145/3264903 78

[53] S. Blanas, J. M. Patel, V. Ercegovac, J. Rao, E. J. Shekita, and Y. Tian. A comparison of join algorithms for log processing in MapReduce. In *SIGMOD*, 2010. DOI: 10.1145/1807167.1807273 44

[54] M. Boehm, D. R. Burdick, A. V. Evfimievski, B. Reinwald, F. R. Reiss, P. Sen, S. Tatikonda, and Y. Tian. SystemML's optimizer: Plan generation for large-scale machine learning programs. *IEEE Data Engineering Bulletin*, 37(3), 2014. 18, 33, 37, 39, 40, 41, 43, 45, 51, 87, 90

[55] M. Boehm, M. Dusenberry, D. Eriksson, A. V. Evfimievski, F. M. Manshadi, N. Pansare, B. Reinwald, F. Reiss, P. Sen, A. Surve, and S. Tatikonda. SystemML: Declarative machine learning on spark. *PVLDB*, 9(13), 2016. DOI: 10.14778/3007263.3007279 18, 36, 38, 42, 43, 46, 54, 55, 57, 62, 73, 74, 75, 87, 90

[56] M. Boehm, A. V. Evfimievski, and B. Reinwald. Efficient data-parallel cumulative aggregates for large-scale machine learning. In *BTW*, 2019. 38

[57] M. Boehm, B. Reinwald, D. Hutchison, P. Sen, A. V. Evfimievski, and N. Pansare. On optimizing operator fusion plans for large-scale machine learning in SystemML. *PVLDB*, 11(12), 2018. DOI: 10.14778/3229863.3229865 47, 49, 50

[58] M. Boehm, S. Tatikonda, B. Reinwald, P. Sen, Y. Tian, D. Burdick, and S. Vaithyanathan. Hybrid parallelization strategies for large-scale machine learning in SystemML. *PVLDB*, 7(7), 2014. DOI: 10.14778/2732286.2732292 43, 52, 58, 60, 61, 62, 67, 68

[59] V. R. Borkar, Y. Bu, M. J. Carey, J. Rosen, N. Polyzotis, T. Condie, M. Weimer, and R. Ramakrishnan. Declarative systems for large-scale machine learning. *IEEE Data Engineering Bulletin*, 35(2), 2012. 89

[60] M. Brantner. Modern stored procedures using GraalVM: Invited talk. In *DBPL*, 2017. DOI: 10.1145/3122831.3125717 52

[61] G. Buehrer and K. Chellapilla. A scalable pattern mining approach to web graph compression with communities. In *WSDM*, 2008. DOI: 10.1145/1341531.1341547 78

[62] Z. Cai, Z. J. Gao, S. Luo, L. L. Perez, Z. Vagena, and C. Jermaine. A comparison of platforms for implementing and running very large scale machine learning algorithms. In *SIGMOD*, 2014. DOI: 10.1145/2588555.2593680 119

[63] Z. Cai, Z. Vagena, L. L. Perez, S. Arumugam, P. J. Haas, and C. M. Jermaine. Simulation of database-valued Markov chains using SimSQL. In *SIGMOD*, 2013. DOI: 10.1145/2463676.2465283 15, 16, 17, 18

[64] A. M. Caulfield, E. S. Chung, A. Putnam, H. Angepat, J. Fowers, M. Haselman, S. Heil, M. Humphrey, P. Kaur, J. Kim, D. Lo, T. Massengill, K. Ovtcharov, M. Papamichael, L. Woods, S. Lanka, D. Chiou, and D. Burger. A cloud-scale acceleration architecture. In *MICRO*, 2016. DOI: 10.1109/micro.2016.7783710 69

[65] S. Chandrasekaran and M. J. Franklin. Streaming queries over streaming data. In *VLDB*, 2002. DOI: 10.1016/b978-155860869-6/50026-3 43

[66] S. Chaudhuri and K. Shim. Including group-by in query optimization. In *VLDB*, 1994. 23

[67] J. Chen, R. Monga, S. Bengio, and R. Józefowicz. Revisiting distributed synchronous SGD. *CoRR*, 2016. 64

[68] L. Chen, P. Koutris, and A. Kumar. Model-based pricing: Do not pay for more than what you learn! In *SIGMOD DEEM Workshop*, 2017. DOI: 10.1145/3076246.3076250 102

[69] L. Chen, P. Koutris, and A. Kumar. Towards model-based pricing for machine learning in a data marketplace. In *SIGMOD*, 2019. 102

[70] L. Chen, A. Kumar, J. F. Naughton, and J. M. Patel. Towards linear algebra over normalized data. *PVLDB*, 10(11), 2017. DOI: 10.14778/3137628.3137633 24, 35

[71] T. Chen et al. TVM: End-to-end compilation stack for deep learning. In *SysML*, 2018. 50, 70

[72] T. Chen, M. Li, Y. Li, M. Lin, N. Wang, M. Wang, T. Xiao, B. Xu, C. Zhang, and Z. Zhang. MXNet: A flexible and efficient machine learning library for heterogeneous distributed systems. *CoRR*, 2015. 47, 63, 75

[73] T. Chen, T. Moreau, Z. Jiang, L. Zheng, E. Q. Yan, H. Shen, M. Cowan, L. Wang, Y. Hu, L. Ceze, C. Guestrin, and A. Krishnamurthy. TVM: An automated end-to-end optimizing compiler for deep learning. In *OSDI*, 2018. 49, 50, 70

[74] Y. Cheng, C. Qin, and F. Rusu. GLADE: Big data analytics made easy. In *SIGMOD*, 2012. DOI: 10.1145/2213836.2213936 14, 17

[75] N. Chohan, C. Castillo, M. Spreitzer, M. Steinder, A. N. Tantawi, and C. Krintz. See spot run: Using spot instances for MapReduce workflows. In *HotCloud Workshop*, 2010. 94, 96

[76] X. Chu, I. F. Ilyas, S. Krishnan, and J. Wang. Data cleaning: Overview and emerging challenges. In *SIGMOD*, 2016. DOI: 10.1145/2882903.2912574 102

[77] B.-G. Chun, B. Cho, B. Jeon, J. S. Jeong, G. Kim, J. Y. Kim, W.-Y. Lee, Y. S. Lee, M. Weimer, Y. Yang, and G.-I. Yu. Dolphin: Runtime optimization for distributed machine learning. In *NIPS MLSys Workshop*, 2016. 90

[78] E. S. Chung, J. Fowers, K. Ovtcharov, M. Papamichael, A. M. Caulfield, T. Massengill, M. Liu, D. Lo, S. Alkalay, M. Haselman, M. Abeydeera, L. Adams, H. Angepat, C. Boehn, D. Chiou, O. Firestein, A. Forin, K. S. Gatlin, M. Ghandi, S. Heil, K. Holohan, A. E. Husseini, T. Juhász, K. Kagi, R. Kovvuri, S. Lanka, F. van Megen, D. Mukhortov, P. Patel, B. Perez, A. Rapsang, S. K. Reinhardt, B. Rouhani, A. Sapek, R. Seera, S. Shekar, B. Sridharan, G. Weisz, L. Woods, P. Y. Xiao, D. Zhang, R. Zhao,

and D. Burger. Serving DNNs in real time at datacenter scale with project brainwave. *IEEE Micro*, 38(2), 2018. DOI: 10.1109/mm.2018.022071131 69

[79] Y. Chung, T. Kraska, S. E. Whang, and N. Polyzotis. Slice finder: Automated data slicing for model interpretability. In *SysML*, 2018. 116

[80] E. Cohen. Structure prediction and computation of sparse matrix products. *Journal of Combinatorial Optimization*, 2(4), 1998. 39, 41, 42

[81] J. Cohen, B. Dolan, M. Dunlap, J. M. Hellerstein, and C. Welton. MAD skills: New analysis practices for big data, vol. 2, 2009. DOI: 10.14778/1687553.1687576 9, 11, 17

[82] C. Coleman, D. Narayanan, D. Kang, T. Zhao, J. Zhang, L. Nardi, P. Bailis, K. Olukotun, C. Ré, and M. Zaharia. DAWNBench: An end-to-end deep learning benchmark and competition. In *NIPS LearningSys Workshop*, 2017. 120

[83] R. Collobert, C. Puhrsch, and G. Synnaeve. Wav2Letter: An end-to-end ConvNet-based speech recognition system. *CoRR*, 2016. 108

[84] T. Condie, P. Mineiro, N. Polyzotis, and M. Weimer. Machine learning for big data. In *SIGMOD*, 2013. DOI: 10.1145/2463676.2465338 5

[85] T. H. Cormen, C. E. Leiserson, R. L. Rivest, and C. Stein. *Introduction to Algorithms*. MIT Press, 2009. DOI: 10.2307/2583667 41

[86] M. Courbariaux, Y. Bengio, and J. David. Low precision arithmetic for deep learning. *CoRR*, abs/1412.7024, 2014. 78

[87] D. Crankshaw, P. Bailis, J. E. Gonzalez, H. Li, Z. Zhang, M. J. Franklin, A. Ghodsi, and M. I. Jordan. The missing piece in complex analytics: Low latency, scalable model management and serving with velox. In *CIDR*, 2015. 38, 118

[88] D. Crankshaw, X. Wang, G. Zhou, M. J. Franklin, J. E. Gonzalez, and I. Stoica. Clipper: A low-latency online prediction serving system. In *NSDI*, 2017. 118

[89] A. Crotty, A. Galakatos, K. Dursun, T. Kraska, C. Binnig, U. Çetintemel, and S. Zdonik. An architecture for compiling UDF-centric workflows. *PVLDB*, 8(12), 2015. DOI: 10.14778/2824032.2824045 36, 49, 50, 55

[90] A. Crotty, A. Galakatos, K. Dursun, T. Kraska, U. Çetintemel, and S. B. Zdonik. Tupleware: "Big" data, big analytics, small clusters. In *CIDR*, 2015.

[91] H. Cui, J. Cipar, Q. Ho, J. K. Kim, S. Lee, A. Kumar, J. Wei, W. Dai, G. R. Ganger, P. B. Gibbons, G. A. Gibson, and E. P. Xing. Exploiting bounded staleness to speed up big data analytics. In *ATC*, 2014. 62

[92] H. Cui, H. Zhang, G. R. Ganger, P. B. Gibbons, and E. P. Xing. GeePS: Scalable deep learning on distributed GPUs with a GPU-specialized parameter server. In *EuroSys*, 2016. DOI: 10.1145/2901318.2901323 75

[93] B. Dally. Hardware for deep learning. In *SysML*, 2018. 69, 70

[94] A. Darte. On the complexity of loop fusion. *Parallel Computing*, 26(9), 2000. DOI: 10.1109/pact.1999.807510 50

[95] A. Das, I. Upadhyaya, X. Meng, and A. Talwalkar. Collaborative filtering as a case-study for model parallelism on bulk synchronous systems. In *CIKM*, 2017. DOI: 10.1145/3132847.3132862 55, 57

[96] J. Dean, G. Corrado, R. Monga, K. Chen, M. Devin, Q. V. Le, M. Z. Mao, M. Ranzato, A. W. Senior, P. A. Tucker, K. Yang, and A. Y. Ng. Large scale distributed deep networks. In *NIPS*, 2012. 56, 62, 64

[97] J. Dean and S. Ghemawat. MapReduce: Simplified data processing on large clusters. In *OSDI*, 2004. DOI: 10.1145/1327452.1327492 54, 89

[98] J. DeBrabant, A. Pavlo, S. Tu, M. Stonebraker, and S. B. Zdonik. Anti-caching: A new approach to database management system architecture. *PVLDB*, 6(14), 2013. DOI: 10.14778/2556549.2556575 73

[99] R. Dechter. Bucket elimination: A unifying framework for reasoning. *Artificial Intelligence*, 113(1–2), 1999. DOI: 10.1016/s0004-3702(99)00059-4 42

[100] J. Deng, W. Dong, R. Socher, L.-J. Li, K. Li, and L. Fei-Fei. ImageNet: A large-scale hierarchical image database. In *CVPR*, 2009. DOI: 10.1109/cvprw.2009.5206848 108

[101] A. Deshpande, Z. G. Ives, and V. Raman. Adaptive query processing. *Foundations and Trends in Databases*, 1(1), 2007. DOI: 10.1561/1900000001 39

[102] A. Deshpande and S. Madden. MauveDB: Supporting model-based user views in database systems. In *SIGMOD*, 2006. DOI: 10.1145/1142473.1142483 19, 29, 39

[103] Dirk Eddelbuettel. CRAN task view: High-performance and parallel computing with R. *R Project*, 2018. cran.r-project.org/web/views/HighPerformanceComputing.html 53, 58

[104] B. Dong, T. Wang, H. Tang, Q. Koziol, K. Wu, and S. Byna. ARCHIE: Data analysis acceleration with array caching in hierarchical storage. *Tech Report*, 2018. DOI: 10.1109/bigdata.2018.8622616 74, 75

[105] J. V. D'silva, F. De Moor, and B. Kemme. AIDA—abstraction for advanced in-database analytics. *PVLDB*, 11(11), 2018. DOI: 10.14778/3236187.3236194 17, 18

[106] S. Duan and S. Babu. Processing forecasting queries. In *VLDB*, 2007. 30

[107] C. Dwork. What's fair? In *KDD*, 2017. DOI: 10.1145/3097983.3105807 117

[108] C. Dwork and A. Roth. The algorithmic foundations of differential privacy. *Foundations and Trends in Theoretical Computer Science*, 9(3–4), 2014. DOI: 10.1561/0400000042 114

[109] G. Efland, S. Parikh, H. Sanghavi, and A. Farooqui. High performance DSP for vision, imaging and neural networks. In *HotChips*, 2016. DOI: 10.1109/hotchips.2016.7936210 69

[110] T. Elgamal, S. Luo, M. Boehm, A. V. Evfimievski, S. Tatikonda, B. Reinwald, and P. Sen. SPOOF: Sum-product optimization and operator fusion for large-scale machine learning. In *CIDR*, 2017. 49

[111] A. Elgohary, M. Boehm, P. J. Haas, F. R. Reiss, and B. Reinwald. Compressed linear algebra for large-scale machine learning. *PVLDB*, 9(12), 2016. DOI: 10.14778/2994509.2994515 34, 43, 76, 77

[112] A. Elgohary, M. Boehm, P. J. Haas, F. R. Reiss, and B. Reinwald. Compressed linear algebra for large-scale machine learning. *VLDB Journal*, 27(5), 2018. DOI: 10.14778/2994509.2994515 77

[113] S. Ewen, K. Tzoumas, M. Kaufmann, and V. Markl. Spinning fast iterative data flows. *PVLDB*, 5(11), 2012. DOI: 10.14778/2350229.2350245 39

[114] W. Fan, J. Li, X. Wang, and Y. Wu. Query preserving graph compression. In *SIGMOD*, 2012. DOI: 10.1145/2213836.2213855 78

[115] X. Feng, A. Kumar, B. Recht, and C. Ré. Towards a unified architecture for in-RDBMS analytics. In *SIGMOD*, 2012. DOI: 10.1145/2213836.2213874 9, 13, 17, 55

[116] M. Feurer, A. Klein, K. Eggensperger, J. T. Springenberg, M. Blum, and F. Hutter. Efficient and robust automated machine learning. In *NIPS*, 2015. 112

[117] U. Fischer. Forecasting in database systems. Ph.D. thesis, Technische Universitaet Dresden, 2014. 30

[118] Z. J. Gao, S. Luo, L. L. Perez, and C. Jermaine. The buds language for distributed Bayesian machine learning. In *SIGMOD*, 2017. DOI: 10.1145/3035918.3035937 9, 18

[119] R. Garcia, V. Sreekanti, N. Yadwadkar, D. Crankshaw, J. E. Gonzalez, and J. M. Hellerstein. Context: The missing piece in the machine learning lifecycle. In *KDD CMI Workshop*, 2018. 114

[120] R. Gemulla, E. Nijkamp, P. J. Haas, and Y. Sismanis. Large-scale matrix factorization with distributed stochastic gradient descent. In *KDD*, 2011. DOI: 10.1145/2020408.2020426 55

[121] L. Getoor. Probabilistic soft logic: A scalable approach for Markov random fields over continuous-valued variables. In *RuleML*, 2013. DOI: 10.1007/978-3-642-39617-5_1 26

[122] L. Getoor and B. Taskar. *Introduction to Statistical Relational Learning (Adaptive Computation and Machine Learning)*. The MIT Press, 2007. DOI: 10.7551/mitpress/7432.001.0001 21, 23, 26

[123] A. Ghoting, R. Krishnamurthy, E. P. D. Pednault, B. Reinwald, V. Sindhwani, S. Tatikonda, Y. Tian, and S. Vaithyanathan. SystemML: Declarative machine learning on MapReduce. In *ICDE*, 2011. DOI: 10.1109/icde.2011.5767930 18, 24, 34, 36, 44, 46, 55, 90, 106

[124] I. Goodfellow, Y. Bengio, and A. Courville. *Deep Learning*. The MIT Press, 2016. DOI: 10.1038/nature14539 107, 108

[125] Google. TensorFlow XLA (accelerated linear algebra). tensorflow.org/performance /xla/ 40, 50

[126] P. Goyal, P. Dollár, R. B. Girshick, P. Noordhuis, L. Wesolowski, A. Kyrola, A. Tulloch, Y. Jia, and K. He. Accurate, large minibatch SGD: Training ImageNet in 1 hour. *CoRR*, 2017. 64

[127] G. Graefe and W. J. McKenna. The volcano optimizer generator: Extensibility and efficient search. In *ICDE*, 1993. DOI: 10.1109/icde.1993.344061 19

[128] G. Graefe and L. D. Shapiro. Data compression and database performance. In *Applied Computing*, 1991. DOI: 10.1109/soac.1991.143840 76

[129] H. P. Graf, E. Cosatto, L. Bottou, I. Durdanovic, and V. Vapnik. Parallel support vector machines: The cascade SVM. In *NIPS*, 2004.

[130] R. Gupta and S. Sarawagi. Creating probabilistic databases from information extraction models. In *VLDB*, 2006. 19

[131] S. Gupta, A. Agrawal, K. Gopalakrishnan, and P. Narayanan. Deep learning with limited numerical precision. In *ICML*, 2015. 78

[132] I. Guyon, S. Gunn, M. Nikravesh, and L. A. Zadeh. *Feature Extraction: Foundations and Applications (Studies in Fuzziness and Soft Computing)*. Springer-Verlag, 2006. 106

[133] S. Hadjis, C. Zhang, I. Mitliagkas, and C. Ré. Omnivore: An optimizer for multi-device deep learning on CPUs and GPUs. *Computing Research Repository*, abs/1606.04487, 2016. 90

[134] N. Halko, P. Martinsson, and J. A. Tropp. Finding structure with randomness: Probabilistic algorithms for constructing approximate matrix decompositions. *SIAM Review*, 53(2), 2011. DOI: 10.1137/090771806 78

[135] S. Han, H. Mao, and W. J. Dally. Deep compression: Compressing deep neural network with pruning, trained quantization and Huffman coding. *CoRR*, 2015. 78

[136] B. Hancock, P. Varma, S. Wang, M. Bringmann, P. Liang, and C. Ré. Training classifiers with natural language explanations. In *ACL*, 2018. 104

[137] H. Zhang, G. Ananthanarayanan, P. Bodik, M. Philipose, P. Bahl, and M. J. Freedman. Live video analytics at scale with approximation and delay-tolerance. In *NSDI*, 2017. 31

[138] A. Harlap, H. Cui, W. Dai, J. Wei, G. R. Ganger, P. B. Gibbons, G. A. Gibson, and E. P. Xing. Addressing the straggler problem for iterative convergent parallel ML. In *SoCC*, 2016. DOI: 10.1145/2987550.2987554 65

[139] A. Harlap, A. Tumanov, A. Chung, G. R. Ganger, and P. B. Gibbons. Proteus: Agile ML elasticity through tiered reliability in dynamic resource markets. In *EuroSys*, 2017. DOI: 10.1145/3064176.3064182 94, 95, 98

[140] J. M. Hellerstein, J. F. andJoseph Gonzalez, J. Schleier-Smith, V. Sreekanti, A. Tumanov, and C. Wu. Serverless computing: One step forward, two steps back. In *CIDR*, 2019. 96

[141] J. M. Hellerstein, C. Re, F. Schoppmann, Z. D. Wang, E. Fratkin, A. Gorajek, K. S. Ng, C. Welton, X. Feng, K. Li, and A. Kumar. The MADlib analytics library or MAD skills, the SQL. *PVLDB*, 5(12), 2012. DOI: 10.14778/2367502.2367510 11, 12, 13, 14, 17, 18

[142] H. Herodotou and S. Babu. Profiling, what-if analysis, and cost-based optimization of MapReduce programs. *PVLDB*, 4(11), 2011. 89

[143] H. Herodotou, H. Lim, G. Luo, N. Borisov, L. Dong, F. B. Cetin, and S. Babu. Starfish: A self-tuning system for big data analytics. In *CIDR*, 2011. 89

[144] Q. Ho, J. Cipar, H. Cui, S. Lee, J. K. Kim, P. B. Gibbons, G. A. Gibson, G. R. Ganger, and E. P. Xing. More effective distributed ML via a stale synchronous parallel parameter server. In *NIPS*, 2013. 64

[145] V. Hodge and J. Austin. A survey of outlier detection methodologies. *Artificial Intelligence Review*, 22(2), 2004. DOI: 10.1023/b:aire.0000045502.10941.a9 101

[146] F. Hohman, M. Kahng, R. Pienta, and D. H. Chau. Visual analytics in deep learning: An interrogative survey for the next frontiers. *CoRR*, 2018. DOI: 10.1109/tvcg.2018.2843369 117

[147] K. Hsieh, G. Ananthanarayanan, P. Bodik, S. Venkataraman, P. Bahl, M. Philipose, P. B. Gibbons, and O. Mutlu. Focus: Querying large video datasets with low latency and low cost. In *OSDI*, 2018. 31

[148] T. C. Hu and M. T. Shing. Computation of matrix chain products. Part II. *SIAM Journal Computing*, 13(2), 1984. DOI: 10.1137/0213017 41

[149] B. Huang, S. Babu, and J. Yang. Cumulon: Optimizing statistical data analysis in the cloud. In *SIGMOD*, 2013. DOI: 10.1145/2463676.2465273 18, 36, 44, 46, 55, 61, 86, 87, 90

[150] B. Huang, M. Boehm, Y. Tian, B. Reinwald, S. Tatikonda, and F. R. Reiss. Resource elasticity for large-scale machine learning. In *SIGMOD*, 2015. DOI: 10.1145/2723372.2749432 18, 52, 87, 90

[151] B. Huang, N. W. Jarrett, S. Babu, S. Mukherjee, and J. Yang. Cumulon: Cloud-based statistical analysis from users' perspective. *IEEE Data Engineering Bulletin*, 37(3), 2014. 18, 90

[152] B. Huang, N. W. Jarrett, S. Babu, S. Mukherjee, and J. Yang. Cümülön: Matrix-based data analytics in the cloud with spot instances. *PVLDB*, 9(3), 2015. DOI: 10.14778/2850583.2850590 92, 93, 95, 97

[153] B. Huang and J. Yang. Cümülön-D: Data analytics in a dynamic spot market. *PVLDB*, 10(8), 2017. DOI: 10.14778/3090163.3090165 18, 90, 94, 95, 97

[154] S. F. Hummel, E. Schonberg, and L. E. Flynn. Factoring: a practical and robust method for scheduling parallel loops. In *SC*, 1991. DOI: 10.1145/125826.126137 59

[155] N. Hynes, D. Sculley, and M. Terry. The data linter: Lightweight, automated sanity checking for ML data sets. In *NIPS MLSys Workshop*, 2017. 103

[156] S. Idreos, M. L. Kersten, and S. Manegold. Database cracking. In *CIDR*, 2007. DOI: 10.1145/2619228.2619232 82

[157] Intel. MKL: Math Kernel library. software.intel.com/en-us/intel-mkl/ 56

[158] R. Jampani, F. Xu, M. Wu, L. L. Perez, C. Jermaine, and P. J. Haas. The Monte Carlo database system: Stochastic analysis close to the data. DOI: 10.1145/2000824.2000828 16, 17

[159] J. Jiang, B. Cui, C. Zhang, and L. Yu. Heterogeneity-aware distributed parameter servers. In *SIGMOD*, 2017. DOI: 10.1145/3035918.3035933 62, 63, 64, 88, 90

[160] J. Jiang, F. Fu, T. Yang, and B. Cui. SketchML: Accelerating distributed machine learning with data sketches. In *SIGMOD*, 2018. DOI: 10.1145/3183713.3196894 78

[161] J. Jiang, L. Yu, J. Jiang, Y. Liu, and B. Cui. Angel: A new large-scale machine learning system. *National Science Review*, 5(2), 2018. DOI: 10.1093/nsr/nwx018 62

[162] R. J. L. John, N. Potti, and J. M. Patel. Ava: From data to insights through conversations. In *CIDR*, 2017. 115

[163] T. Johnson, S. M. Muthukrishnan, V. Shkapenyuk, and O. Spatscheck. Query-aware partitioning for monitoring massive network data streams. In *SIGMOD*, 2008. DOI: 10.1109/icde.2008.4497612 63

[164] J. Tremblay, A. Prakash, D. Acuna, M. Brophy, V. Jampani, C. Anil, T. To, E. Cameracci, S. Boochoon, and S. Birchfield. Training deep networks with synthetic data: Bridging the reality gap by domain randomization. In *CVPR Workshop on Autonomous Driving*, 2018. 104

[165] N. P. Jouppi et al. In-datacenter performance analysis of a tensor processing unit. In *ISCA*, 2017. 69, 70

[166] N. Kabra and D. J. DeWitt. OPT++: An object-oriented implementation for extensible database query optimization. *The VLDB Journal*, 8(1):55–78, 1999. DOI: 10.1007/s007780050074 19

[167] M. Kahng, D. Fang, and D. H. Chau. Visual exploration of machine learning results using data cube analysis. In *SIGMOD HILDA Workshop*, 2016. DOI: 10.1145/2939502.2939503 115

[168] B. Kanagal and A. Deshpande. Efficient query evaluation over temporally correlated probabilistic streams. In *ICDE*. DOI: 10.1109/icde.2009.229 19

[169] D. Kang, P. Bailis, and M. Zaharia. BlazeIt: Fast exploratory video queries using neural networks. *CoRR*, 2018. 31

[170] D. Kang, J. Emmons, F. Abuzaid, P. Bailis, and M. Zaharia. NoScope: Optimizing neural network queries over video at scale. *PVLDB*, 10(11), 2017. DOI: 10.14778/3137628.3137664 118

[171] U. Kang, E. E. Papalexakis, A. Harpale, and C. Faloutsos. GigaTensor: Scaling tensor analysis up by 100 times—algorithms and discoveries. In *KDD*, 2012. DOI: 10.1145/2339530.2339583 42, 46

[172] U. Kang, C. E. Tsourakakis, and C. Faloutsos. PEGASUS: A peta-scale graph mining system. In *ICDM*, 2009. 55

[173] Z. Kaoudi, J. Quiané-Ruiz, S. Thirumuruganathan, S. Chawla, and D. Agrawal. A cost-based optimizer for gradient descent optimization. In *SIGMOD*, 2017. DOI: 10.1145/3035918.3064042 79

[174] V. Karakasis, T. Gkountouvas, K. Kourtis, G. I. Goumas, and N. Koziris. An extended compression format for the optimization of sparse matrix-vector multiplication. *IEEE Transactions on Parallel and Distributed Systems*, 24(10), 2013. DOI: 10.1109/t-pds.2012.290 77

[175] T. Karnagel, T. Ben-Nun, M. Werner, D. Habich, and W. Lehner. Big data causing big (TLB) problems: Taming random memory accesses on the GPU. In *DaMoN*, 2017. DOI: 10.1145/3076113.3076115 70

[176] K. Kennedy and K. S. McKinley. Maximizing loop parallelism and improving data locality via loop fusion and distribution. In *LPPC*, 1993. DOI: 10.1007/3-540-57659-2_18 50

[177] D. Kernert, F. Köhler, and W. Lehner. SLACID—sparse linear algebra in a column-oriented in-memory database system. In *SSDBM*, 2014. DOI: 10.1145/2618243.2618254 29, 56

[178] D. Kernert, F. Köhler, and W. Lehner. SpMacho—optimizing sparse linear algebra expressions with probabilistic density estimation. In *EDBT*, 2015. 39, 41, 42

[179] D. Kernert, W. Lehner, and F. Köhler. Topology-aware optimization of big sparse matrices and matrix multiplications on main-memory systems. In *ICDE*, 2016. DOI: 10.1109/icde.2016.7498293 80, 82

[180] M. A. Khamis, H. Q. Ngo, X. Nguyen, D. Olteanu, and M. Schleich. In-database learning with sparse tensors. In *PODS*, 2018. DOI: 10.1145/3196959.3196960 25, 42

[181] M. A. Khamis, H. Q. Ngo, and A. Rudra. FAQ: Questions asked frequently. In *PODS*, 2016. DOI: 10.1145/2902251.2902280 26, 42

[182] K.-H. Kim, S. Gaba, D. Wheeler, , J. M. Cruz-Albrecht, T. Hussain, N. Srinivasa, and W. Lu. A functional hybrid memristor crossbar-array/CMOS system for data storage and neuromorphic applications. *Nano Letters*, 12(1), 2012. DOI: 10.1021/nl203687n 69

[183] M. Kim and K. S. Candan. TensorDB: In-database tensor manipulation with tensor-relational query plans. In *CIKM*, 2014. DOI: 10.1145/2661829.2661842 24

[184] F. Kjolstad, S. Kamil, S. Chou, D. Lugato, and S. P. Amarasinghe. The tensor algebra compiler. *PACMPL*, 1(OOPSLA), 2017. DOI: 10.1145/3133901 49, 50

[185] J. Knight. Intel Nervana graph beta. `intelnervana.com/intel-nervana-graph-and-neon-3--0-updates/` 48, 71

[186] P. Konda, A. Kumar, C. Ré, and V. Sashikanth. Feature selection in enterprise analytics: A demonstration using an R-based data analytics system. *PVLDB*, 6(12), 2013. DOI: 10.14778/2536274.2536302 108

[187] J. Konecný. Federated learning privacy-preserving collaborative machine learning without centralized training data. `http://jakubkonecny.com/files/2018--01_UW_Federated_Learning.pdf` 65, 66

[188] J. Konecný, H. B. McMahan, F. X. Yu, P. Richtárik, A. T. Suresh, and D. Bacon. Federated learning: Strategies for improving communication efficiency. *CoRR*, 2016. 66

[189] U. Köster, T. Webb, X. Wang, M. Nassar, A. K. Bansal, W. Constable, O. Elibol, S. Hall, L. Hornof, A. Khosrowshahi, C. Kloss, R. J. Pai, and N. Rao. Flexpoint: An adaptive numerical format for efficient training of deep neural networks. In *NIPS*, 2017. 70

[190] K. Kourtis, G. I. Goumas, and N. Koziris. Optimizing sparse matrix-vector multiplication using index and value compression. In *CF*, 2008. DOI: 10.1145/1366230.1366244 77

[191] T. Kraska, M. Alizadeh, A. Beutel, E. H. Chi, A. Kristo, G. Leclerc, S. Madden, H. Mao, and V. Nathan. SageDB: A learned database system. In *CIDR*, 2019. 6

[192] T. Kraska, A. Beutel, E. H. Chi, J. Dean, and N. Polyzotis. The case for learned index structures. In *SIGMOD*, 2018. DOI: 10.1145/3183713.3196909 6

[193] T. Kraska, A. Talwalkar, J. C. Duchi, R. Griffith, M. J. Franklin, and M. I. Jordan. MLbase: A distributed machine-learning system. In *CIDR*, 2013. 112

[194] S. Krishnan, M. J. Franklin, K. Goldberg, J. Wang, and E. Wu. ActiveClean: An interactive data cleaning framework for modern machine learning. In *SIGMOD*, 2016. DOI: 10.1145/2882903.2899409 103

[195] S. Krishnan, M. J. Franklin, K. Goldberg, and E. Wu. BoostClean: Automated error detection and repair for machine learning. *CoRR*, 2018. 103

[196] S. Krishnan and E. Wu. PALM: Machine learning explanations for iterative debugging. In *SIGMOD HILDA Workshop*, 2017. DOI: 10.1145/3077257.3077271 116

[197] J. Krüger, C. Kim, M. Grund, N. Satish, D. Schwalb, J. Chhugani, H. Plattner, P. Dubey, and A. Zeier. Fast updates on read-optimized databases using multi-core CPUs. *PVLDB*, 5(1), 2011. DOI: 10.14778/2047485.2047491 81

[198] A. Kumar, A. Beutel, Q. Ho, and E. P. Xing. Fugue: Slow-worker-agnostic distributed learning for big models on big data. In *AISTATS*, 2014. 55

[199] A. Kumar, M. Jalal, B. Yan, J. Naughton, and J. M. Patel. Demonstration of san-toku: Optimizing machine learning over normalized data. *PVLDB*, 8(12), 2015. DOI: 10.14778/2824032.2824087 24

[200] A. Kumar, R. McCann, J. Naughton, and J. M. Patel. Model selection management systems: The next frontier of advanced analytics. *SIGMOD Record*, 44(4), 2016. DOI: 10.1145/2935694.2935698 109, 110, 112

[201] A. Kumar, J. Naughton, and J. M. Patel. Learning generalized linear models over nor-malized data. In *SIGMOD*, 2015. DOI: 10.1145/2723372.2723713 22, 23

[202] A. Kumar, J. F. Naughton, J. M. Patel, and X. Zhu. To join or not to join?: Thinking twice about joins before feature selection. In *SIGMOD*, 2016. DOI: 10.1145/2882903.2882952 78, 102

[203] A. Kumar and C. Ré. Probabilistic management of OCR data using an RDBMS. *PVLDB*, 5(4), 2011. DOI: 10.14778/2095686.2095691 19, 117

[204] Y. Kwon, M. Balazinska, B. Howe, and J. Rolia. SkewTune: Mitigating skew in MapRe-duce applications. In *SIGMOD*, 2012. DOI: 10.14778/2367502.2367541 89

[205] Q. Le and T. Mikolov. Distributed representations of sentences and documents. In *ICML*, 2014. 107

[206] Y. Lee, A. Scolari, B.-G. Chun, M. D. Santambrogio, M. Weimer, and M. Interlandi. Pretzel: Opening the black box of machine learning prediction serving systems. In *OSDI*, 2018. 118

[207] J. Letchner, C. Ré, M. Balazinska, and M. Philipose. Approximation trade-offs in Markovian stream processing: An empirical study. In *ICDE*, 2010. DOI: 10.1109/icde.2010.5447926 19

[208] F. Li, L. Chen, Y. Zeng, A. Kumar, J. Naughton, J. Patel, and X. Wu. Tuple-oriented compression for large-scale mini-batch stochastic gradient descent. *SIGMOD*, 2019. 77

[209] L. Li, K. G. Jamieson, G. DeSalvo, A. Rostamizadeh, and A. Talwalkar. Hyperband: A novel bandit-based approach to hyperparameter optimization. *Journal of Machine Learning Research*, 18, 2017. 111

[210] M. Li, D. G. Andersen, J. W. Park, A. J. Smola, A. Ahmed, V. Josifovski, J. Long, E. J. Shekita, and B. Su. Scaling distributed machine learning with the parameter server. In *OSDI*, 2014. DOI: 10.1145/2640087.2644155 62, 63, 65, 88

[211] S. Li, L. Chen, and A. Kumar. Enabling and optimizing non-linear feature interactions in linear algebra over normalized data. In *SIGMOD*, 2019. 25

[212] T. Li, J. Zhong, J. Liu, W. Wu, and C. Zhang. Ease.ml: Towards multi-tenant resource sharing for machine learning workloads. *PVLDB*, 11(5), 2018. 113

[213] X. Lian, C. Zhang, H. Zhang, C. Hsieh, W. Zhang, and J. Liu. Can decentralized algorithms outperform centralized algorithms? A case study for decentralized parallel stochastic gradient descent. In *NIPS*, 2017. 64, 65

[214] Y. Lin, S. Han, H. Mao, Y. Wang, and W. J. Dally. Deep gradient compression: Reducing the communication bandwidth for distributed training. *ICLR*, 2017. 66, 78

[215] Z. C. Lipton, J. Berkowitz, and C. Elkan. A critical review of recurrent neural networks for sequence learning. *CoRR*, 2015. 107

[216] W. Liu and B. Vinter. An efficient GPU general sparse matrix-matrix multiplication for irregular data. In *IPDPS*, 2014. DOI: 10.1109/ipdps.2014.47 39, 42

[217] Y. Liu, T. Safavi, A. Dighe, and D. Koutra. Graph summarization methods and applications: A survey. *ACM Computing Surveys*, 2018. DOI: 10.1145/3186727 78

[218] Y. Low, J. Gonzalez, A. Kyrola, D. Bickson, C. Guestrin, and J. Hellerstein. GraphLab: A new framework for parallel machine learning. In *UAI*, 2010. 31

[219] Y. Lu, A. Chowdhery, and S. Kandula. Optasia: A relational platform for efficient large-scale video analytics. In *SoCC*, 2016. DOI: 10.1145/2987550.2987564 31

[220] Y. Lu, A. Chowdhery, S. Kandula, and S. Chaudhuri. Accelerating machine learning inference with probabilistic predicates. In *SIGMOD*, 2018. DOI: 10.1145/3183713.3183751 117

[221] S. Luo, Z. J. Gao, M. N. Gubanov, L. L. Perez, and C. M. Jermaine. Scalable linear algebra on a relational database system. In *ICDE*, 2017. DOI: 10.1109/icde.2017.108 10, 11, 17, 18, 37, 55, 57

[222] E. Ma, V. Gupta, M. Hsu, and I. Roy. dmapply: A functional primitive to express distributed machine learning algorithms in R. *PVLDB*, 9(13), 2016. DOI: 10.14778/3007263.3007268 55, 57

[223] L. Ma, D. V. Aken, A. Hefny, G. Mezerhane, A. Pavlo, and G. J. Gordon. Query-based workload forecasting for self-driving database management systems. In *SIGMOD*, 2018. DOI: 10.1145/3183713.3196908 6

[224] A. Maccioni and D. J. Abadi. Scalable pattern matching over compressed graphs via dedensification. In *KDD*, 2016. DOI: 10.1145/2939672.2939856 78

[225] D. Mahajan, J. K. Kim, J. Sacks, A. Ardalan, A. Kumar, and H. Esmaeilzadeh. In-RDBMS hardware acceleration of advanced analytics. *PVLDB*, 11(11), 2018. DOI: 10.14778/3236187.3236188 17, 18, 69

[226] F. Makari, C. Teflioudi, R. Gemulla, P. J. Haas, and Y. Sismanis. Shared-memory and shared-nothing stochastic gradient descent algorithms for matrix completion. *Knowledge and Information Systems*, 42(3), 2015. DOI: 10.1007/s10115-013-0718-7 55

[227] C. D. Manning, M. Surdeanu, J. Bauer, J. Finkel, P. Inc, S. J. Bethard, and D. Mc-closky. The Stanford CoreNLP natural language processing Toolkit. In *ACL*, 2014. DOI: 10.3115/v1/p14-5010 31

[228] R. Marcus and O. Papaemmanouil. Releasing cloud databases for the chains of performance prediction models. In *CIDR*, 2017. 6

[229] R. Marcus and O. Papaemmanouil. Towards a hands-free query optimizer through deep learning. In *CIDR*, 2019. 6

[230] N. Mateev, K. Pingali, P. Stodghill, and V. Kotlyar. Next-generation generic programming and its application to sparse matrix computations. In *ICS*, 2000. DOI: 10.1145/335231.335240 49

[231] C. Mayfield, J. Neville, and S. Prabhakar. ERACER: A database approach for statistical inference and data cleaning. In *SIGMOD*, 2010. 28 DOI: 10.1145/1807167.1807178

[232] B. McMahan, E. Moore, D. Ramage, S. Hampson, and B. A. Y. Arcas. Communication-efficient learning of deep networks from decentralized data. In *AISTATS*, 2017. 66

[233] P. Mehta, S. Dorkenwald, D. Zhao, T. Kaftan, A. Cheung, M. Balazinska, A. Rokem, A. Connolly, J. Vanderplas, and Y. AlSayyad. Comparative evaluation of big-data systems on scientific image analytics workloads. *PVLDB*, 10(11), 2017. DOI: 10.14778/3137628.3137634 119

[234] X. Meng et al. MLlib: Machine learning in Apache spark. *JMLR*, 17, 2016. 55

[235] H. Miao, A. Li, L. S. Davis, and A. Deshpande. ModelHub: Deep learning lifecycle management. In *ICDE*, 2017. DOI: 10.1109/icde.2017.192 109, 112, 114

[236] H. Miao, A. Li, L. S. Davis, and A. Deshpande. On model discovery for hosted data science projects. In *SIGMOD DEEM Workshop*, 2017. DOI: 10.1145/3076246.3076252 114

[237] T. Mikolov, I. Sutskever, K. Chen, G. Corrado, and J. Dean. Distributed representations of words and phrases and their compositionality. In *NIPS*, 2013. DOI: 10.1101/524280 107

[238] A. Mirhoseini, H. Pham, Q. V. Le, B. Steiner, R. Larsen, Y. Zhou, N. Kumar, M. Norouzi, S. Bengio, and J. Dean. Device placement optimization with reinforcement learning. In *ICML*, 2017. 43, 47

[239] N. Mishra, C. Imes, H. Hoffmann, and J. D. Lafferty. Controlling AI engines in dynamic environments. In *SysML*, 2018. 89

[240] S. Muggleton. Inductive logic programming. *New Generation Computing*, 8(4), 1991. DOI: 10.1007/3-540-63494-0 28

[241] S. Nakandala and A. Kumar. Materialization trade-offs for feature transfer from deep CNNs for multimodal data analytics, 2019. `https://adalabucsd.github.io/paper s/TR_2019_Vista.pdf` 109, 118

[242] S. Nakandala, A. Kumar, and Y. Papakonstantinou. Incremental and approximate inference for faster occlusion-based deep CNN explanations, 2019. `https://adalabucsd.g ithub.io/papers/TR_2019_Krypton.pdf` 39, 116

[243] S. Narayanamurthy, M. Weimer, D. Mahajan, T. Condie, S. Sellamanickam, and K. Selvaraj. Towards resource-elastic machine learning. In *NIPS Biglearn Workshop*, 2013. 65, 93

[244] A. Netz, S. Chaudhuri, J. Bernhardt, and U. M. Fayyad. Integration of data mining with database technology. In *VLDB*, 2000. 19

[245] G. Neubig, C. Dyer, Y. Goldberg, A. Matthews, W. Ammar, A. Anastasopoulos, M. Ballesteros, D. Chiang, D. Clothiaux, T. Cohn, K. Duh, M. Faruqui, C. Gan, D. Garrette, Y. Ji, L. Kong, A. Kuncoro, G. Kumar, C. Malaviya, P. Michel, Y. Oda, M. Richardson, N. Saphra, S. Swayamdipta, and P. Yin. DyNet: The dynamic neural network Toolkit. *CoRR*, abs/1701.03980, 2017. 35

[246] G. Neubig, Y. Goldberg, and C. Dyer. On-the-fly operation batching in dynamic computation graphs. In *NIPS*, 2017. 67

[247] H. Q. Ngo, E. Porat, C. Ré, and A. Rudra. Worst-case optimal join algorithms: [extended abstract]. In *PODS*, 2012. DOI: 10.1145/2213556.2213565 46

[248] M. Nikolic, M. Elseidy, and C. Koch. LINVIEW: Incremental view maintenance for complex analytical queries. In *SIGMOD*, 2014. DOI: 10.1145/2588555.2610519 39

[249] M. Nikolic and D. Olteanu. Incremental maintenance of regression models over joins. *CoRR*, 2017. 39

[250] M. Nikolic and D. Olteanu. Incremental view maintenance with triple lock factorization benefits. In *SIGMOD*, 2018. DOI: 10.1145/3183713.3183758 24

[251] F. Niu, C. Ré, A. Doan, and J. Shavlik. Tuffy: Scaling up statistical inference in Markov logic networks using an RDBMS. *PVLDB*, 4(6), 2011. DOI: 10.14778/1978665.1978669 26, 27

[252] F. Niu, C. Zhang, C. Re, and J. Shavlik. Scaling inference for Markov logic via dual decomposition. In *ICDM*, 2012. DOI: 10.1109/icdm.2012.96 28

[253] J. Nocedal and S. J. Wright. *Numerical Optimization*. Springer, 1999. DOI: 10.1007/b98874 34

[254] NVIDIA. cuSPARSE: CUDA sparse matrix library. `https://docs.nvidia.com/cuda/cusparse/` 56

[255] NVIDIA. TensorRT—programmable inference accelerator. `https://developer.nvidia.com/tensorrt` 48, 71

[256] S. Palkar, J. J. Thomas, D. Narayanan, P. Thaker, R. Palamuttam, P. Negi, A. Shanbhag, M. Schwarzkopf, H. Pirk, S. P. Amarasinghe, S. Madden, and M. Zaharia. Evaluating end-to-end optimization for data analytics applications in weld. *PVLDB*, 11(9), 2018. DOI: 10.14778/3213880.3213890 49, 50

[257] S. Palkar, J. J. Thomas, A. Shanbhag, M. Schwarzkopt, S. P. Amarasinghe, and M. Zaharia. A common runtime for high performance data analysis. In *CIDR*, 2017. 35, 49

[258] X. Pan, S. Venkataraman, Z. Tai, and J. Gonzalez. Hemingway: Modeling distributed optimization algorithms. In *NIPS MLSys Workshop*, 2016. 90, 113

[259] N. Pansare, M. Dusenberry, N. Jindal, M. Boehm, B. Reinwald, and P. Sen. Deep learning with Apache SystemML. *SysML*, 2018. 58, 75

[260] S. Papadopoulos, K. Datta, S. Madden, and T. G. Mattson. The TileDB array data storage manager. *PVLDB*, 10(4), 2016. DOI: 10.14778/3025111.3025117 30, 76, 82

[261] A. Parashar, M. Rhu, A. Mukkara, A. Puglielli, R. Venkatesan, B. Khailany, J. S. Emer, S. W. Keckler, and W. J. Dally. SCNN: An accelerator for compressed-sparse convolutional neural networks. In *ISCA*, 2017. DOI: 10.1145/3079856.3080254 70

[262] Y. Park, J. Qing, X. Shen, and B. Mozafari. BlinkML: Efficient maximum likelihood estimation with probabilistic guarantees. *SIGMOD*, 2019. 36, 79

[263] L. Passing, M. Then, N. Hubig, H. Lang, M. Schreier, S. Günnemann, A. Kemper, and T. Neumann. SQL—and operator-centric data analytics in relational main-memory databases. In *EDBT*, 2017. 19, 55

[264] A. Paszke, S. Gross, S. Chintala, G. Chanan, E. Yang, Z. DeVito, Z. Lin, A. Desmaison, L. Antiga, and A. Lerer. *NIPS Autodiff Workshop*, 2017. 35, 38, 63, 120

[265] A. Pavlo, G. Angulo, J. Arulraj, H. Lin, J. Lin, L. Ma, P. Menon, T. C. Mowry, M. Perron, I. Quah, S. Santurkar, A. Tomasic, S. Toor, D. V. Aken, Z. Wang, Y. Wu, R. Xian, and T. Zhang. Self-driving database management systems. In *CIDR*, 2017. 6

[266] J. Pennington, R. Socher, and C. D. Manning. Glove: Global vectors for word representation. In *EMNLP*, 2014. DOI: 10.3115/v1/d14-1162 107

[267] J. Picado, A. Termehchy, A. Fern, and P. Ataei. Schema independent relational learning. In *SIGMOD*, 2017. DOI: 10.1145/3035918.3035923 29

[268] H. Pirahesh, J. M. Hellerstein, and W. Hasan. Extensible/rule based query rewrite optimization in starburst. In *SIGMOD*, 1992. DOI: 10.1145/141484.130294 19

[269] N. Polyzotis, S. Roy, S. E. Whang, and M. Zinkevich. Data management challenges in production machine learning. In *SIGMOD*, 2017. DOI: 10.1145/3035918.3054782 101

[270] A. D. Popescu, A. Balmin, V. Ercegovac, and A. Ailamaki. PREDIcT: Towards predicting the runtime of large scale iterative analytics. *PVLDB*, 6(14), 2013. DOI: 10.14778/2556549.2556553 90

[271] R. Preissl, T. M. Wong, P. Datta, M. Flickner, R. Singh, S. K. Esser, W. P. Risk, H. D. Simon, and D. S. Modha. Compass: A scalable simulator for an architecture for cognitive computing. In *SC*, 2012. DOI: 10.1109/sc.2012.34 69

[272] I. Psaroudakis, T. Scheuer, N. May, A. Sellami, and A. Ailamaki. Scaling up concurrent main-memory column-store scans: Towards adaptive NUMA-aware data and task placement. *PVLDB*, 8(12), 2015. DOI: 10.14778/2824032.2824043 80

[273] M. Pumperla. Elephas: Distributed deep learning with Keras & Spark. https://github.com/maxpumperla/elephas 62

[274] C. Qin and F. Rusu. Speculative approximations for Terascale analytics. *CoRR*, 2015. 78

[275] C. Qin and F. Rusu. Speculative approximations for Terascale distributed gradient descent optimization. In *SIGMOD DanaC Workshop*, 2015. DOI: 10.1145/2799562.2799563 113

[276] C. Qin and F. Rusu. Dot-product join: Scalable in-database linear algebra for big model analytics. In *SSDBM*, 2017. DOI: 10.1145/3085504.3085512 76

[277] J. R. Quinlan. Learning logical definitions from relations. *Machine Learning*, 5, 1990. DOI: 10.1007/bf00117105 28

[278] E. Rahm and H. H. Do. Data cleaning: Problems and current approaches. *IEEE Data Engineering Bulletin*, 23(4), 2000. 102

[279] R. Raina, A. Madhavan, and A. Y. Ng. Large-scale deep unsupervised learning using graphics processors. In *ICML*, 2009. DOI: 10.1145/1553374.1553486 69

[280] K. Ramachandra, K. Park, K. V. Emani, A. Halverson, C. A. Galindo-Legaria, and C. Cunningham. Froid: Optimization of imperative programs in a relational database. *PVLDB*, 11(4), 2017. 52

[281] R. Ramakrishnan and J. Gehrke. *Database Management Systems*. McGraw-Hill, Inc., 2000. 21, 23

[282] V. Raman and G. Swart. How to wring a table dry: Entropy compression of relations and querying of compressed relations. In *VLDB*, 2006. 76

[283] N. Rao. Intel Nervana neural network processors (NNP) redefine AI silicon. https://ai.intel.com/intel-nervana-neural-network-processors-nnp-redefine-ai-silicon/ 69

[284] A. Ratner, S. H. Bach, H. Ehrenberg, J. Fries, S. Wu, and C. Ré. Snorkel: Rapid training data creation with weak supervision. *PVLDB*, 11(3), 2017. DOI: 10.14778/3157794.3157797 104

[285] A. Ratner, B. Hancock, J. Dunnmon, R. Goldman, and C. Ré. Snorkel MeTaL: Weak supervision for multi-task learning. In *SIGMOD DEEM Workshop*, 2018. DOI: 10.1145/3209889.3209898 104

[286] A. Ratner, B. Hancock, and C. Ré. The role of massively multi-task and weak supervision in software 2.0. In *CIDR*, 2019. 105

[287] C. Ré, J. Letchner, M. Balazinska, and D. Suciu. Event queries on correlated probabilistic streams. In *SIGMOD*, 2008. DOI: 10.1145/1376616.1376688 19

[288] B. Recht, C. Ré, S. J. Wright, and F. Niu. Hogwild!: A lock-free approach to parallelizing stochastic gradient descent. In *NIPS*, 2011. 64, 80

[289] S. Rendle. Scaling factorization machines to relational data. *PVLDB*, 6(5), 2013. DOI: 10.14778/2535573.2488340 24

[290] A. Rheinländer, M. Beckmann, A. Kunkel, A. Heise, T. Stoltmann, and U. Leser. Versatile optimization of UDF-heavy data flows with sofa. In *SIGMOD*, 2014. DOI: 10.1145/2588555.2594517 19

[291] M. T. Ribeiro, S. Singh, and C. Guestrin. "Why should I trust you?": Explaining the predictions of any classifier. In *KDD*, 2016. DOI: 10.18653/v1/n16-3020 117

[292] M. Richardson and P. Domingos. Markov logic networks. *Machine Learning*, 62(1–2), February 2006. DOI: 10.1007/s10994-006-5833-1 26, 27

[293] T. Rohrmann, S. Schelter, T. Rabl, and V. Markl. Gilbert: Declarative sparse linear algebra on massively parallel dataflow systems. In *BTW*, 2017. 55

[294] V. Rokhlin, A. Szlam, and M. Tygert. A randomized algorithm for principal component analysis. *SIAM Journal on Matrix Analysis and Applications*, 31(3), 2009. DOI: 10.1137/080736417 86

[295] F. Rusu and Y. Cheng. A survey on array storage, query languages, and systems. *CoRR*, 2013. 19

[296] F. Rusu and A. Dobra. GLADE: A scalable framework for efficient analytics. *Operating Systems Review*, 46(1):12–18, 2012. DOI: 10.1145/2146382.2146386 14, 17

[297] Y. Saad. SPARSKIT: A basic tool kit for sparse matrix computations—Version 2, CSRD, University of Illinois and RIACS, NASA Ames Research Center, 1994. 56, 77

[298] V. Satuluri, S. Parthasarathy, and Y. Ruan. Local graph sparsification for scalable clustering. In *SIGMOD*, 2011. DOI: 10.1145/1989323.1989399 78

[299] S. Schelter, J.-H. Boese, J. Kirschnick, and T. Klein. Automatically tracking metadata and provenance of machine learning experiments. In *NIPS MLSys Workshop*, 2017. 114

[300] S. Schelter, S. Ewen, K. Tzoumas, and V. Markl. "All roads lead to rome": Optimistic recovery for distributed iterative data processing. In *CIKM*, 2013. DOI: 10.1145/2505515.2505753 93

[301] S. Schelter, A. Palumbo, S. Quinn, S. Marthi, and A. Musselman. Samsara: Declarative machine learning on distributed dataflow systems. *NIPS MLSys Workshop*, 2016. 35, 42, 43, 55

[302] M. Schleich, D. Olteanu, and R. Ciucanu. Learning linear regression models over factorized joins. In *SIGMOD*, 2016. DOI: 10.1145/2882903.2882939 24

[303] C. D. Schuman, T. E. Potok, R. M. Patton, J. D. Birdwell, M. E. Dean, G. S. Rose, and J. S. Plank. A survey of neuromorphic computing and neural networks in hardware. *CoRR*, 2017. 69

[304] F. Seide and A. Agarwal. CNTK: Microsoft's open-source deep-learning Toolkit. In *KDD*, 2016. DOI: 10.1145/2939672.2945397 63

[305] F. Seide, H. Fu, J. Droppo, G. Li, and D. Yu. 1-bit stochastic gradient descent and its application to data-parallel distributed training of speech DNNs. In *INTERSPEECH*, 2014. 63, 78

[306] T. Sellam, K. Lin, I. Y. Huang, C. Vondrick, and E. Wu. "I like the way you think!" Inspecting the internal logic of recurrent neural networks. In *SysML*, 2018. 116

[307] V. Shah, A. Kumar, and X. Zhu. Are key-foreign key joins safe to avoid when learning high-capacity classifiers? *PVLDB*, 11(3), 2017. DOI: 10.14778/3157794.3157804 102

[308] S. Shalev-Shwartz and S. Ben-David. *Understanding Machine Learning: From Theory to Algorithms*. Cambridge University Press, 2014. DOI: 10.1017/cbo9781107298019 106, 110

[309] C. J. Shallue, J. Lee, J. M. Antognini, J. Sohl-Dickstein, R. Frostig, and G. E. Dahl. Measuring the effects of data parallelism on neural network training. *CoRR*, abs/1811.03600, 2018. 66

[310] V. Sharan, K. S. Tai, P. Bailis, and G. Valiant. Fast and accurate low-rank factorization of compressively-sensed data. *CoRR*, abs/1706.08146, 2018. 78

[311] G. Sharma and J. Martin. MATLAB®: A language for parallel computing. *International Journal of Parallel Programming*, 37(1), 2009. 53, 58

[312] P. Sharma, T. Guo, X. He, D. E. Irwin, and P. J. Shenoy. Flint: Batch-interactive data-intensive processing on transient servers. In *EuroSys*, 2016. DOI: 10.1145/2901318.2901319 91, 93, 94, 96

[313] J. Shin, S. Wu, F. Wang, C. De Sa, C. Zhang, and C. Ré. Incremental knowledge base construction using DeepDive. *PVLDB*, 8(11), 2015. DOI: 10.14778/2809974.2809991 28

[314] P. Shivam, S. Babu, and J. S. Chase. Active and accelerated learning of cost models for optimizing scientific applications. In *VLDB*, 2006. 6

[315] J. Snoek, H. Larochelle, and R. P. Adams. Practical Bayesian optimization of machine learning algorithms. In *NIPS*, 2012. 111

[316] E. Sparks, S. Venkataraman, T. Kaftan, M. J. Franklin, and B. Recht. KeystoneML: Optimizing pipelines for large-scale advanced analytics. In *ICDE*, 2017. DOI: 10.1109/icde.2017.109 109

[317] E. R. Sparks, A. Talwalkar, D. Haas, M. J. Franklin, M. I. Jordan, and T. Kraska. Automating model search for large scale machine learning. In *SoCC*, 2015. DOI: 10.1145/2806777.2806945 36, 67, 89, 112, 113

[318] M. Stillger, G. M. Lohman, V. Markl, and M. Kandil. LEO—DB2's LEarning optimizer. In *VLDB*, 2001. 52

[319] M. Stonebraker, D. J. Abadi, A. Batkin, X. Chen, M. Cherniack, M. Ferreira, E. Lau, A. Lin, S. Madden, E. J. O'Neil, P. E. O'Neil, A. Rasin, N. Tran, and S. B. Zdonik. C-Store: A column-oriented DBMS. In *VLDB*, 2005. DOI: 10.1145/3226595.3226638 81

[320] M. Stonebraker, P. Brown, A. Poliakov, and S. Raman. The architecture of SciDB. In *SSDBM*, 2011. DOI: 10.1007/978-3-642-22351-8_1 30, 44, 51, 54, 55, 76

[321] M. Stonebraker, P. Brown, D. Zhang, and J. Becla. SciDB: A database management system for applications with complex analytics. *Computing in Science and Engineering*, 15(3):54–62, 2013. DOI: 10.1109/mcse.2013.19 19

[322] V. S. Subrahmanian and S. Jajodia. *Multimedia Database Systems: Issues and Research Directions*. Springer Publishing Company, Incorporated, 2012. 31

[323] B. Subramaniam, N. Nielsen, C. Doyle, A. Deshpande, J. Knight, and S. Leishman. Abstractions for containerized machine learning workloads in the cloud. In *SysML*, 2018. 79

[324] S. Subramanya, T. Guo, P. Sharma, D. E. Irwin, and P. J. Shenoy. SpotOn: A batch computing service for the spot market. In *SoCC*, 2015. DOI: 10.1145/2806777.2806851 94, 95

[325] A. K. Sujeeth, H. Lee, K. J. Brown, T. Rompf, H. Chafi, M. Wu, A. R. Atreya, M. Odersky, and K. Olukotun. OptiML: An implicitly parallel domain-specific language for machine learning. In *ICML*, 2011. 35, 37, 40

[326] I. Sutskever, O. Vinyals, and Q. V. Le. Sequence to sequence learning with neural networks. In *NIPS*, 2014. 107

[327] R. Taft, M. Vartak, N. R. Satish, N. Sundaram, S. Madden, and M. Stonebraker. GenBase: A complex analytics genomics benchmark. In *SIGMOD*, 2014. DOI: 10.1145/2588555.2595633 120

[328] M. Tepper and G. Sapiro. Compressed nonnegative matrix factorization is fast and accurate. *IEEE Transactions on Signal Processing*, 64(9), 2016. DOI: 10.1109/tsp.2016.2516971 78

[329] A. Thomas and A. Kumar. A comparative evaluation of systems for scalable linear algebra-based analytics. *PVLDB*, 11(13), 2018. DOI: 10.14778/3275366.3275367 120

[330] C. Thornton, F. Hutter, H. H. Hoos, and K. Leyton-Brown. Auto-WEKA: Combined selection and hyperparameter optimization of classification algorithms. In *KDD*, 2013. DOI: 10.1145/2487575.2487629 112

[331] S. Toledo. A survey of out-of-core algorithms in numerical linear algebra. In *DIMACS*, 1998. DOI: 10.1090/dimacs/050/09 75, 76

[332] Unidata. Network common data form (NetCDF). https://unidata.ucar.edu/sof tware/netcdf/docs/netcdf_utilities_guide.html 77

[333] P. Varma, D. Iter, C. De Sa, and C. Ré. Flipper: A systematic approach to debugging training sets. In *SIGMOD HILDA Workshop*, 2017. DOI: 10.1145/3077257.3077263 115

[334] P. Varma and C. Ré. Snuba: Automating weak supervision to label training data. *PVLDB*, 12(3), 2019. 104

[335] M. Vartak, J. M. F. da Trindade, S. Madden, and M. Zaharia. MISTIQUE: A system to store and query model intermediates for model diagnosis. In *SIGMOD*, 2018. DOI: 10.1145/3183713.3196934 78, 114, 116

[336] M. Vartak, P. Ortiz, K. Siegel, H. Subramanyam, S. Madden, and M. Zaharia. Supporting fast iteration in model building. In *NIPS LearningSys Workshop*, 2015. 112

[337] M. Vartak, H. Subramanyam, W.-E. Lee, S. Viswanathan, S. Husnoo, S. Madden, and M. Zaharia. ModelDB: A system for machine learning model management. In *SIGMOD HILDA Workshop*, 2016. DOI: 10.1145/2939502.2939516 114

[338] N. Vasilache et al. Tensor comprehensions: Framework-agnostic high-performance machine learning abstractions. In *CoRR*, 2018. 50

[339] S. Venkataraman, E. Bodzsar, I. Roy, A. AuYoung, and R. S. Schreiber. Presto: Distributed machine learning and graph processing with sparse matrices. In *EuroSys*, 2013. DOI: 10.1145/2465351.2465371 55

[340] P. Viola and M. Jones. Rapid object detection using a boosted cascade of simple features. In *CVPR*, 2001. DOI: 10.1109/cvpr.2001.990517 118

[341] D. Z. Wang, M. J. Franklin, M. Garofalakis, J. M. Hellerstein, and M. L. Wick. Hybrid in-database inference for declarative information extraction. In *SIGMOD*, 2011. DOI: 10.1145/1989323.1989378 15, 16

[342] D. Z. Wang, E. Michelakis, M. N. Garofalakis, and J. M. Hellerstein. BayesStore: Managing large, uncertain data repositories with probabilistic graphical models. *PVLDB*, 1(1), 2008. DOI: 10.14778/1453856.1453896 19

[343] H. Wang and C. Zaniolo. ATLaS: A native extension of SQL for data mining. In *ICDM*, 2003. DOI: 10.1137/1.9781611972733.12 19

[344] H. Wang, C. Zaniolo, and C. Luo. ATLaS: A small but complete SQL extension for data mining and data streams. In *VLDB*, 2003. 19

[345] L. Wang, J. Ye, Y. Zhao, W. Wu, A. Li, S. L. Song, Z. Xu, and T. Kraska. SuperNeurons: Dynamic GPU memory management for training deep neural networks. In *PPoPP*, 2018. DOI: 10.1145/3178487.3178491 47, 75

[346] X. Wang, Y. Luo, D. Crankshaw, A. Tumanov, F. Yu, and J. E. Gonzalez. IDK cascades: Fast deep learning by learning not to overthink. *CoRR*, 2018. 118

[347] X. Wang, C. Olston, A. D. Sarma, and R. C. Burns. CoScan: Cooperative scan sharing in the cloud. In *SoCC*, 2011. DOI: 10.1145/2038916.2038927 89

[348] Z. Wang, F. Bayer, S. Lee, K. Narendran, X. Pan, Q. Tang, J. Wang, and C. Li. A demonstration of TextDB: Declarative and scalable text analytics on large data sets. In *ICDE*, 2017. DOI: 10.1109/icde.2017.196 30

[349] P. Watcharapichat, V. L. Morales, R. C. Fernandez, and P. R. Pietzuch. Ako: Decentralised deep learning with partial gradient exchange. In *SoCC*, 2016. DOI: 10.1145/2987550.2987586 65

[350] T. Westmann, D. Kossmann, S. Helmer, and G. Moerkotte. The implementation and performance of compressed databases. *SIGMOD Record*, 29(3), 2000. DOI: 10.1145/362084.362137 76

[351] S. Williams, L. Oliker, R. W. Vuduc, J. Shalf, K. A. Yelick, and J. Demmel. Optimization of sparse matrix-vector multiplication on emerging multicore platforms. *Parallel Computing*, 35(3), 2009. DOI: 10.1145/1362622.1362674 79

[352] S. Williams, A. Waterman, and D. A. Patterson. Roofline: An insightful visual performance model for multicore architectures. *Communications of the ACM*, 52(4), 2009. DOI: 10.1145/1498765.1498785 67

[353] M. Winslett. Interview with Pat Selinger. *SIGMOD Record*, 32(4), 2003. 52

[354] M. Winter, D. Mlakar, R. Zayer, H. Seidel, and M. Steinberger. faimGraph: High performance management of fully-dynamic graphs under tight memory constraints on the GPU. In *SC*, 2018. 75

[355] F. Wolf, I. Psaroudakis, N. May, A. Ailamaki, and K. Sattler. Extending database task schedulers for multi-threaded application code. In *SSDBM*, 2015. DOI: 10.1145/2791347.2791379 29, 62

[356] X. Wu, F. Li, A. Kumar, K. Chaudhuri, S. Jha, and J. F. Naughton. Bolt-on differential privacy for scalable stochastic gradient descent-based analytics. In *SIGMOD*, 2017. DOI: 10.1145/3035918.3064047 114

[357] J. Xiang, H. Meng, and A. Aboulnaga. Scalable matrix inversion using MapReduce. In *HPDC*, 2014. DOI: 10.1145/2600212.2600220 55

[358] D. Xin, L. Ma, J. Liu, S. Macke, S. Song, and A. G. Parameswaran. Accelerating human-in-the-loop machine learning: Challenges and opportunities. In *SIGMOD DEEM Workshop*, 2018. DOI: 10.1145/3209889.3209897 113, 115

[359] E. P. Xing, Q. Ho, W. Dai, J. K. Kim, J. Wei, S. Lee, X. Zheng, P. Xie, A. Kumar, and Y. Yu. Petuum: A new platform for distributed machine learning on big data. In *KDD*, 2015. DOI: 10.1109/tbdata.2015.2472014 62, 64

[360] E. P. Xing, Q. Ho, P. Xie, and W. Dai. Strategies and principles of distributed machine learning on big data. *CoRR*, abs/1512.09295, 2015. DOI: 10.1016/j.eng.2016.02.008 62

[361] E. Yablonovitch. Deep learning: The reincarnation of analog computing. *Brain Storming EECS Colloquium*. 69

[362] D. Yan, Y. Bu, Y. Tian, and A. Deshpande. Big graph analytics platforms. *Foundations and Trends in Databases*, 7(1–2), 2017. DOI: 10.1561/1900000056 5

[363] D. Yan, Y. Bu, Y. Tian, A. Deshpande, and J. Cheng. Big graph analytics systems. In *SIGMOD*, 2016. DOI: 10.1145/2882903.2912566 5, 31

[364] D. Yan, Y. Tian, and J. Cheng. *Systems for Big Graph Analytics*. Springer Publishing Company, Incorporated, 2017. DOI: 10.1007/978-3-319-58217-7 31

[365] W. P. Yan and P.-A. Larson. Eager aggregation and lazy aggregation. In *VLDB*, 1995. 23

[366] L. Yu, Y. Shao, and B. Cui. Exploiting matrix dependency for efficient distributed matrix computation. In *SIGMOD*, 2015. DOI: 10.1145/2723372.2723712 34, 43, 55

[367] Y. Yu, M. Tang, W. G. Aref, Q. M. Malluhi, M. M. Abbas, and M. Ouzzani. In-memory distributed matrix computation processing and optimization. In *ICDE*, 2017. DOI: 10.1109/icde.2017.150 37, 39, 42, 45, 51, 55

[368] R. B. Zadeh, X. Meng, A. Ulanov, B. Yavuz, L. Pu, S. Venkataraman, E. R. Sparks, A. Staple, and M. Zaharia. Matrix computations and optimization in Apache spark. In *KDD*, 2016. DOI: 10.1145/2939672.2939675 43, 44, 55, 57, 58

[369] M. Zafer, Y. Song, and K. Lee. Optimal bids for spot VMs in a cloud for deadline constrained jobs. In *CLOUD*, 2012. DOI: 10.1109/cloud.2012.59 95, 97

[370] M. Zaharia, M. Chowdhury, T. Das, A. Dave, J. Ma, M. McCauly, M. J. Franklin, S. Shenker, and I. Stoica. Resilient distributed datasets: A fault-tolerant abstraction for in-memory cluster computing. In *NSDI*, 2012. 42, 54, 57, 73, 77, 89, 91

[371] M. D. Zeiler and R. Fergus. Visualizing and understanding convolutional networks. In *ECCV*, 2014. DOI: 10.1007/978-3-319-10590-1_53 117

[372] Q. Zeng, J. M. Patel, and D. Page. QuickFOIL: Scalable inductive logic programming. *PVLDB*, 8(3), 2014. DOI: 10.14778/2735508.2735510 28

[373] C. Zhang, A. Kumar, and C. Ré. Materialization optimizations for feature selection workloads. In *SIGMOD*, 2014. DOI: 10.1145/2588555.2593678 67, 79, 108

[374] C. Zhang, A. Kumar, and C. Ré. Materialization optimizations for feature selection workloads. *ACM Transactions on Database Systems*, 41(1), 2016. DOI: 10.1145/2588555.2593678 108, 113

[375] C. Zhang and C. Ré. Towards high-throughput Gibbs sampling at scale: A study across storage managers. In *SIGMOD*, 2013. DOI: 10.1145/2463676.2463702 27, 28, 74, 76

[376] C. Zhang and C. Ré. DimmWitted: A study of main-memory statistical analytics. *PVLDB*, 7(12), 2014. DOI: 10.14778/2732977.2733001 79

[377] C. Zhang, C. Re, A. Abbas Sadeghian, Z. Shan, J. Shin, F. Wang, and S. Wu. Feature engineering for knowledge base construction, *IEEE Data Eng. Bull.*, 37, 2014. 28, 109

[378] H. Zhang, J. Li, K. Kara, D. Alistarh, J. Liu, and C. Zhang. ZipML: Training linear models with end-to-end low precision, and a little bit of deep learning. In *ICML*, 2017. 78

[379] J. Zhang, Z. Zhang, X. Xiao, Y. Yang, and M. Winslett. Functional mechanism: Regression analysis under differential privacy. *PVLDB*, 5(11), 2012. DOI: 10.14778/2350229.2350253 114

[380] M. Zhang, Y. Wu, K. Chen, T. Ma, and W. Zheng. Measuring and optimizing distributed array programs. *PVLDB*, 9(12), 2016. DOI: 10.14778/2994509.2994511 43, 50

[381] Y. Zhang, H. Herodotou, and J. Yang. RIOT: I/O-efficient numerical computing without SQL. In *CIDR*, 2009. 8, 9, 10, 17, 18, 35, 41, 55, 74, 76, 81

[382] Y. Zhang, M. L. Kersten, and S. Manegold. SciQL: Array data processing inside an RDBMS. In *SIGMOD*, 2013. DOI: 10.1145/2463676.2463684 19

[383] Y. Zhang, K. Munagala, and J. Yang. Storing matrices on disk: Theory and practice revisited. *PVLDB*, 4(11), 2011. 75, 81

[384] Y. Zhang and Q. Yang. A survey on multi-task learning. *CoRR*, 2018. 104

[385] Y. Zhang, W. Zhang, and J. Yang. I/O-efficient statistical computing with RIOT. In *ICDE*, 2010. DOI: 10.1109/icde.2010.5447819 8, 17, 18

[386] Z. Zhang, L. Cherkasova, and B. T. Loo. Exploiting cloud heterogeneity to optimize performance and cost of MapReduce processing. *ACM SIGMETRICS Performance Evaluation Review*, 42(4), 2015. DOI: 10.1145/2788402.2788409 89, 94

[387] A. C. Zhou, B. He, and C. Liu. Monetary cost optimizations for hosting workflow-as-a-service in IaaS clouds. *IEEE Transactions on Cloud Computing*, 4(1), 2016. DOI: 10.1109/tcc.2015.2404807 94, 95, 96

[388] C. Zhu, S. Han, H. Mao, and W. J. Dally. Trained ternary quantization. *CoRR*, abs/1612.01064, 2016. 78

Authors' Biographies

MATTHIAS BOEHM

Matthias Boehm is a professor at Graz University of Technology, Austria, where he holds a BMVIT-endowed chair for data management. Prior to joining TU Graz in 2018, he was a research staff member at IBM Research – Almaden, CA, USA, with a focus on compilation and runtime techniques for declarative, large-scale machine learning. He received his Ph.D. from Dresden University of Technology, Germany in 2011 with a dissertation on cost-based optimization of integration flows. His previous research also includes systems support for time series forecasting as well as in-memory indexing and query processing. Matthias is a recipient of the 2016 VLDB Best Paper Award, and a 2016 SIGMOD Research Highlight Award.

ARUN KUMAR

Arun Kumar is an Assistant Professor at the University of California, San Diego. He received his Ph.D. from the University of Wisconsin-Madison in 2016. His research interests are in the intersection of data management, systems, and ML, with a focus on making ML-based data analytics easier, faster, cheaper, and more scalable. Ideas from his work have been adopted by many companies, including EMC, Oracle, Cloudera, Facebook, and Microsoft. He is a recipient of the Best Paper Award at SIGMOD 2014, the 2016 CS dissertation research award from UW-Madison, a 2016 Google Faculty Research Award, and a 2018 Hellman Fellowship.

JUN YANG

Jun Yang is a Professor of Computer Science at Duke University, where he has been teaching since receiving his Ph.D. from Stanford University in 2001. He is broadly interested in databases and data-intensive systems. He is a recipient of the NSF CAREER Award, IBM Faculty Award, HP Labs Innovation Research Award, and Google Faculty Research Award. He also received the David and Janet Vaughan Brooks Teaching Award at Duke. His current research interests lie in making data analysis easier and more scalable for scientists, statisticians, and journalists.

Printed in the United States
by Baker & Taylor Publisher Services